D1378290

AFTER THE SALE

*How to Manage Product Service
for Customer Satisfaction
and Profit*

OTHER BOOKS BY JOSEPH D. PATTON

Instrument Maintenance Manager's Sourcebook (EDITOR)

Logistics Technology and Management: The New Approach

Maintainability and Maintenance Management (THREE EDITIONS)

Preventive Maintenance (TWO EDITIONS)

Service Management: Principles and Practices (WITH WILLIAM H. BLEUEL, SUPERCEDED BY AFTER THE SALE)

Service Parts Handbook

Service Parts Management (SUPERCEDED BY SERVICE PARTS HANDBOOK)

AFTER THE SALE

How to Manage Product Service for Customer Satisfaction and Profit

Joseph D. Patton
& William H. Bleuel

 New York: THE SOLOMON PRESS

AFTER THE SALE
How to Manage Product Service for Customer Satisfaction and Profit
by Joseph D. Patton & William H. Bleuel

© 2000 by Joseph D. Patton & William H. Bleuel

THE SOLOMON PRESS
98-12 66th Avenue, Suite #2
Rego Park, NY 11374, USA

or

Joseph D. Patton
36 Blue Heron Point
Hilton Head, SC 29926, USA
843-689-6650
jdpatton@aol.com
www.supportparts.com

This book was designed by Raymond Solomon and Sidney Solomon,
and typeset by Eve Brant in Baskerville, Eurostile, and Times New Roman type faces.

ISBN: 0-934623-63-5

This book is dedicated to all service managers with the hope that it will contribute positively to their professional development

Preface

*W*e rely so much on automobiles, computers, copiers, electrical power, farm equipment, industrial plants, medical instruments, jet planes, telecommunications, and television that we take these durable resources for granted. After the sale, they all require product service to install and maintain their related equipment in effective operating condition. Satisfied customers and profits are usually supporting—but sometime conflicting—goals. Many customers would be very happy with cheap service, but the organization providing that support would not be in business very long without profit to reinvest in the enterprise.

Service management has developed considerably since the Industrial Revolution, when large capital expenditures were first made for equipment, and the need for service to protect the capital investment was established. Today, product service management is one of the fastest growing segments of the world economy. Support of durable equipment over its life cycle is now a major profit center for many organizations. For many companies, product service is far more profitable than is the manufacturing of the original capital goods. The value of service on high-technology equipment alone is estimated at over $700 billion per year as we enter the 21st century.

As service management of durable equipment evolved, most people in the profession came up through service ranks or were salespeople who were told to also manage the service function. This transition led to good people running service organizations, but they have little experience or formal training in how to effectively manage the business of service. Professional managers are now being made responsible for the product service function. In fact, independent service organizations (ISOs) that specialize in only product service are becoming a major factor in the support of durable equipment.

This book, *After the Sale: How to Manage Product Service for Customer Satisfaction and Profit*, is built on a foundation of three editions of the classic work, *Service Management: Principles and Practices*, published from 1978 to 1994. The authors, Joseph Patton and William Bleuel, took over the original copyrights from the Instrument Society of America to extensively update the book. The title is changed to be more descriptive and to avoid confusion with service as applied to banks, fast-food restaurants, and insurance companies. Do note, however, that those industries contain many durable hardware products, which are the subject of this book, and there are many topics in this book that are applicable to non-hardware service enterprises.

One purpose of this book is to provide a new emphasis to service management. The emphasis is on management of the function, rather than intimate technical knowledge of the products being serviced. Most service operations represent an opportunity to increase the profitability of the product serviced, and ultimately of the company. Service thus directly affects the company's cash position and profits. Application of information systems, management science, statistics, and general management skills provide major benefits to the service operation. The authors' experience shows the need for a book that translates general management techniques into specific topics for the service manager.

The service manager, who may be familiar with specific hardware, plant operations, or sales has typically not had experience in such diverse areas as customer satisfaction, organizational development, manpower planning, information systems, capital and expense budgets, and controls. In addition, the service manager's understanding of inventory theory and physical distribution is typically developed by the seat of the pants without any specific acquaintance with analytical inventory theory. Effective understanding of the economics of the service business is the weakest area seen during the authors' many years in service management. The ability to translate service activities and service needs into return on investment and profit figures that can be clearly understood by corporate management is not typical of the service management operation. This book covers such topics as needed by service management personnel.

The material presented is organized into four segments. Chapters 1 and 2 introduce the language, principles, terms, and objectives of service management. The next two chapters apply to service management and planning. They give the service manager topical coverage of the various factors to be taken into account when developing service manpower and financial plans. The third group of chapters concerns service operations and the specific topics related to managing those service operations. The subject matter covers manpower development, organizing, training, maintenance, and basic technology available for service. Chapters on inventory management and physical distribution are followed by two chapters on service support and customer satisfaction. These chapters, which cover the broad range of service operations, have been written to apply both to field service operations and to in-plant service operations. The final chapters outline the basis for control of the service function. In particular, Chapter 14 discuses modern information systems in the service operation. This is obviously an area of rapid change. Note that support of software is covered along with hardware, since many hard parts are today being replaced with software. Chapter 15 overviews the economics of the service business; namely, how to financially analyze service performance. Chapter 16, on the marketing function, emphasizes sensitivity to serving and satisfying both corporate and human needs. Chapter covers service quality and its many facets. The final chapter overviews the professional services that are profitable additions to hardware service.

This book is designed for any person interested in product service, whether in a plant operation or in a field service organization, at the level of CEO or as a technician. The principles are applicable around the world, since similar products require service in every part of our global economy. *After the Sale* is also designed to be used in the undergraduate classroom. The management techniques and service concepts presented are applicable to virtually every type of service organization. The management functions discussed can meet the needs of both large and small service organizations. The text material is arranged in such a manner that the service manager who uses this text on a day-to-day basis can easily find a topic of concern. Although the book cannot exhaustively cover the breadth and depth of service management, it takes a major step toward bringing the service manager or the student to a level of competence that will lead to better decisions about the direction and operation of the product service function.

Special thanks to Eve Brant, Raymond Solomon, and Sidney Solomon of The Solomon Press, who applied their skills almost around the clock to prepare our words for publication.

Susan O. Patton gets special recognition for her tolerance, understanding, and support when her husband wrote one more than "the last book."

–J.D.P.

–W.H.B.

Contents

8 SERVICE TRAINING   145

Computers, telecommunications, video conferencing and other modern techniques offer opportunity for improved learning. Service technicians must transition to new products without requiring classroom training, often just minutes before encountering a new product.

9 MAINTENANCE TECHNOLOGY   157

There are fundamental differences between logical diagnostics and shot-gunning problems. Like the five fingers on your hand, maintenance relationships can be classed as Improvement, Corrective, and three Preventive: on-condition, condition monitor, and scheduled.

10 INVENTORY MANAGEMENT   181

Parts have now passed labor as the most expensive item in product service. Fundamentals of inventory carrying and order costs are explained along with the *Top Ten Techniques for Managing Service Parts.*

11 PHYSICAL DISTRIBUTION 207

Parts control and costs are minimized with centralization. However, same-day response requires that expensive parts be stocked a few hours from critical sites. Balancing time and costs with channels of distribution are outlined as service management decisions.

12 CALL MANAGEMENT 239

Explains how management varies for support that falls into two distinctly different categories: rapid-reaction, time-driven support for critical repair needs, and cost-driven support for less critical equipment, installation, changes, and preventive maintenance.

13 CUSTOMER SATISFACTION 249

As inclusion in the subtitle emphasizes, pleasing customers and their varied desires is a key to retaining them as paying clients.

14 INFORMATION SYSTEMS 293

Computers are prevalent in service, both as product components and for data collection and analysis. Many readers will be like the shoemaker's children because they do not have adequate computer support to guide requirements and acquisition of new systems.

15 ECONOMICS, ACCOUNTING, AND FINANCE   313

Money is the common denominator by which nearly all service efforts can be measured and compared. Finance as applied to the service business is outlined because it is one of the weakest subjects for neophyte managers, and is critical to their success.

16 SERVICE MARKETING   335

Only recently is service marketing developing separately from selling products. The significant differences and need to interest top management are emphasized along with distinction between simple price competitiveness and value-added for better margins.

17 SERVICE QUALITY   363

Recognition of service quality by the national Baldrige Award, ISO certifications, and state quality competitions provide service organizations an opportunity to stand out from competitors. Benefits as well as costs are enumerated to provide high quality service.

1

Introduction

*M*ore than 70% of the American gross national product and eight out of ten jobs now come from the performance of service rather than the production of products. Business managers in our global economy confront many barriers. Walls between nations are crumbling, but they still establish boundaries between national markets, local practices, or social, economic, and political systems. Barriers between companies and the society in which they exist often draw sharp distinctions between corporate interests and social interests. Conflicts threaten to separate those activities that involve earning a living from those that constitute just plain living. And finally, the company often fails to communicate clearly with its employees, shareholders, venture partners, suppliers, and customers.

Global markets, instant communications, travel at the speed

of sound, political realignments, changing demographics, technological transformations in both products and production, corporate alliances, and flatted organizations are changing the structure of service organizations.

It is startling to note that we have gained as much knowledge in the last 50 years as from the time of Julius Caesar to the end of World War II. A child entering college ten years from now is projected to have only two percent of his or her knowledge based on information prior to this time. How can organizations cope, make sense of, and manage such dynamic and challenging times?

Experts who look ahead at the 21st century predict that pacesetting corporations will compete successfully in several key ways. Leading organizations will: 1) anticipate market changes and respond to customers' needs, 2) focus on areas of distinctive competence and provide value-added services, 3) use quality guidelines and benchmarks as standards for operations, 4) emphasize speed and simplicity, and 5) innovate and experiment.

Research confirms repeatedly that organizations that deliver high-quality service increase or maintain market share and have a higher return on sales than do their competitors. Further, companies that excel in delivering perceived quality can charge about nine percent more for those services, and they tend to grow twice as fast as the competitors. Clearly, service quality is critical for success.

Most of us can cite daily occurrences and dozens of experiences of mediocre or poor service in this country. Why is service so bad when we know it's so important? Ron Zemke, president of Performance Research Associates and author of several books and numerous articles on the subject, suggests, "The emerging answer seems to be that we try to manage, produce, and deliver services the same way that we manage, produce, and deliver products."

Product service is the process as much as the results. Service has to occur in real time. Time passed by while waiting for assistance can never be reclaimed. If contracted times are exceeded then extraordinary efforts are usually required to placate the customer. This requires a different approach to management. One element that highlights that difference is measurement. In manufacturing, product specifications are the source of the measurement. High quality is a three-step process: 1) determine what the customer wants, 2) develop written specifications, and 3) measure your finished products against the specifications. If the specifications are completely met than you have perfect quality. In service delivery, the specifications are in the heads of individual customers. Service providers must adjust their delivery to satisfy every customer.

In his book, *Selling the Invisible*, Harry Beckwith sets out three stages for the possible service. In stage one, the driving force is *meeting minimum acceptable standards*. Stage two is market-driven in which *answering customer needs* becomes paramount. Then in the rarely achieved stage three superior service companies surprise the customer with imagination-driven possible service that customers love.

Two basic concepts form the basis of product service. First, a customer buys a product to gain capability and productivity far beyond the collection of parts. The purpose of product service is to assist the customer to optimize continuous product performance. Second, from a marketing perspective, product service has become obligatory to ensure that the product delivers the promised level of performance. Many products bear an additional responsibility to perform in a system of which it is a part.

One of the fundamental differences between product and service management involves the issue of outcomes. Most manufacturing organizations strive to decrease product cost, achieve shipment schedules, and increase product quality ("zero defects"). Service companies tend to measure success by achieving high First Call Fix Rate, responding to problems within specified time limits, and providing high operational availability. Good performance on these measures is expected to improve customer retention with related revenue and profits. Service organizations find that those expectations are not always met. The relationships are much more complicated. There are many ways by which product and service companies achieve success and profitability. The ways that they measure quality, manage customers, and select employees reflect some critical differences. The term "service heart" summarizes a major personality trait that separates service people from the population is general. To illustrate, a manager interviewing a potential service person will purposefully drop a handkerchief in view of the candidate. Many people will walk on by and say nothing. Some people will say, "You dropped something." Others will pick up the dropped handkerchief and hand it back to the manager. Which person do you think has the best attitude toward helping other people and will be the best service person?

To manage service effectively, one needs to understand some of the distinguishing characteristics, which are in Table 1-1.

The formulation of an effective product service policy must take into account a number of important issues: 1) technical complexity of the product; 2) degree of product uniqueness or

TABLE 1-1
Product versus service characteristics.

Product	Service
Customer owns tangible hardware	Customer experiences intangible memory
Product production drives uniformity	Service promotes uniqueness to help customer feel special
Product can be stored & retrieved	Service is created as needed and time is lost if not used
Customer is the user & is not involved in the production process	Customer is partner in interactive exchange
Quality is determined by measurement against specification	Customer evaluates quality by comparison with experience
Product can be recalled if improperly produced	If service is improperly performed, apologies and credits are the only recourse
High automation to assemble components from around the world.	Morale of Service associates is critical.

innovation; 3) conditions of use; 4) possible economic loss to the customer from product defects that cause failure; and 5) possible sources of customer dissatisfaction. For example, the product may be so inexpensive that no corrective action would be warranted. Conversely, the product may represent such a large financial investment that extensive service provisions may be required to preclude hardship or economic loss to the customer. Complex or distinctive products may require greater emphasis on service than on standardized parts. Commercial products generally require more service than consumer products.

A commitment to strategic service involves much more than using service as a marketing tool to enhance customer satisfaction. Service should stimulate product sales efforts and contribute to profits. Organizations need a totally integrated approach to use service as an effective barrier to increasing competitive threats from manufacturers, third-party organizations, and in-house operations. A commitment to strategic service management provides a framework for both the inculcation of a corporate service culture and the creation of a strategic servicing organization.

In his article, "Strategic Service Management," Rick Roscit describes the concept of strategic service management as "creating a customer service culture that permeates throughout the corporation and whose service and marketing parameters are much more pervasive than a combination of actively selling service contracts and developing a proactive service policy. Providing servicing to the customer base takes into account a wide variety of activities as compared to product sales; well beyond transitional installation and maintenance." As business shifts from marketing equipment and supplies to the marketing of service, requirements for service become a major factor in product development strategies. While focusing on service is not a panacea, it can provide a vital tool to achieve customer satisfaction and retention. Service offerings have become an important point of differentiation for customers and corporations, especially since increased value for service can result in profit margins significantly higher than from product sales.

In order for the strategic service management umbrella to support a corporate service culture, several elements must be considered:

I. *Traditional Role of Service.* Typically the traditional role of service has been to install and maintain equipment sold by the sales staff and takes one of several forms: A) preventive maintenance according to a predetermined schedule contained in a contract; B) contractual agreement for service as required; and C) no service contract; manufacturer performs and bills for service as requested. Historically, minimal effort was made to sell service contracts. Then service companies realized that service can provide high-margin profit. Now, service contracts are on a decline as equipment is generally more reliable and fault-tolerant, with less preventive maintenance, so customers no longer feel the need for agreements to do routine service. On the other hand, servicers and other critical equipment that can cause significant loss of productivity in case of failure are often supported by service level agreements (SLAs) that require two- or four-hour response and fast restoration time.

II. *Competitive Product and Service Factors.*

    A. Competition for service contracts has intensified between manufacturers as profit margins decline on equipment sales. As product technology equalizes, acquisition costs become a major factor in purchase decisions. Companies eager to gain market share lower prices, which erodes their already weak profit margins.

    B. In many instances in technology-intensive industries, product performance, reliability, and uptime have become critical. More and more customers must now consider the quality of service and support in addition to acquisition costs when selecting a vendor. As customers broaden their purchase decision criteria to include "cost of ownership" issues, service organizations that can provide superior quality and cost on post-sales service will prevail.

C. As the value of total system uptime increases, the necessity for simple, reliable, cost-effective solution increases proportionately. Many major manufacturers have earned substantial new revenue by responding with "account control" programs that include serving competitive products. This is known as multi-vendor servicing (MVS).

D. Third-party independent service companies continue to grow in number and scope. Coincident with this development, buyers and maintenance managers have initiated and expanded internal cost-reduction programs. Often small service organizations can provide more rapid service delivery and more local flexibility than larger providers.

E. Some companies have achieved significant cost reductions by performing most service functions themselves and outsourcing the complicated tasks. Manufacturers find these customers reluctant to purchase or renew full-service contracts on new equipment.

III. *Strategic Service Management.* Companies that "market" service contribute to and support the marketing efforts of the company. With strategic service management, servicing plays a central role in the organization. The corporate focus includes comprehensive customer servicing and support that integrate the product management, marketing, sales, design, material management, engineering, production, and service divisions into a synergistic team committed to building an ongoing relationship with the customer. The extent and nature of fully supporting the customer will depend upon the customer's servicing needs, sophistication, and competition. Pace-setting corporations manage and market their service capabilities with the same fervor once reserved for selling equipment. This approach requires a corporate philosophy, mission, and culture that embodies a superior service attitude in which, regardless of functional roles, customer service is a prime responsibility of every employee.

IV. *Service Policy Audit.* In order to establish a foundation on which to build a strategic service culture, a thorough audit of an organization's individual service policies within the overall structure will determine the extent of effort required to implement a more broad-based strategy. A company's service orientation could be classified into four categories: no formal policy, traditional/reactive, proactive, and strategic. Key issues in the audit process include:

   A. Mission. Upper management must direct and support the concept of strategic service focused on building ongoing, interactive service relationships with the customer.
   B. Image. The internal and external service image must be congruent; no discrepancies! What do employees and customers expect from the organization with respect to service?
   C. Customer Perception. Measure and understand thoroughly the customer's perceptions as compared with competition
   D. Financial Integrity. Ensure that service financial measurement and management systems are integrated and link corporate executive reports to field work performance reports. Profit center, contribution center, or cost center approaches will work effectively.
   E. Service Quality. Use ongoing quantitative research to ensure that the organization delivers quality service that focuses on customer's needs and expectations as compared to the competition.
   F. Competitive Intelligence. All divisions of the company that interact with the customer should contribute competitive information into a formalized intelligence-gathering process. This process provides the ammunition to anticipate market changes and customer needs, which translates into significant competitive advantage.
   G. Human Resources. Front-line service employees should receive careful screening with devices such as: 1) customer contact role-play simulations, 2) biographical inventories including previous customer

experiences, and 3) service orientation inventory to understand candidates values and beliefs relative to customer service. The "service heart" concept mentioned earlier is illustrative of this type of evaluation. Employees will work in service groups or teams, because servicing the customer involves implementing shared client relationships with all people who serve and interact with the customer.

H. Service Portfolio. A company should have the flexibility to customize their service offerings to accommodate the specific requirements of each customer. This includes traditional types of maintenance and service as well as responding to and anticipating customer needs and wishes discovered through the development and enhancement of the ongoing relationship.

I. Relationship Management. The audit should achieve a comprehensive understanding of two distinct areas: customer relationships and the internal relationships of the service team. This includes all people who share responsibility for servicing the customer.

J. Technology Utilization. Examine the potential for using technology to improve efficiency, quality, and costs such as system software, diagnostic software, computer-controlled monitoring systems, and communication equipment.

V. *Recommendations for Operation.* Consider the following tactical issues to develop a strategic servicing organization:

A. A Service Tour as Part of Management Development. Face-to-face contact with the customer is vital to understand the customer's perspective of service. Include field service and sales in order to develop managers who understand the total experience of customer contact, including initial sale, after-market service, maintenance, and relationship management.

B. Strategic Business Units. Service managers must identify target market segments in order to address spe-

cific customer needs, devise an effective operating
strategy, and design a service delivery system. Organize appropriate strategic business units to serve and
compete in each key market. Develop specific expertise within each target area to provide rapid delivery,
predictive capabilities, relevant customer databases,
company-wide service support, hotline support, delivery of unique products and services, flexibility, and
the ability to compete effectively. Establish measurements that hold each business unit accountable for
service results, customer satisfaction, and profit contribution.

C. One-Stop-Shopping. Customers want the convenience, productivity, and savings provided by dealing
with only one source for service and maintenance.

D. Market Service. Create an awareness of service
through customer education; make your customer a
business partner. To improve customer satisfaction,
improve the customer's perception. A marketing
effort involves informing customers of: 1) advertising
and public relations efforts that emphasize a corporate service image; 2) the best times to call customer
service; 3) how to get problems solved and/or questions answered; 4) how a product can work with
another supplier's; 5) customer service improvements, new products, and services; 6) product training; 7) reasons that problems exist; and 8) functions
of different areas of the company.

E. Product Differentiation. In some industries, actual
product differentiation has become negligible. When
customers perceive a product as essentially generic,
superior service can provide the added value that
increases customer retention and earns customer
loyalty.

F. Additional Business. In an organization committed to
the delivery of excellent service, each employee will:
1) seek new product and service opportunities, 2)

uncover additional and/or incremental customer needs, 3) anticipate customer needs and wishes, 4) have a mechanism in place to report these discoveries, and 5) have a support system that will welcome and respond to each suggestion.

G. Accountability. Each person within the organization should serve the customer or support someone who does. Each person should understand clearly the corporate mission, the commitment, and the measurement of their customer satisfaction performance.

H. Service Profitability. The successful company needs to provide exemplary customer service while combating competitive threats and containing costs. Success derives from simultaneous emphasis on customer value and service productivity, hence the need for financial integrity and accountability. Customer satisfaction includes the customer's perception of service quality in comparison to the competition. Customer satisfaction frequently converts to customer loyalty (customer retention) when the company has successfully resolved a problem for a customer. Service productivity is defined as the percentages of time service people spend engaged in "customer support" or "customer contact" as opposed to internal, administrative, or overhead activities. Thus, higher service productivity should result in increased profits. However, customer dissatisfaction occurs when the customer interaction does not meet or exceed expectations. Consequently, the service division must monitor vigilantly all factors that simultaneously contribute to service productivity and customer satisfaction. Technical service employees must never discount or ignore the customer satisfaction aspects of the transaction.

The challenge of achieving excellent customer loyalty with profitability requires an optimal blend of: 1) customer operations knowledge, 2) superior service field work, 3) increased customer contact, 4) service personnel training, 5) staff support, 6) engineering and technical backup, 7) hotline support, 8) prompt service deployment, and 9) a variety of substantive service offerings matched to a unique market segment.

So, why build a case for the unique aspects of service management? We can certainly make too much of the differences between product and services businesses because most organizations offer both; a bit of product and a lot of service. The quality of service counts for automobile manufacturers and consumers just as product-like specifications, such as filling prescriptions accurately, are critically important to quality healthcare providers. One of the most distinctive aspects of service management is the need to manage not only employees and processes, but customers as well. Service organizations must find ways to effectively manage their customer's perceptions of processes and outcomes. However, in service delivery, the "fix" sometimes lies in doing a better job of managing the customer, not in improving the core process or the performance of the people delivering the service. A case in point is *waiting time.* Disneyland works hard to minimize waiting time as well as to minimize the *perception* of waiting time by diverting customer attention from concentrating on the wait. Another example of waiting time complaints comes from the health care field. A recent study found that if the doctor or primary care provider made immediate, direct, and friendly contact with the patient, estimates of time spent waiting decreased by half. Customer education and information giving are frequently used customer management techniques.

Even though both manufacturers and service providers want every customer to come back and buy again (zero defections) and both crave faultless output (zero defects), when treated as either/or positions, they impose unnecessary constraints on the quality effort. Ron Zemke provides a succinct overview of the differences between product and service when he outlines his view of quality service (see Table 1-2).

Service satisfaction results from a dynamic, not static interaction. Service is intangible. It can't be created in advance of delivery, shelved, and inventoried. Quality control of service involves measuring perceptions and processes rather than hard goods. The customer's expectations, not the producer's intentions, determine the customer's level of satisfaction. Peter Drucker, dean of American management theorists, reminds organizations that the purpose of a business is to attract and retain customers. Focusing on service quality, according to recent research, is a highly effective customer retention strategy. Committing all levels of the organization to delivering superior

TABLE 1-2
Differences between products and services.

Zero Defects is About...	Zero Defections is About...
Technical quality	Customer quality
Precise standards and performance	Transactions that delight the customer
Treating errors as mortal sins	Treating errors as opportunities to excel
Minimizing the human element	Capitalizing on the human element
Creating standards and protocols for every aspect of a transaction	Standards for technical quality, empowerment and recovery strategies for customer quality
No surprises, standard operating procedures, rote, and drill	Speed, flexibility, and ability to respond reliably to unique demands
Production quality	Performance quality
Developing satisfactory and mutually beneficial relationships	Building lasting, creative customer partnerships
Customer satisfaction	Customer retention
Reworking every policy and procedure to perfection, creating an absolutely seamless performance	Experimenting, leapfrogging the competition, taking measured risks, and then learning from them

customer service produces bottom-line results.

Exemplary organizations let nothing deter them from responding efficiently and effectively to their customers' wants and needs. These companies have core products and services that customers want. They make it easy for prospects and customers to do business with them. They define standards of quality and customer service, measure results, and reward performance. Of equal importance, these organizations have made a commitment to hire the right people, train and develop them carefully, and support and reward them in their efforts to achieve the marketplace image and service quality results that are focused on by the organization. Superior service organizations regard their front-line and staff support personnel as valuable and reliable resources who are equal in importance to customers for quick and efficient determination of how the organization is performing in the marketplace. Employees are the internal customers who can discover what obstacles exist to maintaining and enhancing the reputation and results that the organization regards as important to long-term service success. Superior employees not only identify problems, they suggest solutions and take the initiative to retain a valued customer.

Questions

1. What are the fundamental differences between product and service management?

2. What are characteristics of pace-setting corporations in the 21st century?

3. Describe the essence of product service.

4. Describe the key elements of an effective product service policy.

5. What are the key elements of strategic service management?

6. What role does service play in the sales process?

7. Who is the most important person in the service system? Why?

8. Describe the concepts underlying a "zero defects" and "zero defections" view of quality service.

9. Describe the characteristics of exemplary service organizations.

10. Describe the elements necessary to achieve a balance between superior customer service and profitability.

2

Terms
and Definitions

*T*his chapter on terms and their definitions establishes the meanings of words commonly used within the profession of product service management. The delineation of this vocabulary also helps to describe and bound the broad area of service management for durable products, and provides a basis for discussion and further detailing.

The vocabulary of service has its roots in many other activities—economics, finance, statistics, operations research, engineering, manufacturing, marketing, software—all have contributed words and meanings. Government and the military have also contributed terms, because they as a group comprise the largest service-oriented organization in the world.

Certain words or terms may have several meanings. This glossary contains those definitions commonly accepted by the product service profession. Terms and definitions are rapidly changing, the better to suit the communication needs of an emerging profession. There are over 30 new terms and many more changes in the two years since this list was last published.

Glossary

Access—To gain entry in order to contact part of a system.

Acquisition Costs—Financial and other investments made to obtain a new product or idea.

Administration—The conduct, direction, or internal management of an organization.

Advance Exchange—Method of quickly obtaining a good part, whereby the supplier immediately provides a good part and the technician returns the defective core part as soon as it is replaced with the good part.

Alignment—The placing of a variable setting to a condition within tolerance.

Allocation—Assignment or distribution for a specific purpose or to particular persons or things.

Analog—Representation for the real item or also signals which vary in amplitude directly as the strength of the input. For example, AM radio waves and a clock with hands to show hours and minutes. Opposed to digital where the signals are either 0 (off) or 1 (on). A digital instrument would show the specific readout numbers.

Authorized Stock List (ASL)—Parts that a stock location should have good on hand.

Availability—The probability that a system or equipment will, when used under specified conditions, operate satisfactorily and effectively. Also, the percentage of time or number of occurrences for which a product will operate properly when called upon. Inherent Availability (Ai) is "pure, as designed," and considers only corrective maintenance time. Achieved Availability (Aa) includes preventive maintenance time, but with an ideal support environment. Operational Availability (Ao) considers total down time, which includes administrative and supply times.

Backorder—An order for items not now available that will be shipped when possible.

Bar Code—A series of vertical bars and spaces that can be scanned to machine-read the letters and numbers designated by the code. Bar codes are used to identify equipment, parts, and other items, and produce a much lower error rate and faster read that does key entry by humans.

Beeper—Wireless receiver (and sometimes also transmitter) often worn on a technician's belt so a message and phone number can be quickly transmitted to the technician. The device often "beeps" a sound, which gives the pager its common name.

Break-Even—Financial point of a product or project at which the revenue in equals the fixed costs plus variable costs out.

Built-In Test Equipment (BITE)—Diagnostic and checkout devices integrated into equipment design to assist operation and service.

Calibrate—To verify the accuracy of equipment and assure performance within tolerance, usually by comparison to a reference standard that can be traced to a primary standard.

Call Management—Total process of handling a customer's request for assistance from start to satisfactory completion.

Calls Per Year—Activity measure, which may be expressed in other units of time, such as Calls Per Day, or in operating units, such as Calls Per Million Copies. This activity usually cascades from the customer to the call management center to the help desk to technician dispatch and other resources necessary to satisfy the customer.

Capital–Durable items with life or value that allows them to be used a long time. An accounting classification, contrasted to expense.

Carrying Costs–Expense of keeping an item in stock including space, handling equipment, environmental controls, data systems, people, insurance, taxes, and the cost of money. Typically about 30% per year of the unit cost. Also termed *Holding Costs.*

Cellular Phone–Commonly called a "cell phone." A hand-carried communications wireless telephone means of communicating voice and data messages where a wired phone is not available.

Change Impact Analysis–The logic and reasoning process used to predict the outcome of a change in quantifiable terms before the change is attempted.

Channels of Distribution–The transactions and processes through which goods and services flow from producer to consumer.

Checkout–Determination of the working condition of a system.

Component–A constituent part.

Concept–Basic idea or generalization. The concept phase is often the first phase in program planning. See also *Maintenance Concept.*

Configuration–Arrangement and contour of the physical and functional characteristics of systems, equipment, and related items of hardware or software; the shape of a thing at a given time. The specific parts used to construct a machine.

Consumables–Materials used up during a product's operation, as are gasoline and oil in a car. The cost of consumables is normally expensed.

Contractor–Any individual or organization having a formal agreement with a procuring agency to furnish things or services at a specified price or rate.

Corrective Maintenance—Unscheduled maintenance or repair actions performed as a result of failures or deficiencies, to restore items to a specified condition. See also *Unscheduled Maintenance* and *Repair.*

Cost-Effectiveness—A measure of system effectiveness versus lifecycle cost.

Courier—Delivery service, often connected to a warehouse for parts and equipment, which can rapidly deliver the ordered items to the point of need.

Critical—Describes items especially important to product performance and more vital to operation than noncritical items.

Critical Path Method (CPM)—A logical method of planning and control that analyzes the events, the times required, and the interactions of the process considered.

Customer—Person or organization who purchases a service or commodity, usually frequently and systematically.

Customer Relationship Management (CRM) or *Customer Management System (CMS)*—Computer software and supporting processes that enable a company to receive calls from customers and quickly see and use information about the customer and equipment to facilitate meeting the customer's total needs.

Dead on Arrival (DOA)—Term applied to parts that are unusable for any reason including manufacturing defects, shipping damage, wrong configuration ordered, and wrong part shipped.

Depreciation—Financial recovery of investment that allows a company to expense a portion of a durable item's cost each period. For example, an $1,800 personal computer used for business might be depreciated over 18 months at $100 per month.

Diagnostics—Tests using software, logic, measurement tools, and sometimes parts, to determine the source of a problem so that corrective action may be applied.

Digital—Signals that are either 0 (off) or 1 (on), which enable modern communications and computer logic to operate at high speeds and accuracy.

Direct Costs—Any expenses associated with specific products, operations, or services.

Disposal—The act of getting rid of excess or surplus property under proper authorization. Disposal may be accomplished by such processes as transfer, donation, sale, abandonment, destruction, or recycling.

Distribution—Dispensing of materials, supplies, equipment, products, or services according to need, requisition, orders, or plans, including the authorized delivery of such things.

Down Time—That portion of calendar time during which an item or equipment is not in condition to fully perform its intended function.

Economic Order Quantity (EOQ)—The amount of an item that should be acquired at one time to get the lowest combination of inventory carrying cost and order/production cost.

Economic Repair—A repair that will restore the product to sound condition at a cost less than the value of its estimated remaining useful life.

End Article or *End Item*—An entity of hardware capable of performing an operational function, which is not intended to be installed in or as part of another piece of equipment. Examples of end items are an automobile, an electric drill, a hammer, and a television set.

End User—The individual or organization that employs an article or system to accomplish the purpose for which it was designed and intended.

Engineering—The profession in which knowledge of the mathematical and natural sciences is applied with judgment to develop ways to utilize economically the materials and forces of nature.

Environment—The aggregate of all conditions influencing a product or service, including physical location, operating characteristics of surrounding or nearby equipment, actions of people, conditions of temperature, humidity, salt spray, acceleration, shock, vibration, radiation, and contaminants in the surrounding area.

Equipment—All items of a durable nature capable of continuing or repetitive utilization by an individual or organization.

Essentiality—Importance of an item to mission performance.

Expense—Cost incurred for items that are directly charged as a cost of doing business since they are used over a specific period of time.

Exponential Distribution—Statistical distribution of logarithmic form that often describes the pattern of events over time.

Facilities—Physical plants such as real estate and the improvements thereto including buildings and associated equipment.

Failure—Inability to perform the basic function or to perform it within specified limits. Malfunction.

Failure Analysis—The logical, systematic examination of an item or its design, to identify and analyze the probability, causes, and consequences of real or potential malfunction.

Failure Modes, Effects and Criticality Analysis (FMECA)—Failure analysis of what items are expected to fail and the resulting consequences of failure.

Failure Rate—The number of failures per unit measure of life (cycles, time, miles, events, etc.) as applicable for the item.

Feedback—The utilization of part of the output of one phase of an activity as input to another phase, to influence the final or eventual output.

First In-First Out (FIFO)—The practice of choosing the oldest item in inventory for each next use. Contrasts with *Last In-First Out (LIFO)*.

First in-Still Here (FISH)—Not an accounting category, but rather the undesirable items that cost money but have never been used. They are probably excess and should be discarded.

First Call Fix Rate (FCFR)—Percentage of service calls completed on the first visit. The opposite of broken calls.

First Pass Fill Rate (FPFR)—Percentage of parts available and issued on the initial attempt to meet requests.

Fixed Costs—Expenses such as office facilities and training that do not vary directly with activity rates.

Forecast—To calculate or predict some future event or condition, usually as a result of rational study and analysis of pertinent data.

Fractionation of Inventory—A supply management process whereby stocked items are classified as to relative rate of issue, cost, or other significant factors.

Function—A separate and distinct action required to achieve a given objective, to be accomplished by the use of hardware, computer programs, personnel, facilities, procedural data, or a combination thereof; or an operation a system must perform to fulfill its mission or reach its objective.

Functional Levels—Rankings of the physical hierarchy of a product. Typical levels of significance from smallest to largest are part, subassembly, assembly, subsystem, and system.

Gantt Chart—Display of events and their times, used for planning and control.

General and Administrative (G&A)—A category of expense, usually added as a percentage of direct labor and material costs, to cover support and management costs.

General Support Equipment (GSE)—Equipment that has maintenance application to more than a single model or type of equipment. See *Support Equipment.*

Gross Weight–The combined weight of a container and its contents, or of a vehicle including fuel, lubricant, coolant, on-vehicle material, payload, and operating personnel.

Hardware–A physical object or physical objects, as distinguished from capability or function. A generic term dealing with physical items of equipment–tools, instruments, components, parts–as opposed to funds, personnel, services, programs, and plans, which are termed "software."

Human Engineering–The application of knowledge about human capabilities and limitations to the planning, design, development, and testing of systems, equipment, and facilities to obtain the best mix of safety, comfort, and effectiveness compatible with established requirements.

Human Factors–All scientific biomedical and sociological facts and considerations that constitute characteristics of mankind. These include principles and applications in the areas of human engineering, personnel selection, training, life support, job performance aids, and human performance evaluation.

Identification–Means by which items are named or numbered to indicate that they have a given set of characteristics. Identification may be in terms of name, part number, type, model, specification number, drawing number, code, stock number, or catalog number. Items may also be identified as part of an assembly, a piece of equipment, or a system.

Independent Service Organization (ISO)–Service company not involved with creating or marketing the items it supports. Synonymous to *Third Party Maintainer (TPM)*.

Indirect Costs–Expenses not directly associated with specific products, operations, or services, usually considered as overhead.

Industrial Engineering–A composite of activities responsible for the design and development of a production or a support capability.

Installation—A fixed or relatively fixed facility location together with its real estate, buildings, structures, utilities, equipment, etc. Also, that period of initial setup, adjustment, and checkout of a product in the customer's environment.

Insurance Items—Stocked articles or material that may be required occasionally but are not subject to periodic replacement or wearout, for which prudence requires some stock on hand at certain central points, because of the essentiality or time involved in their procurement.

Integrated Logistics Support (ILS)—A composite of the elements necessary to assure the effective and economical sustaining of a system or equipment, at all levels of maintenance, throughout its programmed life cycle. It is characterized by the harmony and coherence obtained between each of its elements and levels of maintenance.

Integrated Logistics Support Planning—Planning that during acquisition requires management of the following selected activities or elements: maintainability and reliability, maintenance planning, support and test equipment, supply support, transportation and handling, technical data, facilities, personnel and training, funding, and management data.

Interface—A common boundary between two or more items, characteristics, systems, functions, activities, departments, or objectives. That portion of anything that impinges upon or directly affects something else.

Intermittent—Failure that occurs sporadically, which makes it difficult to diagnose until the defective condition is observed.

Isolation—Separation of the good from the bad in order to repair the bad.

Inventory—All items on hand by physical count, weight, volume, money value, or other measurement.

Inventory Control—That phase or function of logistics that includes management, cataloging, requirements determination, procurement, distribution, overhaul, and disposal of material.

Inventory Management—The management activity that plans and controls the input, availability, and disposal of items within the total owned by any organization. Similar to, but slightly broader than *Inventory Control* in that management should include forecasting and planning.

Item—A generic term used to identify a specific entity under consideration. Items may be parts, components, assemblies, subassemblies, accessories, groups, equipment, or attachments.

Item of Supply—An article or material that is recurrently purchased, stocked, distributed, and used and is identified by one distinctive set of numbers or letters throughout the organization concerned. It consists of any number of pieces or objects that can be treated as a unit.

Just in Case (JIC)—Stocking of service parts against the probability that they will be needed, but where the time of need can not be determined in advance.

Just in Time (JIT)—Delivery of items when they are needed, rather than before, in order to reduce carrying costs.

Labor—Work done by people.

Labor Costs—Expenses for labor including wages, taxes, benefits, and overhead.

Last In-First Out (LIFO)—Use newest inventory next. Contrasts with *First In-First Out (FIFO)*.

Lead Time—The allowance made for that amount of time required to accomplish a specific objective.

Less Than Truck Load (LTL) and *Less Than Carload (LCL)*—Transportation category rated as higher cost than for full truckload (TL). The absolute weight or volume varies by commodity.

Level of Supply—Quantity of an item authorized or directed to be kept on hand at a storage or distribution point to meet predictable and anticipated future demands.

Life Cycle—The series of phases or events that constitute the total existence of anything. The entire "womb-to-tomb" scenario of a product from the time concept planning is started until it is finally discarded.

Life-Cycle Cost—All costs associated with the system life cycle including research and development, production, operation, support, and termination.

Life-Cycle Profits—A concept that expands on *Life-Cycle Costs* by including the benefits received from the system under consideration, all evaluated in monetary terms.

Logistics—The art and science of management, engineering, and technical activities concerned with requirements, design, and planning and maintaining resources to support objectives, plans, and operations.

Logistics Engineering—The professional art of applying science to the optimum planning, handling, and implementation of personnel, materials, and facilities, including life-cycle designs, procurement, production, maintenance, and supply.

Logistics Management—The process by which human efforts are systematically coordinated to create economic and effective support throughout the planned life cycle of equipment and operations.

Long-Range Planning—The process of making decisions expected to affect an organization, usually beyond one year. The period of long-range plans is often set at three, five, or ten years. Contrast with short-range planning, which normally includes from the present to one year in the future.

Lower of Cost or Market—Conservative accounting valuation, which uses the lower of what was paid for an item or what it could be sold for now.

Maintainability (M)—The inherent characteristic of a design or installation that determines the ease, economy, safety, and accuracy with which maintenance actions can be performed, Also, the ability to restore a product to service or to perform preventive maintenance within required limits.

Maintainability Engineering—The application of applied scientific knowledge and methods and management skills to the development of equipment, systems, projects, or operation with the inherent ability to be effectively and efficiently maintained.

Maintenance—The function of keeping items or equipment in serviceable condition or restoring them to serviceable condition. It includes servicing, testing, inspection, adjustment/ alignment, removal replacement, reinstallation, troubleshooting, calibration condition determination, repair, modification, overhaul, or building, and reclamation. Maintenance includes both corrective and preventive activities.

Maintenance Concept—Statements and illustrations that define the theoretical means of maintaining equipment. It relates to tasks, techniques, tools, and people.

Maintenance Engineering—Developing concepts, criteria, and technical requirements for maintenance during the conceptual acquisition phases of a project. Providing policy guidance for maintenance activities and exercising technical and management direction and review of maintenance programs.

Management—The effective, efficient, economical leadership of people, and use of money, materials, time, and space to achieve predetermined objectives. It is a process of establishing and attaining objectives and carrying out responsibilities that include planning, organizing, directing, staging, controlling, and evaluating.

Material—All items used or needed in any business, industry, or operation, as distinguished from personnel.

Mean, Arithmetic–An average of a series of quantities or values; specifically, their sum divided by the number of items in the series. Sometimes simply called "mean."

Median–An average of a series of quantities of values; specifically, the quantity or value of that item so positioned in the series, when arranged in order of numerical quantity or value, that there are an equal number of greater magnitude and lesser magnitude.

Methods Engineering–The aspect of analyzing operations in terms of effectiveness and cost. Includes setting methods, time and cost standards, analysis of operations, skill requirements, and changes for improvement.

Mean Down Time (MDT)–Average time a system cannot perform its mission; including response time, active maintenance, supply time, and administrative time.

Mean Time Between Failure (MTBF)–The average time/distance/events a product delivers between breakdowns.

Mean Time Between Maintenance (MTBM)–The average time between both corrective and preventive actions.

Mean Time to Repair (MTTR)–The average time it takes to fix a failed item.

Model–Simulation of an event or process or product physically, verbally, or mathematically.

Modification–Change in configuration.

Modularization–Separation of components of a product or equipment into physically and functionally distinct entities to facilitate identification, removal, and replacement utilization.

Moving Average–A method of considering recent events. For example, averaging the last three months shipments, or the average item cost of the last ten items added to inventory.

Normal–Statistical distribution commonly described as a "bell curve." Mean, mode, and median are the same in the normal distribution.

No Trouble Found (NTF) or *No Problem Found (NPF)*—Situations in which the difficulty reported by a customer or technician can not be verified. *NTF* is a major challenge when returned parts pass all screening tests and repair personnel can not completely determine if the parts contain intermittent problems or if they are really good parts. Also called *Could Not Determine (CND)*.

Operations Research (OR)—Use of modern scientific techniques to solve complex problems arising in the direction and management of large systems of people, machines, common materials, and money. Its distinctive approach is to develop a scientific model of the system involved, incorporating measurement factors such as chance and risk, with which to predict and prepare the outcomes of alternative decisions, strategies, or controls, to help management determine its policy and actions scientifically.

Operations Research Techniques—Techniques that include but are not limited to mathematical programming, inventory model, simulation, queuing model, and critical path analysis.

Operating Costs—Expenses of using an item. Not incurred when the item is acquired but not used.

Operating and Support (O&S) Costs—The costs for all user activities after acquisition.

Order Costs—Expenses associated with a material order to identify the item, obtain quotes, select the best supplier, place the purchase order, receive the material, pay the invoice, and complete the transaction.

Original Equipment Manufacturer (OEM)—Company that produced the basic components or even the entire system that another company labels as its own. There may be several levels of *OEM*s in modern products where many product companies are assembly plants or outsource production, rather that being vertically integrated to make all components.

Outsource—Arranging for another company to provide goods and services that are not part of the partner company's core competency. For example, outsourcing organizations often provide computing power, payroll, telephone communications, and warehousing.

Overhead—Costs that are not directly traceable to products, operations, or services. Indirect.

Packaging—The use of protective wrappings, cushioning, inside containers, and complete identification marking, up to but not including the exterior shipping container.

Packing—The application or use of exterior shipping containers or any other shipping medium, such as pallets, and assembling of items or packages thereof, together with necessary blocking, bracing, cushioning, weatherproofing, exterior strapping, and marking the shipment.

Pallets—Low, portable platforms of wood, metal, or other material used to facilitate handling, storage, and transportation of individual items or groups of items.

Parameter—A common factor or characteristic element.

Part—Functional component of a product that is usually handled as a line item or stock-keeping unit, with a unique part number. Parts are combined to make up sub-assemblies, assemblies, and whole units of equipment.

Personnel—Employees. Also, the name of the organization concerned with people.

PERT—Acronym formed from the initials *Program Evaluation Review Technique*, a planning method based on a product-oriented work breakdown structure and time-dependency network.

Physical Distribution—Term describing the wide range of activities concerned with the movement of raw materials from the source of supply to the beginning of the production line and the movement of finished products from the end of the production line to the consumer. Activities included are freight, transportation, materials handling, market forecasting, packaging, protection, warehousing, and customer service.

Pipeline—Channel of support by means of which material or personnel flow from sources of procurement to their point of use.

Preventive Maintenance—Actions performed in an attempt to keep an item in a specified operating condition by means of systematic inspection, detection, and prevention of incipient failure.

Procurement—The process of obtaining personnel, services, supplies, materials, and equipment or facilities. Procurement may consist of borrowing, consignment, loan, advance exchange, demanufacture, and other methods beyond direct purchase.

Production—A term used to designate manufacturing or fabrication in organized enterprise.

Project/Program Management—A concept for the business and technical management of specified projects or programs based on a designated, centralized management authority, or Project/Program Manager who is responsible for planning, directing, and controlling the definition, research, development, acquisition, and support necessary to provide a balanced project or program that will effectively accomplish the objectives.

Provisioning—The process of determining and selecting the varieties and quantities of repair parts, spares, special tools, tests, and support equipment that should be procured and stocked to sustain equipment and systems for specified periods of time.

Queuing—Pattern of demand placed on any activity. If many activities are ahead in a queue, a wait for service usually occurs.

Random—Any change whose occurrence is not predictable with respect to time or events.

Reaction Time or *Response Time*—The time required between the receipt of an order or impulse triggering some action and the initiation of the action.

Rebuild Recondition—Total tear down and reassembly of a product, usually to the latest configuration.

Redundancy—Two or more parts, components, or systems joined functionally so that if one fails, some or all of the remaining components are capable of continuing with the function accomplishment. Fail-safe, backup.

Refurbish—Clean and replace worn parts on a selective basis to make product usable to a customer. Less involved than rebuild.

Reliability (R)—The probability that an item will perform its intended function without failure for a specified time period under specified conditions.

Reorder Point (ROP)—Quantity of product that triggers a replacement order when usage decreases the good quantity to that point. Calculated as the number of parts that will be used during the procurement lead-time, plus safety stock.

Repair—The restoration or replacement of components of facilities or equipment as necessitated by wear, tear, damage, or failure. To return the facility or equipment to efficient operating condition.

Repair Parts—Individual parts or assemblies required for the maintenance or repair of equipment, systems, or spares. Such repair parts may be repairable or nonrepairable assemblies or one-piece items. Consumable supplies used in maintenance, such as wiping rags, solvent, and lubricants, are not considered repair parts.

Repairable Item—Durable item determined, by application of engineering, economic, and other factors, to be restorable to serviceable condition through regular repair procedures.

Replacement Item—Hardware that is functionally interchangeable with another item but that differs physically from the original part to the extent that installation of the replacement requires such operations as drilling, reaming, cutting, filing, or shimming in addition to normal attachment or installation operations.

Resources—Manpower, funds, materials, equipment, tools, space, and time available for or required to accomplish specific objectives.

Retrofits—Modifications to a machine to correct a deficiency or modernize it or improve performance.

Return on Investment (ROI)—Financial evaluation that measures the reward expected if an investment is made at a specified time.

Safety—Elimination of hazardous conditions that could cause injury. Protection against failure, breakage, and accident.

Safety Stock—The quantity of an item, in addition to the normal level of supply, required to be on hand to permit continuing operation with a specific level of confidence if resupply is interrupted or demand varies in an unpredictable manner.

Salvage—The saving or reuse of condemned, discarded, or abandoned property, and of materials contained therein for reuse or scrapping. As a noun, it refers to property that has some value in excess of its basic material content but is in such condition that it has no reasonable prospect of original use, and its repair or rehabilitation is clearly not practical.

Scheduled Maintenance—Preplanned actions performed to keep an item in a specified operating condition by means of systematic inspection, detection, and prevention of incipient failure. Sometimes called *Preventive Maintenance.*

Scrap—Property or items, discarded as far as original use is concerned, which have no reasonable prospect of value except for the recovery value of basic material content.

Serial Number—Number or letters that uniquely identify an item.

Service—Helpful acts. Useful labor that does not produce a tangible commodity. The repair and maintenance and support of equipment and operation.

Service Contract—Contract calling directly for a contractor's time and effort rather than for a specific end product.

Serviceability—Characteristic of an item, equipment, or system that makes it easy to maintain after it is put into operation. Similar to *Maintainability.*

Service Technician—Person who installs and maintains equipment. Also called Customer Engineer, Field Service Representative, Technical Representative, or Service Engineer.

Shelf Life—The period of time during which an item can remain unused in proper storage without significant deterioration.

Shipment—An item or group of items from one place, released to a carrier for transportation to a single destination.

Software—Efforts, plans, or paperwork to sustain or support projects, operations, equipment, assemblies, or items including such things as engineering and design, technical data, plans, schedules, and computer programs. Software excludes physical parts, materials, equipment, and tools. Contrasts to *Hardware.*

Spares—Common term for parts and equipment that are completely interchangeable with like items and can be used to replace items removed during maintenance. The word "spare" carries the connotation of being excess, so "service part" is preferred.

Specifications—Documents that clearly and accurately describe the essential technical requirements for materials, items, equipment, systems, or services; including the procedures by which it will be determined that the requirements have been met. Such documents may include performance, support, preservation, packaging, packing, and marking requirements.

Standards—Established or accepted rules, models, or criteria by which the degree of user satisfaction of a product or an act is determined, or against which comparisons are made.

Standard Deviation—A measure of average dispersion (departure from the mean) of numbers, computed as the square root of the average of the squares of the differences between the numbers and their arithmetic means.

Standard Item—An item described accurately for common use by a standard document or drawing.

Standardization—The process of establishing greatest practical uniformity of items and of practices, to insure the minimum feasible variety of such items and practices and to effect optimum interchangeability.

Statistics—The collecting, classifying, summarizing, and interpreting of numerical facts by other than accounting methods.

Stock—The supply of physical items kept on hand at storage points in a supply system to meet anticipated demand.

Stock Control—The process of maintaining inventory data on the quantity, location, and condition of items; to determine quantities available, required, or both, and to facilitate distribution and management of stock.

Stock Due In—The quantity of items expected to be received under outstanding procuring and requisitioning documents, and the quantity expected from other sources such as transfer, reclamation, and recovery.

Stock Due Out—The quantity of items requisitioned by ordering or using activities that is not immediately available for issue, but which is reported as a commitment for future issue. Backorder.

Stock-Keeping Unit (SKU)—A uniquely part-numbered line item that differs in form, fit, or function from other parts or equipment.

Stock Number—Number assigned by the stocking organization to each group of articles or material treated as if identical within the using supply system.

Subcontractor—Any supplier, distributor, vendor, or firm that enters into a formal contract to furnish items, services, parts, or supplies to a prime contractor.

Sunk Costs—Past costs, already incurred, which are therefore irrelevant to consideration of alternative courses of action.

Supervision—The guidance, leadership, and control of the efforts of a group of individuals towards some common goal.

Supply—The procurement, maintenance in storage, distribution, and salvage of items that are consumed in use or become part of other items, thus losing their identity.

Supply Support—All the spare parts, repair parts, consumables, and related materials and documents necessary for scheduled and unscheduled maintenance; taking into consideration location, transportation, time, and overall availability to insure maximum continuity and effectiveness of operations.

Supply System—The organizations, offices, facilities, methods, techniques, and trained personnel utilized to provide supplies and equipment to users or consumers and to take care of requirements, computations, planning, procurement, inventory control, distribution, maintenance in storage, issue, and salvage or disposal of items and materials.

Support—Action to sustain or complement anything to keep it effective by furnishing it with whatever it needs.

Support Equipment—Items required to maintain systems in effective operating condition under various environments. Support equipment includes general and special-purpose vehicles, power units, stands, test equipment, tools, or test benches needed to facilitate or sustain maintenance action, to detect or diagnose malfunctions, or to monitor the operational status of equipment and systems.

System—Assemblage of correlated hardware, software, facts, principles, doctrines, ideas, methods, procedures, and people, or any combination of these, all arranged or ordered toward a common objective.

System Effectiveness—The probability that a system can successfully meet an overall operational demand within a given time, when operated under specified conditions; the ability of a system to do the job for which it was intended; a measure of the degree to which a system can be expected to achieve its objectives or purpose.

Systems Engineering—The application of scientific and engineering methods to the study, planning, design, construction, direction, and evaluation of man-machine systems and system components.

Technical Data and Information—Includes but is not limited to production and engineering data, prints and drawings, documents such as standards, specifications, technical manuals, changes in modifications, inspection and testing procedures, and performance and failure data.

Test and Support Equipment—All special tools and checkout equipment, metrology and calibration equipment, maintenance stands, and handling equipment required for maintenance. Includes external and built-in test equipment (BITE) considered part of the supported system or equipment.

Third Party Maintainer (TPM)—Early term for an *Independent Service Organization*. Third party meant that the servicer was neither the first party owner nor the second party provider of the devices being supported.

Trade-Off—Action or decision generally concerned with the evaluation of alternatives and with compromises to obtain the best mix of support characteristics, system performance, and real cost.

Training—The pragmatic approach to supplementing education with particular knowledge and assistance in developing special skills. Helping people to learn to practice an art, science, trade, profession, or related activity. Basically more specialized than education and involves learning what to do rather than why.

Troubleshooting—Locating or isolating and identifying discrepancies or malfunctions of equipment and determining the corrective action required.

Turnaround Time—Interval between the time a repairable item is removed from use and the time it is again available in full serviceable condition.

Transportation and Handling Support—Special provisions, planning, reusable containers, and training necessary to help insure adequate packaging, preservation, storage, handling, and transportation of materials, parts, equipment, personnel, data, and facilities.

Unscheduled Maintenance (UM)—Emergency maintenance (EM) or *Corrective Maintenance (CM)* to restore a failed item to usable condition.

Value Engineering—An organized, applied scientific effort directed at analyzing the design, construction, procurement, inspection, installation, operation, and maintenance of an item to achieve the necessary performance, reliability, and maintainability at the lowest overall cost.

Variable Costs—Costs that change as a function of units of time or resources.

Vendor Items—Items or parts acquired by the equipment manufacturer or prime contractor without the acquisition of the design rights; where the prime contractor's source or the manufacturer of the item for that source has and retains proprietary rights with respect to design and processes.

Warehousing—Those operations and storage activities concerned with the receipt, storage, care, preservation, packaging, packing, marking, issue of items, and documentation and record keeping incidental to such operations.

Warranty—Guarantee that an item will perform as specified for at least a specified time.

Wireless—A communications device that operates using airwaves and does not require wires to pass the signals. Service wireless devices include pagers, cell phones, radio frequency (RF) modems, and radios to provide continuous mobile communications.

Zero Defects—Quality effort to eliminate all defects and provide items 100% good.

Zero Defections—Retaining of all contracts and customer business.

Questions

1. Should a customer be more concerned with inherent availability (Ai) or operational availability (Ao)?

2. What is the difference between capital and expense items?

3. What other names are given to corrective maintenance (CM)?

4. Give some examples of end items.

5. What is an OEM?

6. Give some examples of general support equipment (GSE) and of special test and support equipment.

7. How does hardware differ from software? Give some examples of each.

8. A product's life cycle includes all events from the first idea through final disposition. Why is this important to service management?

9. What is the difference between maintainability and maintenance?

10. Give examples of five different kinds of models.

3

Service Objectives, Responsibilities, and Measurement

*A*n astronaut has been quoted as saying, "One of my most sobering experiences was realizing that we were blasting off to the moon in a machine composed of thousands of parts, all made by the lowest bidder." Although, as he knew, NASA had paid a lot of money for the high reliability built into the spacecraft components, manned spacecraft have over 5.6 million parts. At even a 99.99% level of reliability, over 560 failures are expected on each mission. The success of the Challenger space shuttle programs has proved that reliability can be obtained with specific programs, formal efforts, and adequate funding. It also proved that failures could be fatal. There will always be failures to be corrected and many preventive maintenance efforts to be sustained. Service is a vital part of the space program.

We are all familiar with the luxuries and problems associated with the technology that has invaded our lives. The many labor-saving devices in our homes, the modern jet aircraft that whisk us to faraway places, the automobile that lets us create our own travel schedules, and the computer that controls production facilities—all perform dependably, but all need service. Maintaining the heat, light, clean air, food and shelter you take for granted requires service. Service may be the user changing a light bulb or a service technician modifying a huge computer installation. Virtually every item or machine will break down sometime. One of the axioms of modern life is, "Things seem to break down just when you need them most." It is certainly true that we recognize failures when we call on equipment to perform.

Objectives

Technical service has three major objectives:

◆   Satisfy customers
◆   Earn profits
◆   Care for company property

Service must strive to give the customer satisfactory performance that is commensurate with the price the customer pays, while maintaining expenses in line with company profit objectives. Some organizations will place profits above customer satisfaction. However, as anyone who has been in the service business very long will recognize, the sequence is generally customer satisfaction first, which will then lead to profits. Satisfied customers are vital if a company is to have any business from which to profit. Certainly, in government, military, or non-profit service organizations, the idea of profit implies minimizing expenses. Most service organizations strive to attain happy, delighted customers who are pleased beyond being satisfied.

Service can be used both to protect and to promote. Protective service ensures that equipment and all company assets are well maintained and give the best performance of which they are capable. Protective service goals for the technician may include the following:

- Install equipment properly.
- Teach the customer how to use the equipment capability effectively.
- Provide functions that the customer is unable to supply himself.
- Maintain quality on installed equipment.
- Gain experience on servicing needs.
- Investigate customer problems and rapidly solve them to the customer's satisfaction.
- Preserve the end value of the product and extend its useful life.
- Observe competitive activity.
- Gain technical feedback in order to correct problems.

Promotional service will increase sales by projecting a desirable image that gives the customer confidence in the product. Promotional service goals include the following:

* Meet decision-makers of the customers' organization.
* Increase the use of installed equipment.
* Expand the uses and needs in order to sell other products.
* Support demonstrations and trade shows.
* Meet the competition.
* Contribute positively to the company's reputation.
* Introduce new products and concepts to the customer.
* Keep the customer aware of the value of service.

Do you recall the Maytag washing machine ad that pictures a serviceman sitting glumly on his tool kit, complaining that no machines require his attention? That's a good ad, because it points out that the quality of the product almost eliminates the need for service. But, the message continues, if a genuine need occurs, it can be met by the ready serviceman.

We normally use the term "service technician" to include both men and women. Although some abilities, such as lifting heavy weights, are predominantly ascribed to men; and others, such as manual dexterity and color vision, to women, service technicians may be of either sex. Synonymous terms include "field engineer" (FE), "customer service representative" (CSR), and variations on those titles.

The typical service technician has to care for company property, ranging from a company vehicle and tool kit through expensive instruments, technical documentation, service parts, and communications devices. Organizations typically invest many thousands of dollars in equipping each service technician. One of the concerns of service management is assuring that company property is utilized where it should be and not abused or siphoned off for personal gain.

SETTING OBJECTIVES

The heart of any management system is the establishment of the objectives that must be met. Once the objectives are determined, plans, budgets, and other parts of the management process can be brought into play. Too often service management fails to take the time to establish clear objectives and goes off half-cocked, often in the wrong direction. As service may contribute a majority of a company's revenues and profits, that can be a very expensive mistake.

Objectives should be:

⇒ Written
⇒ Understandable
⇒ Challenging
⇒ Achievable
⇒ Measurable

It is not economically feasible to provide a 100% level of service. That would require customer engineers continually on the alert at every site where breakdowns might occur, with complete stocks of replacement parts, tools, and information. That would be too expensive for the vast majority of situations. Situational objectives may be developed to provide very fast but expensive service when time is critical; and to deliver slower, less expensive service when low cost is the driver.

Influences

Many factors influence the objectives of service. Influences may be classified initially as external, meaning outside the organization, and internal, meaning under the control of organizational management.

External influences include:

Customer Changes:
* Account relationships
* Capability more important than product
* Single-point contact
* Comprehensive support desired
* Systems integrator
* Happiness beyond satisfaction
* International considerations
* 24 hour x 7 days per week coverage
* Independent and self-service increasing
* Quality emphasis
* Information plays important role

Competitive Changes:
* Acquisitions and mergers
* Market growth slowing
* Competition growing
* Price cutting
* Intangible, value-add
* Profits high but decreasing
* Legal concerns
* Vertical market niches
* Managing versus doing

- Warranties and contracts
- Competitor = Collaborator = Customer

Technology Changes
- ♦ Communications integration
- ♦ Predictive PM
- ♦ Component reliability
- ♦ Software importance
- ♦ Diagnostics enhanced
- ♦ Support tools
- ♦ Micro emphasis
- ♦ Systems complexity
- ♦ Open systems
- ♦ Transport faster
- ♦ Parts importance increasing

Business Changes
- ■ Emphasis on assets and cash
- ■ Labor rates increase
- ■ Information Systems (IS) guidance
- ■ Organization broad and short
- ■ Outsourcing
- ■ Partnerships form
- ■ Products develop fast and short
- ■ Profit centers
- ■ Revenue and profits high
- ■ Service selling self
- ■ Support expensive & invisible
- ■ Tax and accounting changes
- ■ Technician travel reduced
- ■ Technician skill shifts
- ■ Trade technology for labor

Internal interfaces include:

- ◊ Advertising
- ◊ Control*
- ◊ Credit and billing*

◊　Design engineering
◊　Finance*
◊　Human factors*
◊　Legal
◊　Maintainability*
◊　Packaging
◊　Personnel
◊　Procurement
◊　Production
◊　Program office
◊　Quality assurance
◊　Rebuild/reconditioning*
◊　Reliability*
◊　Safety
◊　Sales

Starred functions may vary between a service organization and other internal organizations.

To a considerable extent the external influences identify an organization's opportunities and obstacles. These external forces do not remain static. At all times they make up a set of changing factors that affects the service organization. Consequently, service management is expected to make decisions under dynamic conditions involving variables that are often inadequately identified or understood. Many problems and many decisions that have to be made depend on conditions that cannot be controlled by the service organization or its management. Lack of control does not suggest that management should disregard the external influences. On the contrary, lack of control should cause management to be continually vigilant over the forces that may have an impact on the service organization. Continual surveillance of the external environment is an important part of service management. Proaction is a word used to describe the opposite of reaction. Service is by necessity often reactive to customer and equipment needs. A major challenge is to anticipate probable events and proactively plan to handle them to your advantage.

Customer

The number-one influence on service objectives is the customer. The person who uses or consumes the product is most interested in service. The customer establishes the need, whether real or perceived. Customers are generally aware that any equipment must have maintenance to keep it running properly. Customers are sensitive to service because they often find it hard to get maintenance for common items such as a car, icemaker, TV, or clothes washer.

Competition

Other companies that provide the same products or services we provide are our competition. When there is no competition, giving us a monopoly, we simply tell customers to "take it or leave it." Their demand can be met only by our supply of goods and services. The regulated public utilities, such as electric and telephone companies, operate that way, although under severe government regulation. Beyond the public utilities, however, the real world, stimulated particularly by the United States Government and its antitrust actions, has brought about great competition. Service organizations should research their competitors' strengths and weaknesses carefully and then identify areas of need not being adequately met by competing organizations.

Technology is certainly one way to take advantage of openings. Look, for example, at America Online, which is based on the Internet; Xerox, which is based on the dry reproduction process; and electronics companies that are founded on solid-state devices. All these organizations offered customers initial advantages that no competitor could match. Many such high-technology organizations find, however, that other companies quickly close the technology gap and that future success depends mainly on the strength of their sales and service organizations. This is especially true in the personal computer (PC) marketplace, where the products are often "me-too" commodities and service offers the main competitive difference.

GOVERNMENT

The governments of the United States, states, and municipalities have increasing impact on service management. One General Service Administration (GSA) or government agency contract often amounts to a large portion of a company's business. The government has, in effect, created entire industries, predominantly in aerospace, weapons, and social services. Politics is a major factor in who wins those procurements. There are many "set-aside" contracts that must give preference to small, minority-owned, and high unemployment-area service businesses.

Government also acts as a regulatory body, to make and enforce regulations on income, labor relations, noncompetitive practices, and the like. The Justice Department's decisions to charge IBM with monopolizing the computer industry, Judge Green's breakup of AT&T, and the antitrust suits of third-party independent services against Kodak, Grumman, Data General, Microsoft, and other technology companies indicate that government is very interested in regulating business in the nebulous area of "restraint of trade," leading to antitrust legislation.

Certainly, every service organization is bound by the minimum wage laws, working hours, overtime requirements, and taxes-income, social security, and worker's compensation. The National Labor Relations Board (NLRB) is the major body that oversees labor policies and unions. The service manager of a nonunion organization that wishes to stay that way must keep abreast of governmental actions that regulate the organization's allowable responses to personnel actions. Unionized service organizations must be aware of the same things, since the union may initiate legal problems that have to be decided by the courts instead of by a vote of their workers. The Occupational Safety and Health Administration (OSHA) and related acts of legislation regulate many aspects of service, ranging from the wearing of hard hats through the size and number of toilet facilities.

Present regulations require that any organization with ten or more employees must adhere to all OSHA regulations. The intent of most of these regulations is to assure worker safety by preventing injuries and contact with hazardous substances, such as asbestos and small airborne paint particles, which could cause severe damage after years of exposure. Most large corporations will have a staff experienced in OSHA regulations that can be called upon to assist service management. Smaller service organizations may get assistance from their insurance agent, who is interested in eliminating the same hazards, or by contacting the local OSHA representative for copies of the regulations. The Environmental Protection Agency (EPA) also oversees manufacturing and repair operations that might involve any hazardous wastes or other environmental concerns.

Another government organization with great influence on service management is the Equal Employment Opportunity Commission (EEOC). The EEOC requires equal opportunity for persons of all races, creeds, colors, ages, and sexes. It also requires that organizations with government contracts or at the size of approximately 25 employees and $100,000 yearly business must practice affirmative action. The company must not only allow equal opportunity to disadvantaged potential employees, but also must search them out to fill employment openings. As a general rule, the percentage of such employees in a service organization's work force must be approximately equal to their percentage in the local population. Implications for service management include the need to assure that equipment is designed to be serviced equally well by people with a wide range of size, strength, and capability.

Government regulations concerning restraint of trade should be understood by all service personnel. For example, service technicians must understand that they cannot make disparaging statements about a competitor's product. A statement such as, "I just can't fix this lousy Brand-X flow meter. You should have purchased one of ours," could easily result in a lawsuit by the competitor whose reputation was demeaned.

Prices charged to customers are regulated by the requirement that the price must be the same for each customer, unless it can be proven that economies of scale allow significant savings. For example, an hour of service for General Motors must be charged at the same rate as an hour for the Rinky Dink Manufacturing Company. Transportation savings for parts and consumables by purchase of bulk quantities may be justified, and transportation expenses may be covered; but basically, pricing must be uniform, and the same pricing plans must be available to all.

Warranties, too, are regulated. They must be either full or limited, with specific statements of exactly what they provide. Warranties are covered with more detail in Chapter 12.

Quantitative Measures

We have established that service should have objectives, including customer satisfaction, profit making, and protection of company property, and that those objectives should be written, understandable, challenging, achievable, and measurable.

Table 3-1 displays some samples of quantitative service specifications. Note that the specifications will differ depending on whether service is being provided by a resident technician, an "on call" agreement, a contract rate agreement, a lease agreement, warranty service, or demand time and materials service. The following discussion shows the sources of the factors written into such specifications.

AVAILABILITY

Reliability (R) and maintainability (M) interact to form availability (A), which may be defined as the probability that equipment will be in operating condition at any point in time. Three main types of availability are inherent availability, achieved availability, and operational availability. Service management is not particularly interested in inherent availability, which assumes an ideal support environment without any preventive maintenance, logistics, or administrative down time. In other words, inherent availability is the pure laboratory availability as viewed by design engineering. Achieved availability also assumes an ideal support

TABLE 3-1
Sample quantitative service specifications.

---

1. Installation will be complete in ____calendar days, with commissioning and process evaluation to follow for a minimum of ____days and maximum of ____days.

2. Availability of equipment will be a minimum ____% of required operating hours, as detailed in the following scenario. (Use conditions should be carefully detailed.)

3. Mean time between failures (MTBF), measured in appropriate units of time, volume, weight, distance, or other relevant factor, will be ____.

4. Response time will be a maximum (or average) of ____hours from the time the support organization is notified by the customer until the service technician arrives at the customer's location. 95% of all service requests will be answered within ____hours.

5. Mean time to repair (MTTR) will average less than ____hours, with 95% of all repairs accomplished within a maximum of ____hours.

6. Mean downtime (MDT) will average less than ____hours, including response time, mean time to repair, and time necessary to obtain information, test equipment, tools, and replacement parts.

7. First call fix rate (FCFR) will exceed ____%.

8. Ongoing service cost for corrective and preventive maintenance will not exceed $____ per hour, gallon, mile, or other applicable dimension.

---

environment with everything available.

Operational availability (Ao) is vital to service management because that is the availability of the product in the real customer environment. The formula for operational availability is:

$$Ao = \frac{MTBM}{MTBM + MDT}$$

where MTBM is mean time between maintenance and MDT is mean down time. MDT includes time for active maintenance, logistics supply, and administration

FAILURES

The most important parameter is failure rate, as a product needs corrective action only if it fails. The main service objective for reliability is mean time between failure (MTBF), with "time" stated in units most meaningful for the product. Those units could include:

✓ Time: hours, days, weeks, and so on
✓ Distance: miles, kilometers, fathoms, and so on
✓ Events: cycles, gallons, impressions, landings, and so on

It is important to realize that equipment use in customer locations should be anticipated in the design. Coffee spilled in a keyboard, a necklace dropping into a printer, and panic pushing of buttons by frustrated users add more calls for help. Half of the calls to a service organization typically are operating concerns by inexperienced users. What the customer perceives as a failure may vary from technical definitions, but the customer is right by business definition. The engineer who says that he has "idiot-proofed" a product has probably underestimated the quality of the "idiot" who will try to use the equipment.

We have all heard stories about new users complaining that the foot pedal (which happens to be a mouse) is difficult to operate with the left foot. Joe Patton was listening on a help line when a store manager was told to cut the power to his computer. There was a loud yell of pain when the manager used scissors to cut the 110-volt power cord. Just this week a report came of a new boat owner who radioed the marina that his fancy speedboat just would not perform as advertised. He took a long time to arrive at the marina, which was no surprise since the boat was still firmly strapped to the submerged trailer!

MAINTENANCE

Statistically based objectives are necessary for all activities in the corrective maintenance cycle, as shown in Figure 3-1. Each activity performed during corrective maintenance should be quantitatively specified. As a minimum, numerical time objectives should be set on mean time to repair (MTTR), mean down time (MDT), mean corrective time (MCT), mean preventive time (MPT), and mean maintenance time (MT).

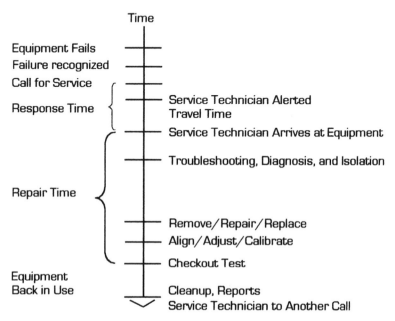

FIGURE 3-1
Typical service call events.

SPECIAL EVENTS

Every product has special events of significance to the service organization that require detailed specifications. Special events may include:

- ◆ Calibration
- ◆ Configuration management
- ◆ Credit for returned items
- ◆ Customer training
- ◆ Engineering change orders

- Help desk assistance
- Installation
- Inventory locations
- Parts availability
- Removal
- Service personnel training
- Site planning
- Software revisions
- Tools

Specifications for installations, for example, should include in detail the amount of time required, any checks and adjustments necessary, special tools or fixtures required, the number of personnel, any required outside assistance, and certification tests to be completed.

Performance Measurement and Reporting

As service management encompasses many facets of business, no unique or single performance measurement has been accepted within the service/maintenance profession. However, a number of performance measures have found wide acceptance for measurement and control. In this chapter the measurements are divided into two categories: field service and plant service. The reason for this split is to provide direct coverage for service management of a field service operation and an in-plant service operation. Before discussion of the specifics for each operation, it is worthwhile to discuss the generic elements common to both. The five elements are presented in Table 3-2. Although these elements are not totally independent or mutually exclusive, they will identify the inherent strengths and weaknesses of the service function. The drawback of these measures of performance is the time and effort that must be expended to document and complete the actual values.

TABLE 3-2
Service elements and performance measures.

Element	Definition	Performance Measurements
Anticipation	Prediction of the needs of the customer in terms of service required and the ability to provide	The percentage of all expected problems for which service was adequately provided
Accuracy in problem definition	The mutual agreement with the customer on the precise problem for which service is required	The average number of contacts between the service organization and the customer necessary to reach mutual agreement
Completeness	The service capability available to customers	The percentage of all customer requests for service that can be adequately handled
Responsiveness	The timeliness of the response of the request for service	The average time elapsed between the customer request and the initiation of service activity on the customer's problem
Problem-solving efficiency	The relative ability of the service organization to complete	Average time required to satisfactorily develop a satisfactory service solution compared to the planned time

Field Service Performance Measures

The field service performance factors are many, but, when intelligently reported, controlled, and interpreted, they can be used as controls. It is important to view performance measures from the perspective of your customers, who may be technicians or may be the end-users. Standard measures are being gradually accepted throughout industry. Each company must develop its own performance measures. Fifty performance measures currently in use include the following:

Asset Measures—Equipment, Parts, and Tools

A1. Support Level $= \dfrac{\text{Total Quantity Issued}}{\text{Total Quantity Demanded}}$

A2. Demand Accommodation $= \dfrac{\begin{array}{c}\text{SKUs on Authorized}\\ \text{Stock List (ASL)}\end{array}}{\text{SKUs Demanded}}$

A3. Demand Satisfaction $= \dfrac{\text{Total Quantity of ASL Parts Issued}}{\begin{array}{c}\text{Total Quantity}\\ \text{of ASL Parts Demanded}\end{array}}$

A4. Turnover $= \dfrac{\text{Quantity (or Value) Issued per Year}}{\text{Average Quantity (or Value) on Hand per Year}}$

A5. Emergency Rate $= \dfrac{\text{Quantity (or Value) Expedited}}{\text{Total Quantity (or Value) Demanded}}$

A6. Assets % $= \dfrac{\text{\$ Book Value of Assets}}{\begin{array}{c}\text{\$ Value of Work, Revenue,}\\ \text{Total Costs, or Profits}\end{array}}$

A7. Repair Cycle = Hours from failure until usable on hand. (Note that this may be divided into the technician's days to return and the repair time once the decision is made to repair the defective part.)

A8. Parts per Unit Repair $= \dfrac{\text{Sum of All Costs of Parts Used}}{\text{Number of Repairs}}$

A9. Repair Cost Ratio $= \dfrac{\text{Cost to Repair Defective Unit}}{\text{Cost of a New Unit}}$

A10. No Trouble Found (NTF) = $\dfrac{\text{Count of Units with No Defects Found}}{\text{Total Alleged Failures}}$

All. Dead on Arrival (DOA) Rate = $\dfrac{\text{Quantity Defective for All Causes}}{\text{Total Quantity Processed}}$

Cost Measures

Cl. Total Maintenance Costs = Sum of Labor \$ + Parts \$
+ Travel \$ + Direct \$ + Indirect \$
+ G&A

C2. Labor Costs = Labor Hours x Loaded Cost per Hour

C3. Parts and Materials Cost = Parts, Expendables, and Consumables Direct + Indirect Costs

C4. Production Loss (Revenue Loss) = \$ Foregone Revenues and/or Cost to Obtain Substitute Capability

C5. Figure of Merit (FOM) = $\dfrac{\text{Consumption}}{\text{Use}}$

C6. Actual versus Estimated = $\dfrac{\text{Actual \$, Time, Events}}{\text{Estimated \$, Time, Events}}$

C7. Revenue per Person = $\dfrac{\text{\$ Total Revenue}}{\text{Number of People}}$

C8. Expense to Revenue Ratio = $\dfrac{\text{\$ Expenses}}{\text{\$ Revenue}}$

C9. Break-Even Quantity: Revenue = Fixed Costs
+ Variable Costs

C1O. Return on Investment (ROI) $= \dfrac{\text{Net Payback}}{\text{\$ Invested}}$

Equipment Measures

E1. Availability (Uptime): $Ai = \dfrac{\text{MTBF}}{\text{MTBF} + \text{MTTR}}$

$$Aa = \dfrac{\text{MTBM}}{\text{MTBM} + \text{M}}$$

$$Ao = \dfrac{\text{MTBM}}{\text{MTBM} + \text{MDT}}$$

E2. Mean Down Time (MDT) $= \dfrac{\text{Sum of All Down Time}}{\text{Number of Failure Occurrences}}$

E3. Mean Time Between Failures $= \dfrac{\text{Total Time}}{\text{Number of Failure Occurrences}}$

E4. Mean Time Between Maintenance $= \dfrac{\text{Total Time}}{\text{Total of Corrective + Preventive Occurrences}}$

E8. Installation Time = Hours and minutes from installation start until useable.

May calculate Mean (MIT) $= \dfrac{\text{Total of All Installation Times}}{\text{Number of Installations}}$

Preventive Measures

P1. PM Rate $= \dfrac{\text{PM Events, Time}}{\text{Total Events, Time}}$

P2. PM Completion Ratio $= \dfrac{\text{PM Events Completed}}{\text{PM Events Due}}$

$$\text{P3. Mean Preventive Time} = \frac{\text{Sum of All PM Times}}{\text{Number of PM Occurrences}}$$

P4. Minimize Total Costs = Minimum Sum of
    (Preventive Costs + Corrective Costs + Lost Revenue)

$$\text{P5. Defect Detection Rate} = \frac{\text{Total Number of Defects Reported}}{\text{Number of Inspections}}$$

Human Measures

H1. Response Time = Hours and minutes from request for
    assistance until expected effort is started.

H2. Restore Time = Time from notification of failure until
    operable.

$$\text{H3. First Call Fix Rate} = \frac{\text{Quantity Satisfied at First Attempt}}{\text{Total Requests}}$$

$$\text{H4. Callback Rate} = \frac{\text{Number of Repeat Attempts}}{\text{Total Attempts}}$$

$$\text{H5. Attempts per Incident} = \frac{\text{Total Attempts}}{\text{Number of Incidents}}$$

$$\text{H6. Maintenance Hours per Operating Hour (MH/OH)} = \frac{\text{Total Support Hours}}{\text{Total Equipment Operating Hours}}$$

$$\text{H7. Administration \& Support Ratio} = \frac{\text{Support People Number, Costs}}{\text{Total People Number, Costs}}$$

$$\text{H8. Overtime \%} = \frac{\text{Overtime Hours, \$}}{\text{Total Labor Hours, \$}}$$

H9. Emergency versus Planned Calls and Time =
$$\frac{\text{Repair Work Number, Time, Costs}}{\text{Total Work Number, Time, Costs}}$$

H10. Backlog Days $= \dfrac{\text{Demand Total Work Hours}}{\text{Supply Work Hours per Day}}$

H11. Operational Productivity $= \dfrac{\text{Utilized Time}}{\text{Total (Paid) Time}}$

H12. Achieved Productivity $= \dfrac{\text{Standard Units Output}}{\text{Total (Paid) Time}}$

H13. Effectiveness $= \dfrac{\text{Standard Units Output}}{\text{Utilized Time}}$

PRODUCTIVE TIME

The typical performance measure of productive time is the ratio of actual time supporting customers in revenue-producing activity compared with the total time available to the technician. Productive time typically includes actual on-site work time and travel time to and from the site. It must be noted that travel time is wasteful. Telephone guidance that enables a user to achieve the desired capability and remote diagnostics that identify the need for parts without a second trip can reduce travel and, at the same time, gain customer satisfaction. Total technician time available includes time spent in the office, in training sessions, and on sick leave or vacation.

The productive time ratio may be based on a 40-hour week, with overtime either excluded or included as a part of the productivity measurement. In either case, individual performance standards for your particular organization should be established. Whereas some companies are very pleased with utilization of 60%, that is, a ratio of actual performance time to total time of 60%, others feel that 80% should be achieved.

Utilization time beyond 80% is virtually impossible to realistically obtain. When the organization provides two or three weeks paid vacation plus as many as 10 paid holidays, then any office time for meetings, for upgrade training, or for general management activities very quickly reduces the available time for productive activity to approximately 80%. Utilization of 80% represents, then, virtually no idle time in the standard workday for a service technician. When effectiveness (doing the right thing well, which is more than mere efficiency) is included, productivity is often about 65%. This offers great opportunity for improvement.

RESPONSE TIME

Another measure of the adequacy of the field service organization is the measurement of the response time provided for emergency demands. Response time is a measurement of the time required to comply to a request for service and is typically measured from the time the call is received until the technician arrives at the location ready to perform the service activity. This measurement represents the flexibility of the service organization and its ability to meet the customer emergency needs.

For operations where downtime is not critical, the need for a highly responsive service organization is not critical. However, for process operations where the integrated production is directly related to the performance of the instruments, control systems, or any other part of the process, downtime can be directly related to the revenue-generation potential of the plant. Under these conditions, response time represents revenue to the plant itself. Thus, plants that would have revenue generation capacity of $10,000 worth of product per hour, operating in a 24-hour day, 7-day week environment, would be losing approximately $240,000 of revenue for every day that the plant is shut down. A 24-hour response time for plants of this type would be completely unsatisfactory. On the other hand, if a process plant that operates on a batch basis has no immediate need to complete the batch because of the scheduling of other products, then a 24 hour response time may very well be satisfactory.

Staffing of the field service organizations that support these two diametrically opposite needs would obviously be equally different, the latter requiring very little idle time in its force, the former needing technicians always ready to respond to a service call. The measurement of response time of the field service technicians provides a direct measure of the ability of the service organization to respond to an emergency demand. The use of response time as a performance measure is not only a significant parameter to measure for operational control but may also be used as an organizational objective. Do note that even though response may be stated and measured as the average, customers expect it to be the maximum, latest time in which someone will start working on their need. Situational goals can be established that react quickly to critical needs and more slowly to less important concerns.

CALLBACKS

The measurement of the number of callbacks provides an evaluation of the technical capability of the service personnel. A callback represents a service call caused by the inadequacy of an original service visit. These are often termed *broken calls*. The callback measure evaluates the problem-solving efficiency of the service organization. The key concern in identifying which service calls can be counted as contributing to a measure of callbacks is to define the period of time between the original call and the callback. In some instances the callback is defined as being a call for the same problem as late as 30 days after the original service call. In other instances, a service call is considered to be a callback only if the customer responds within 24 hours. In some events the customer might need the equipment for production, and a call must be suspended. Thus, the definition of a callback as inadequate service performed is a discretionary value that should be responsive to the demands of the marketplace and the perception of the customer.

CALL DURATION

The measurement of the duration of each field service call is another key element in measuring the problem-solving efficiency of the field service personnel. The variability of call duration is evident from employee to employee in the field service organization. It may be a measure of the differences in the education or training of individual employees. It may also be a measure of workload, recognizing that a technician with a large number of emergency calls waiting to be answered will probably spend less time solving a problem than a technician who has no emergency calls waiting.

The measurement of call duration does not always uniquely reflect the capability of the field service technician. Other factors may also influence call duration. A service call into a plant where all the tools and test equipment may be easily located and the equipment to be repaired is easily accessible will typically have a much shorter call duration than the plant where accessibility to the equipment to be repaired is hindered by obstacles, which may be anything from steam pipes to a clean room environment requiring a "bunny suit" to poor placement of the equipment. In fact, an expert technician may have longer call times than the average technician since she or he will be given the most difficult assignments. Call duration will, however, exhibit a central tendency for typical service activity, and significant deviations from that by any one individual should be given serious consideration for corrective action.

PARTS USAGE

Measurement of the usage of replacement parts provides an indication of the technician's ability to repair equipment rather than to swap equipment. Technicians who feel inadequate in diagnosing equipment that must be disassembled typically require that the device that needs repair be completely replaced with another one. Their service parts usage will be significantly less than usage by technicians with good diagnostic skills and discipline. If you think that logic is backward, remember that the technicians are now replacing entire, expensive products, rather than just the faulty component parts. That situation is an example of why service managers need to look beyond just statistics to the complete event. On the other hand, particularly when mechanical repairs are considered, many technicians, rather than use new parts, will try to repair damaged parts when it would be both to their advantage and to the customer's advantage to replace the part. When faced with angry customers and undiagnosed problems other technicians will change parts haphazardly, which is called "shotgunning." So extremely low or high usage of spare parts can flag poor diagnostic skills, a high availability customer environment, or deficient training and coaching. These considerations must be taken into account when analyzing parts usage. First Call Fix rate (or its converse *Broken Calls*), equipment down waiting for parts, and parts turnover rates are useful measures for evaluating individual technicians.

TIMELINESS AND COMPLETION OF REPORTS

A measure of the practices and procedures of service operation can be obtained by measuring the timeliness and completeness of service reports. As operations shift to real-time communications, entry of the data at the time it occurs becomes critical. This electronic entry does eliminate the paperwork that technicians despise. Timeliness of reporting can also reflect the morale of the service organization. Reports that are continually late may represent a technician who doesn't care, or may indicate a technician who knows the system isn't built to respond quickly to his field service reports and, therefore, does not find it necessary to submit them on time. Thus, the field service report submitted to the headquarters operation can provide clues to the operational procedures of the organization and their effectiveness as well as a measure of the level of morale of the people in the field.

The element of completeness is a very difficult one to measure in the field. If a customer request is not handled adequately by the field service organization the first time, there may never be a second chance for that particular customer. The percentage of all customer requests that are adequately handled represents only those customers who do come back or customers who give you one more chance. For a true measure of completeness one would have to know how many customers calls for service were diverted to other service organizations because of past experience with your service organization. The fact that this is not readily available is the key to why this cannot be adequately measured. Periodic market surveys provide the best way to determine this performance parameter.

PRODUCTION LOSSES FROM EQUIPMENT MALFUNCTION

In-plant service performance is primarily directed at supporting the plant operations. As most equipment failures in a plant represent production loss, the measurement of the amount of loss that results from inaccurate or improper service is a key element to the measurement of the service operation. As other parameters can affect production loss, only by noting the relationship of production losses caused by equipment malfunction to production losses caused by such other variables as operator error, poor engineering, or random failures can a true performance of the service function be assessed. By maintaining long-term records of such data, the success of the service department can be visualized by noting the percent of the total production loss that results from inadequate or improper service. The production loss attributable to maintenance also represents a specific performance measure of the generic element of accuracy in problem definition.

GENERAL OBJECTIVES

The general objectives of the service organization as perceived by operations personnel will measure the level of personnel satisfaction with the service organization. While not quantified as easily as the other generic elements, cooperation, ability, professionalism, dress, reliability, dependability, and cleanliness are important to evaluating performance of the service team. The amount of management time that is spent expediting parts or soothing customers is not often reported in any data collection system, but can be a major drain of valuable time.

Questions

1. List the five characteristics of good objectives.

2. What are the three main objectives of technical service? Discuss each as applied to your business.

3. Select a product and trace the events of a typical corrective maintenance call on it.

4. What external factors influence service in your selected industry?

5. How does competition influence your service objectives?

6. Are both superior technical ability and customer relations ability usually found in the same person? What can be done to obtain skills in both technical and human relations areas?

7. Determine the percentage that productive time is of total time for the typical service technician in your organization.

8. What factors reduce productive time below eight hours a day in a typical service organization?

9. What is the effect of rapid response time to technicians' idle time in a service organization?

10. List the five performance measures that would be most valuable for controlling your service organization.

4

Budgets, Plans, and Controls

*F*inancial budgets, plans, and controls are the basic foundation of good service management. Any such operation will survive only if it is profitable over the long term. Plans are usually divided into two groups by time. Short-term plans, often called tactical or operating plans, are supported by the current year's budget. Although the fiscal year may cover any 12-month period, it typically runs from January 1 through December 31.

The long-range plan, often called the strategic plan, picks up after the operating plan and carries forward to a long-term horizon of three, five, or even ten years.

An organization's plans are established to meet its objectives and goals, which were discussed in the previous chapter. The long-range plan must precede the short-range plan, as the organization should decide first where it wants to be and then decide how it is going to get there. An analogy is a person who has the long-range objective of driving from New York City to San Francisco.

She must determine what general direction she wants to take, what major locations are to be visited en route, and then establish short-range, specific plans for each travel segment. Long-range planning is usually subdivided by quarters or even by years. Short-range plans should be subdivided by months and quarters, and may have specific elements detailed by weeks or even days. Financial plans and controls are meant to be management aids that can detect significant deviation from the plan and provide corrective guidance. At the same time, service plans must be flexible to react to changes in customer desires, new products, catastrophes, and other changes in business conditions.

Planning and controlling a service business is much like sailing a boat. You establish a destination to aim toward and then calculate the effects of tides, wind, weather, boat design, and crew capabilities to determine the proper tactics to get to your destination. Sometimes you can run with the wind at your back and a strong current pushing you to good speed. Other times you are fighting both tide and wind dead ahead so you must either tack at angles to the wind, or if not racing and in a narrow channel, then furl the sails and motor on the engines.

Financial Concepts

Elaboration of several definitions provided in Chapter 2 will help to better explain the budgeting process. Service organizations generally prepare two classes of budgets at the same time, expense and capital. The expense budget will include all items directly charged as a cost of doing business, usually those expended over a short period of time. Major expense items in a service budget will include:

Labor
  Wages
  Taxes
    Social Security
    Medicare
    Unemployment
  Pension
  Insurance
    Health
    Life
    Disability
    Worker's compensation
Communications
  Telephone
  Pager
  Cell phone
Tools
Training
Transportation
Facilities
  Rent
  Utilities
    Electricity
    Heating, ventilating, and air conditioning
    Water and sewer

Capital items are those durable enough to last several years (usually more than three, but as few as 18 months for PCs) or of high value (usually over $500). Items are classed as capital both for tax purposes, because their depreciation may be included as an expense deduction, and for security and record-keeping purposes. Capital items such as furniture, typewriters, calculators, oscilloscopes, and other valuable equipment that could be misplaced or stolen should be indelibly marked with the organization's name and given a specific serial number. Typical capital goods include furniture, office equipment, test equipment, special or valuable tools, cars, and buildings.

Within the expense classification, costs are usually listed as fixed or variable. Fixed costs are those required regardless of the activity level, such as facilities, equipment, and training. Variable costs usually increase directly in proportion to the activity time or usage or units.

One of the basic calculations for any business organization is the break-even point.

$$\text{Break-Even Point} = \frac{\text{Fixed Costs} + (\text{Variable Costs per Unit x Number of Units})}{\text{Profit per Unit x Number of Units}}$$

An organization's break-even point does not remain constant. If the fixed costs rise, the break-even point will rise, which requires more sales income to make the same profit, as is shown in Figure 4-1.

A price rise will produce the opposite effect, but a rise in material and/or labor cost will mean that the line representing variable cost will rise more steeply than anticipated.

It is important to compare the projections of the break-even points for various projects or organizations with the actual breakeven point during the year. If this is not done, management will lack the facts on which to base important decisions. One example of what can happen is shown in Figure 4-2. A large service organization called in a consultant to determine why one of its divisions was losing money. It was expected than an increase in sales volume would be recommended. When the consultant drew the break-even chart, however, it was evident that under prevailing circumstances the company could not stop losing money even if it could sell enough to keep the plant operating at capacity. Parallel lines meet only at infinity!

The reason was two-fold. Income had dropped because of increased competition, and material and labor costs increased. The question to be answered was not how the division could increase its sales, but rather whether the company should eliminate the division entirely or take the chance that prices could be increased enough or costs reduced enough to make it profitable.

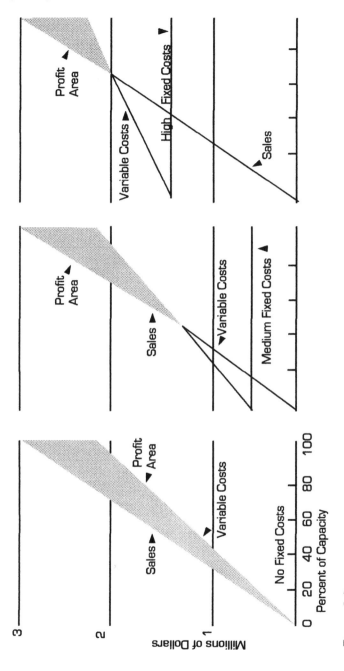

FIGURE 4-1
Break-even diagrams showing the effect of fixed and variable costs on profits.

Dependent and independent costs are categories of expense, related to both fixed and variable costs. Dependent costs will vary directly as production or activity. For example, if an installation takes five hours of labor and each hour of labor costs $45.00, one installation costs $225.00; two installations cost $550.00; and so on. Costs that change as continuous or step functions, such as one service manager for every twelve technicians, are considered variable or dependent. Independent costs are those expenses that don't have a clear relationship to activity or are too small to be worth individually enumerating.

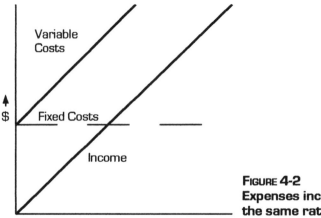

FIGURE 4-2
Expenses increasing at the same rate as income.

The Budget Process

Operating plans and budgets are normally created once a year. If the organization's fiscal year runs from January 1 through December 31, planning should begin formally around August so that the approved budget will be ready before January. The amount of planning time depends primarily upon the amount of effort the organization must put into creating the budget and the time required for each level of approval.

Like most service processes the budget process requires inputs and their processing to yield outputs. The major inputs to service budgets will come from sales, engineering, manufacturing, and top management. Sales will be primarily responsible for projecting activity levels (see Chapter 5, Forecasting). Sales must project the number of current installations that will continue to need service, the number of new sales that will require installation, the amount of activity projected on major accounts, and any new modifications to be installed.

Engineering can advise on the reliability of equipment, how well new products and modifications are expected to perform, and the level of support that they will be able to provide. Manufacturing will be the source of information on quality levels, whether they plan to change configuration or anything else during the future year that will affect performance, and any special field trials or other activities that might affect service. Top management must be responsible for establishing or affirming objectives such as availability and specifically for establishing the profit desired and level of spending to be allowed during the coming year.

There are two schools of thought on whether budgeting and planning should be done from the bottom up or the top down. The answer seems to be that a balance of both is required. Management must set targets and insist on the overall expected level of achievement and constraints from the top down. The detailing of how those targets will be met must come from the bottom up with full participation of all affected persons. Structure should be provided by a financial control group so that all organizations participating in a planning exercise follow the same guidelines and use the same forms.

Budget activities submissions should be classified both by type and by priority. Service budget activity types will include:

- Existing contracts
- Continuing level of "as required, time and materials" business
- Expected new business
- Organizational activities like training, which are expected to increase productivity

Each type of activity should have the related assumptions described in detail. For example, "The XYZ Petrochemical contract will continue with the existing level of effort plus a 10% increase, which will amount to a requirement for twelve full-time equivalent service technicians."

Priorities should separate needs from wants. An A, B, C system is recommended, with items labeled A being vital to the organization's success, B items profitable and desirable but not absolutely mandatory, and C items helpful to operations but movable to a later date if resources are not available this year.

BUDGET GAMESMANSHIP

An axiom of service budgeting is that the initial submission will always be too high and must be reduced. Experienced service management, being aware of this situation, can take one of two approaches. They can either 1) submit a budget that is 10% too high in order to end up with what they want after the typical 10% cut is made, or 2) budget exactly what they feel is required, justify it in detail, and fight tooth and nail to keep what was asked for. Management and profits would certainly be better if the second option were followed.

Preparing the detailed justification usually results in an organization trimming the fat from its own budget so that it will stand up under scrutiny. Confident management and an effective financial control organization can operate very well in this situation. However, the majority of managers, either lazy or not technically competent in detailed budgeting, prefer to make edicts like "Everybody cut 15%." This causes all activities to suffer equally. In an equal-cut situation the activity with a padded budget probably comes out with more money than the activity presenting an effective budget to begin with. A few encounters with this type of budget activity will lead to budget padding in the future.

Thoughtful management will pick and choose priority items to be fully supported and may eliminate some items completely to balance the budget. Unlike the Federal Government, but just like you and me, a service business organization must have funds available from profits and investors that will balance the money out versus the money in.

Service management would be very wise to indoctrinate financial and control personnel with the details of their operation. The comptroller should assign financial people specifically to the service function. These people should be taken into the confidence of service management and shown the details that effect service performance. In affect the service comptroller becomes a lobbyist for service management interests to assure them their share of the money and also to help produce profits.

Workload

Many service organizations attempt to plan workloads for people on the basis of quantitative factors similar to those used for machine loading. The first step is to define good production in terms of time and effort. The time is based on available work hours calculated for most organizations as 40 hours per week for 52 weeks per year, or 2,080 hours as a normal maximum. From this must be subtracted typically 10 holidays (80 hours), vacation days (now averaging 15 days or 120 hours and increasing), and sick time. Additional time is necessary for training, meetings, and other "overhead." An organization is doing well to get 1,800 productive hours from a person in a year, and active hours for a service technician are often less than 50% of the possible total.

The capabilities of a person can be measured to determine how many machines can be repaired in a day or how much time it takes to repair one machine. If the average or mean active maintenance time $(\overline{M})$ is 1.5 hours and travel takes an average of .5 hours, an efficient customer engineer should repair 4 machines in an 8-hour day. Since travel time is a major consideration, geographic density of products to be serviced has a great influence on service effectiveness. In some territories such as inside the Chicago Merchandise Mart or the New York World Trade Center, technicians can do eight or more calls in a day.

Several service organizations use "workload points," which

are essentially measured in minutes required to do an operation. Every activity such as installation, customer training, retrofits, removals, refurbishing, and preventive (scheduled) and corrective (unscheduled) maintenance receives points proportional to the time normally required for its completion. Examples are shown in Table 4-1.

The amount of activity available in the organization is also converted to points. Divided by the point capacity of each person, this determines the number of persons necessary. Naturally, the system must be modified by the learning curve of individuals, with a new, inexperienced person allowed more time

TABLE **4-1**
Typical service time allowances and activity factors.

Hours Used per Month	Work Hours for Scheduled Maintenance	Work Hours for Unscheduled Maintenance
0-9	.025	.13
10-19	.075	.38
20-29	.125	.62
30-39	.175	.88
40-49	.225	1.12
100-109	.525	2.10
200-224	1.06	3.70
300-349	1.63	4.60

Event	Hours per Event
Installation	
Service Technician Trains Operator	4.2
Service Technician Does Not Train	2.7
Removal	.5
Refurbishing	
Level A	7.0
Level B	4.0

	Hours per Retrofit Installation
Negative Ground Strap Mod	2.4
Steering Dust Cover	.9
Lamp Heater	3.2

than a skilled worker. Travel conditions and particular customer characteristics must also be considered. Long travel time between service calls means fewer calls per time period. Particularly difficult customers who require a higher amount of attention than usual should be given extra assistance if that is cost effective.

Workload planning factors allow various alternatives to be evaluated prior to trial in actual operation. The workload factors also illustrate for the reliability and maintainability people the effects of their efforts on service people. However, the service organization and its operational policies are in control the majority of the time, often about 65%, with the minority variable being design change.

Similar workload planning can be done with other logistics functions. For example, field engineering can set factors for evaluation of engineering orders (e.g., a one-hour average) and time spent on direct telephone advice to field customer engineers (e.g., 15 minutes on the phone plus 35 minutes researching the solution). Each task in document preparation can be time-defined. These factors should be determined for every organization and every job so that work is distributed equitably and all workers compensated fairly for their efforts.

There will be a split between exempt and non-exempt salaried and hourly personnel. Non-exempt personnel are under the protection of labor laws that require overtime pay for more than 40 hours work per week, break periods, and other regulated treatment. The exempt people are normally management and professional specialists who are required by the nature of their work to put in whatever time is necessary to do their job. All service associates, non-exempt and exempt, are guided by the same motivational factors that affect other workers.

Activity Requirements

Determining the amount of work required to complete the activities is described in the generalized flow chart shown in

Figure 4-3. The activities can usually be broken into three groups: event-related, use-related, and special. Event-related activities include installations, modifications, removals, and refurbishing.

If a new product is purchased, it must be installed, and time will be required to perform that activity. Use-related activities would be based on miles driven, flight hours, items processed, and the like. Special events would include hours spent in training, demonstrations, trade shows, and special shift coverage. Typical service time allowances and activity factors are shown in Table 4-1.

Scheduled maintenance is usually based on calendar time or usage. In the case shown in Table 4-1, scheduled preventive maintenance was required every 200 hours and took one hour each time. It can be easily seen that if product 310-B were to be used 100-109 hours per month, then 105 / 200 = .525 work hours would be needed for scheduled maintenance. If the scheduled maintenance had been based on calendar time, it would be constant for every product regardless of hours used per month.

The work hours for unscheduled maintenance are based on curves for reliability and maintenance time for the particular product. Reliability for product 310-B improves with higher usage. At low usage this product will require an average of two hours of service for every 80 hours used. As hours-per-month usage increases, reliability almost doubles, so that at a high usage of 550 hours per month, two hours of service are required about every 160 operating hours. The time for each event or special item can also be listed.

These times should be based on field experience for established equipment, and for new equipment on test experience modified by practical engineering judgment. Revisions should be made whenever experience shows the actual figures to be different from the allowance.

There should also be allowances for experience, based on learning curves for the organization. A reasonable range is probably 20%, with a trained person of a few experiences

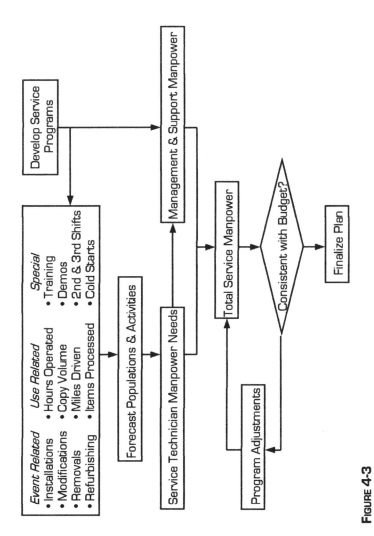

FIGURE 4-3
Development of labor needs.

operating at about a .8 factor and a very experienced person at perhaps 1.2. This means that the average times would be divided by .8 to establish the standards for a novice. A person with one or two years' experience should operate with a factor of close to 1.0. Carrying the figures to three decimal places is done only because so many of the increments will be added to compile a complete workload. The true accuracy is certainly not valid to thousandths of an hour. There may also be adjustments necessary for travel time or peculiarities of the particular customers. For example, if a person is servicing a particularly critical account that will require excessive time, she should be given a special allowance. On the other hand, if a service technician services accounts that are mostly not critical and will therefore fall well under the standard, her factors could be tightened. Likewise, a specialist concentrating on a narrow product line would be expected to perform faster than a generalist who must work on many different products. The factors form a good starting point, but they must be adjusted for specific people by attentive management.

Reports

Good decision making requires up-to-date, relevant information. Service organizations operate in both the internal and the external environments. They must receive accurate information from design and production to provide the proper support equipment and trained people, and they must also relate to the customer in order to satisfy his needs. Every service organization should have a reporting system including routine reports, exceptions, and specials.

At least once a month a budget summary should be issued, indicating the amount budgeted, the actual amount expended, and the variance for the month as well as for the year to date. People will grasp the meaning and magnitude better if the numbers are also shown in graphics. This is easily done today with most spreadsheet programs and report writer software.

It is of fundamental importance that service management design the type and details of reports they will be receiving. Information gathering is expensive. From the perspective of many managers, reporting does not rate a high priority in the firm or in the employees' job description. Fortunately, most service organizations appreciate the value of information and are willing to determine what is necessary and spend the money to get good information.

Backup reports should provide increasing levels of detail behind the summary reports. Top management is interested in summary information. Lower levels of management will typically be interested in increasing amounts of detail, and certainly service technicians will want to know the use, performance, and cost of every piece of equipment they are responsible for so that they can better manage their activities.

Reporting systems have many limitations, including timeliness, cost, relevance, reliability, quality, validity, redundancy, and insufficiency. Every reporting system should be reviewed for each of those limitations to insure that the best possible balance of cost to value is obtained.

Exception reports are used for special events like fires, floods, safety hazards, or defects showing up in an initial group of machines after a change has been made. Exception reports should be accommodated through special forms and a telephone "hotline" to headquarters.

Special reporting systems are often necessary for events like special reviews and initial field trials, when the level of detail and timeliness of existing systems may not be adequate. These special reporting systems are usually used on a small, select group of people and machines with those sampling results transformed to predict the entire population.

Questions

1. Should the long-range plan come before the short-range operating plan? Why?

2. List the major expense items in your service organization.

3. What capital items does your service activity require?

4. What fixed costs are incurred by your organization?

5. Why is it desirable to minimize fixed costs?

6. What organizations should provide input to your service budget process?

7. Would you prefer to budget and plan from "bottom up" or from "top down?" Why?

8. Discuss at least two budget "games" that you have experienced.

9. Calculate the number of productive hours you work in a year. Calculate the percentage these hours are of the total possible hours.

10. What groups of customers require special attention in your business?

5

Service
Forecasting

Service managers today consider some kind of forecast in virtually every decision they make. Sound predictions of demands and trends are no longer luxury items. Managers must cope with seasonalities, sudden changes in demand level, new strategies of the competition, strikes, large swings in the economy, and changes in what customers want.

The past is beyond control. A service organization must start where it is and prepare for the future. To do this it is necessary to predict, assume, or otherwise estimate what is going to happen from now on. Thus, an organization's "success" can be equated with the accuracy of their forecasting techniques, as shown in Figure 5-1.

Forecasting can be defined as the estimating, calculating, and predicting of the values, changes, or even the existence of variables affecting the service process. In a static situation, where the future is a mere extension of the present, forecasting would be unnecessary; what happened today would happen tomorrow. But change does occur. Economic activity is not static, and therefore managers must make predictions if planning for the future is to be successful.

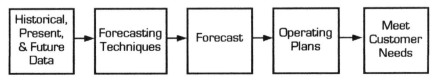

FIGURE 5-1
Steps of the forecasting process.

Time Horizons

Forecasting requirements can be generally classified into three different time horizons, requiring different assumptions and technology, with different objectives.

1. Long-term forecasts cover from one year in the future to three, five, or even ten years into the future. These are required for long-term decisions on facility locations, capacities, and tactical changes. They involve studies of customer preferences, technology, social changes, government regulations, and the economy.

2. Short-term forecasts cover the current year in order to make operating decisions. Short-range forecasts are based on analysis of the various factors that affect the current operation of service organizations, among which are demand, operating costs, work-force requirements, unemployment rates, equipment requirements and availability, and the probable states of nature.

3. Forecasts for the immediate future are the predictions of what is going to happen tomorrow and perhaps next week. They require knowledge of patterns, such as predicting that customers will not call for service on Friday afternoon but that there will be

an extra-heavy load on Monday morning because of both the Friday calls and those accumulated over the weekend. Forecasting a high sickness rate on the first day of trout season, and increasing car mileage during the summer and a high disappearance rate for technicians' tools that are useful around the house are typical of service forecasts.

The sequential relationship between forecasting and planning is often confusing. In forecasting an estimate of economic activity, for example, the sequence is:

$$FORECAST \rightarrow PLAN$$

Plans of a single organization have a negligible effect on the economy and therefore the organization's plans will fluctuate according to the forecast of the economy. That sequence is not valid, however, if the forecast is for some factor influenced by the action of the organization, such as the impact of a marketing program on the company's sales. In this case, the correct sequence would be:

$$PLAN \rightarrow FORECAST$$

Principles

The principles of forecasting include:

1. Large groups of items may be forecast more accurately than small groups.
2. Short periods of time are forecast more accurately than long periods.
3. The immediate future may be forecast more accurately than a longer term.
4. An estimate of error should be included in every forecast.
5. Testing should be done on a forecasting method before it is applied to a system.

Although techniques and tools are available to improve the art and science of forecasting, the amount of money and effort put into applying such tools rapidly reaches the point of diminishing returns. Beyond this point it is far more profitable to develop flexibility to cope with forecasting accuracy instead of trying to improve the forecast. The best solution is to develop an economical forecasting system and a service management system to detect and measure forecast errors and react quickly to correct for such errors.

Overview of Methods

The general methods available to service forecasters are shown in Table 5-1. Mechanical methods of forecasting may be defined as unsophisticated and unscientific projections based on guesses or on mechanical extrapolations of historical data. These methods of prediction may range from simple coin tossing to determine an upward or downward movement to the projection of trends, correlation analysis, and other more seemingly complex mathematical techniques. Typically they are distinguished from other forecasting methods in that they are essentially mechanical and not closely integrated with relevant economic theory. Nevertheless, they are widely used by professional forecasters, probably because they seem to the mathematically naïve to lend an air of sophistication and precision.

TABLE 5-1
Basic forecasting techniques.

Mechanical Methods	Barometric Methods	Survey Methods	Causal Methods
Factor Listing	Leading Indicators	Market Research	Econometrics
Time Series Analysis	Pressure Indices	Polling	Linear Regression
Historical Analogy		Delphi	Input/Output Analysis
		Panel Consensus	

Some of the more widely used mechanical methods are factor listing and time series analysis. Factor listing is one of the earliest forms of forecasting and is still a useful process. The factor listing method is a forecasting procedure whereby the analyst simply enumerates the favorable and unfavorable conditions that will affect business activities as he sees them, with no provision for the quantitative evaluation of the factors and their role in influencing business activities. True factor listing largely ignores the true forces that have a bearing on business change and is therefore essentially an unscientific method. It may obviously be improved by assigning appropriate weights to each of the factors considered.

Time series analysis examines a sequence of events corresponding to particular points or periods or time. Data such as sales, production, and prices when arranged chronologically are referred to as a time series. Figure 5-2 shows how a time series is plotted. In analyzing a time series, the problem is to discover and measure the forces that have caused the series to exhibit its particular fluctuation, in the hope that the causal factors may be projected into the future. Time series procedures are useful if the causal factors are understood.

Service Forecasting

Time series decomposition attempts to break down time series data into trend, cycle, seasonal, and residual components.

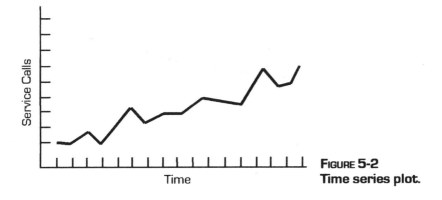

FIGURE 5-2
Time series plot.

The trend is often obtained by using the method of least squares to determine the best curve through all relative historical data points in the time series.

Moving averages are better for time series analysis than are single-point estimates. A moving average forecast is obtained by summing the data points over the desired number of periods. For service, common periods are three, five, and 21 days for moving averages. Extending the moving average to include more periods increases the smoothing effect but decreases its sensitivity to recent data. As shown in Table 5-2, the moving average trend line for the most recent three periods is computed simply by summing the data for the last three periods and dividing the total by three.

TABLE 5-2
Calculating a moving average.

Data	Three-Period Moving Average
190	
370	
300	287
220	297
280	267
420	307
310	337

An average has the problem that is just that—only the mean of a distribution. Many things in service such as parts use trend up or down, but rarely stay level. Weighting the most recent events heavier than past events will give more emphasis to more recent numbers. A common practice is to weight the most recent month's data as 60%, the second oldest month's data 30%, and the oldest 10%. Using the numbers from Table 5-2 gives ((300 x .6) + (370 x .3) + (190 x .1)) = (180 + 114 + 19) = 323. Table 5-3 illustrates the rest of the calculations. Notice that the weighted average picks up changes in trend direction much faster than does normal averaging, but may still lag a turn in the trend. There is considerable judgement required to balance the desire to react immediately to a perceived change in data direction versus realizing that the change may be routine statistical bounce. It can be especially helpful to label data as either recurring or non-recurring. For example, parts ordered for initial stocks of new technicians might cause a peak in needs for those parts, but should not be mistaken for an increase in equipment failures.

TABLE 5-3
Weighted averages.

Data	Three-Period Weighted .6/.3/.1 Averages
190	
370	
300	323
220	259
280	264
420	358
	340

Exponential smoothing, which uses a constant to put emphasis on recent demand, may also be used The formula is:

$$F_n = \alpha\,(Y_{n-1}) + (1 - \alpha)\,F_{n-1}$$

where F_n = forecast for the next period, F_{n-1} = forecast for previous period, α = a smoothing constant, and Y_{n-1} = actual value for previous period. Values for α must be between zero and one. If $\alpha = 0$ there will be no change since the previous period's forecast. If $\alpha = 1$, the next forecast is the same as the most recent data. In general, α is some value between .3 and .7.

Barometric techniques are based on the idea that the future can be predicted from certain happenings in the present, as contrasted with the assumption underlying the mechanical method that the future is an extension of the past. Specifically, barometric methods usually involve the use of statistical indicators that, when used in conjunction with one another or combined in certain ways, indicate the direction in which the economy or a particular service situation is heading. The series chosen thus serve as barometers of change. Two particular applications of the barometric approach commonly employed are leading series and pressure indices. Although to some extent they may overlap, they are discussed separately here.

Leading indicators tend to reflect future changes in economic activity. The movements of the series point to various economic factors that tend to move through the course of the business cycles in consistent but different time sequences. A number of leading series are available in different publications, such as the *Business Conditions Digest* published by the U.S. Department of Commerce. Leading series may be useful but have the following limitations:

1. They are not always consistent in their tendency to lead.

2. It is not always possible to tell whether the series is signaling an actual turning point or merely exhibiting an unimportant variation.

3. They indicate only the direction of future change but disclose little or nothing about the magnitude of the change.

In conclusion it may be said that leading indicators are at best a supplement of other forecasting devices.

Pressure indices are based on the idea that amplitude differences play a significant role in the analysis of business cycles. Economists have developed various ratios and difference measurements called pressure indices as guides to forecasting. Some examples are:

1. The ratio of raw material inventories to new orders for finished goods as a forecaster of raw material prices.

2. The spread between common stock yields and corporate bond yields as a forecaster of stock prices.

3. The difference between the rate of growth in need for petrochemical products and the number of refineries under construction as a predictor of the demand for new process instrumentation.

Pressure indices are valuable as warning signals of impending developments but do not forecast the magnitude of change. When used in conjunction with other forecasting methods, pressure indices can help establish guideposts for better prediction.

Survey methods are subjective methods of prediction, amounting largely to weighted or unweighted averaging attitudes or expectations. The results are often arrived at by asking people who are directly involved about their expectations as to future happenings.

Economic forecasting, for example, surveys businessmen's intentions to spend for plants and equipment. Pricing forecasting will ask service managers from various organizations what they expect to charge for their services in the future. Survey methods may provide good results if the subjects being polled have valid, justifiable opinions on the topic in question. It is important too that actual decision-makers be queried, rather than persons who may have opinions but no authority. Survey methods are usually expensive and time-consuming procedures.

Causal methods include various mathematical formulas used to make predictions. Input/output analysis is a technique developed in economics to study the levels of interdependence of the input and output to predict the changes that would occur in the requirements of one situation given a known change in another. Econometrics and linear regression are based on the idea that changes in activity can be explained by a set of relationships between variables. Econometrics explains past economic activity and predicts future economic activity by deriving mathematical equations that will express the most probable interrelationships among a set of economic variables. The equations are a simplified extraction of a real situation and are employed as a predictive system that will yield good numerical results. It is more analytical in nature and more process-oriented in approach than any other method because its chief concern is to identify and measure changing cause-and-effect relationships through time. It is the only approach logically suitable for incorporating the best features of the other techniques in a model. Many hand calculators and spreadsheet programs available today will compute linear regressions using the least squares method, illustrated in Figure 5-3.

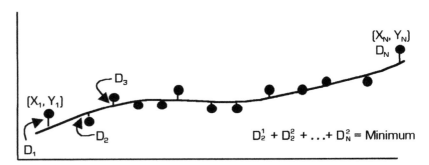

Figure 5-3
Least squares regression line.

Technological Forecasting

Technological forecasting is taking its place alongside other methods of forecasting that aid modern service management. To be useful, technological forecasts do not need to predict the precise form technology will take. Like other forecasts their purpose is to help evaluate the probability and significance of future developments so that managers can make better decisions.

"Technology" is not a single piece of hardware or chemistry, but rather the knowledge of physical relationships applied systematically. This knowledge can range from initial glimmerings of how a basic phenomenon can be applied to the solution of a practical problem, to an end product in an operating system. The performance characteristics of any operating system are normally improved in small increments over time. What may appear to be a step function advance in technology is usually nothing more than an accumulation of small changes not worth individual attention until the total makes a significant contribution.

It is usually futile for a forecaster to try to predict exact technological developments, but he may predict ranges of characteristics likely to occur in the future and can often present the factors on which they depend. Forecasts made in this manner help to identify potential problems and opportunities; advance action may then be taken to improve the organization's position when the projected events occur. Forecasts, no matter how accurate, are useless unless they influence action.

The major techniques of technological forecasting are demand assessment, theoretical limits, parameter analysis, surveys of scientific effort, competitive evaluation, and asking, "What if?" Studies suggest that demand, not excess technological capacity, is the driving force behind technological change. In fact, a technology will be utilized only if it responds to a need. Otherwise it remains a capability and never becomes a functioning reality.

The theoretical limits test asks what will happen if known apparatus or phenomena are pushed to their theoretical limits. For example, laser transmission of energy from the sun can be envisioned and the necessary advances determined. A good way to check the logic of forecasts is to have a group of experts refine their estimates through successive approximations both individually and then collectively. This is called the "Delphi" approach.

Parameter analysis evaluates whether technical systems can reach or exceed key levels or parameters of performance by some future date. It may include predicting technological changeover points, analyzing unique properties of a product, and analyzing substitution growth curves.

Surveys of scientific effort made by the National Science Foundation, the Instrument Society of America, the Institute of Electrical and Electronic Engineers, and other information sources provide information on what areas of science are receiving most attention. Published papers and technical symposia provide guidance in "state of the art" developments and methods.

Competitive evaluations include the monitoring of advertisements, press releases, patents, component ordering, and new product announcements. Technological forecasting can improve decision making through better understanding of probable future events, driving forces, and critical parameters. The payback usually exceeds the cost many times, and the information can be used to make better, more profitable decisions.

Testing

One of the most common areas of neglect in management today is failure to compare what we thought would happen with what actually does happen. Forecasts are valid only if they predict the real world.

A good way to test forecasting techniques is to make the prediction based on past data and then check its outcome against today's real information.

Errors in data used to make forecasts are the most common type of error. Typically, conflicts in motivation may bias the inputs. For example, salesmen will tend to be optimistic about the amount of equipment they are going to place. Manufacturing, on the other hand, will be pessimistic about the amount they can build. Comparison of statements made in the past with the actual occurrences will allow correction factors to be used, thus making the information more accurate.

Models

Types of models include the iconic, verbal, analog, schematic, and mathematical. Iconic models are usually three-dimensional hardware representations of the real thing. A product mock-up is a good example. Verbal models use word descriptions to describe the real thing. Maps that use blue to indicate water and green to show grassland are analog models. A wiring diagram is schematic. Mathematical models use numerical equations to predict outcomes. They are very useful for forecasting, especially with the power of spreadsheet and database software to aid in processing the mathematics.

The calculating power of the modern computer gives service management the ability to rapidly manipulate many factors and provide accurate forecasts. Life cycle cost (LCC) models, for example, allow the prediction of a product's acquisition, operating, and support costs before that product is built. Life-cycle costing can be a very valuable technique, as data from the aerospace industries shows that 70% of a product's life-cycle cost are bounded by the end of concept phase, 85% by the end of development, and 95% by the end of formal design. Level of repair analysis allows a maintainability engineer to determine the best level—operational, intermediate, or depot—at which to repair equipment. Spares models predict the quantity and cost requirements for service parts. Service parts is the specialty area of LPA software, Management Metrics Services, and Servigistics. Many service organizations have built complex models that predict all the major events in a product's life scenario, including failure predictions, downtime predictions, and all related costs. Such a computer model may be quickly run to simulate many products in operation and assure that plans are based on realistic requirements.

In summary, the ability to make and utilize forecasts brings a vital technique to the service managers' skills inventory. Service managers consider some type of forecast in virtually every decision they make. Accurate forecasts are vital to accurately plan the future.

Questions

1. What forecasts are necessary for your organization?

2. Why can large groups be forecast more accurately over a short period of time than small groups can be forecast over a long period?

3. Mechanical methods of forecasting are called unsophisticated and unscientific. Should they therefore be disregarded? Why?

4. Product service normally has fluctuations that are a function of time. What fluctuations exist in your service business?

5. What values does technological forecasting have for service?

6. Why do we say that forecasts are useless unless they influence action?

7. What kinds of forecasting information would you expect to get from professional publications such as *Instrumentation Technology, IEEE Spectrum,* and *Quality Progress?*

8. Why is it vital to compare what we forecast with what actually does happen?

9. What should be done if you find that actual results vary from those forecast?

10. How can mathematical models help manage service?

6

Personnel
and Motivation

Successful organizations have undergone a metamorphosis as sophisticated managers understand that service is much more than a routine equipment maintenance program. Service has become a strategic marketing tool to enhance customer satisfaction, stimulate sales efforts, and contribute profits. Successful companies provide a framework for a corporate service culture that permeates the corporation.

Many organizations have made significant changes in their human resource management strategy as a direct response to competitive pressure. According to a research team at the University of Warwick's Centre for Corporate Strategy and Change in the U.K. (Drs. Chris Hendry and Paul Sparrow and Professor Andrew Pettigrew), some significant business developments that have driven the need for corporate environmental changes are: competitive restructuring, decentralization, internationalization, mergers and acquisition, "total quality" processes, technological change, and new concepts of service management. The management of these internal and external changes includes a broad range of personnel activity such as skill supply, training, organization restructuring, work systems, culture management, human resource development, selection and retention, employee relations, and rewards management. Service organizations have a critical need to integrate business and technical resources and requirements with human resource needs and skills.

Service often differentiates one company from another. In the new millennium, consumers assume that products will work. Customer delight results more from how the products is sold and serviced than how the company responds to inquiries and solves problems. According to Robert A. Peterson, a professor of business administration at the University of Texas in Austin, "Customer satisfaction is not a goal, it is an obligation." His findings indicate that, in most customer satisfaction surveys, about 85% of a company's customers claim to be "satisfied" with the service they receive but will still defect to other vendors given the right circumstances. Companies need to evaluate successful service not by the number or quality of products shipped but by customers' memories and perceptions of their experience the last time they patronized the business.

We know that it costs five times as much to attract a new customer as it does to retain an existing one. Thus, focusing on service quality provides an effective customer retention strategy and barrier to competitive threats. This means that each employee within the company must recognize that if they're not directly helping a customer, then they're helping an employee who is. Thus, effective service quality standards consider employee behaviors as well as customer perceptions. Employees serve a very different function in a service business than in a manufacturing company. Production workers are a means to an end to produce a finished product. Front-line employees in a service business are the ends in themselves. When performance is the product, people are critical!

Since research shows consistently that the quality of service directly impacts revenues, improving customer retention becomes critical and is contingent upon the performance of front-line employees. Employees are the company at the point of customer contact. Individuals must excel at their behind-the-scenes roles, or the entire effort can collapse if just one person fails to do a job on which everyone else depends. As Ken Blanchard, author of *The One Minute Manager* series, says, "In the service world, the front-line service person must now be at the top of the organization pyramid... responsible for the customer. Managers must learn to respond to the needs of the front line."

Well-managed, successful service companies operate with human resources as a focus. Professors Leonard Schlesinger and James Heskett of the Harvard Business School wrote in the *Harvard Business Review*, "In companies that are truly customer-oriented, management has designed the business to support front-line workers' efforts and to maximize the impact of the value they create." The human contact aspects of service delivery weigh heavily on the customer's evaluation of quality. Research has repeatedly demonstrated a direct correlation between high employee job satisfaction and high customer satisfaction and, conversely, between low job satisfaction and lack of customer satisfaction. As a result, it is important to look within the organization to assess its treatment of employees (internal customers) and how well they are helping employees to serve customers.

Professors Schlesinger and Heskett suggest some important elements to consider:

1. Value investments in people as much as investments in technology. Don't rush the process. Invest the time and effort needed to get the right person.

2. Use technology to support, not replace, front-line employees. Great service employees must be able to create a relationship with their customers because every customer encounter is "live" and unique.

3. Emphasize selection and training for front-line employees as much as for managers and executives. Good service employees must have styles of personal interaction that seem natural, friendly, and appropriate to the situation.

4. Link compensation and performance for employees at every level.

Great service employees must have the skill to handle pressure. They must acknowledge the customer's problems and demonstrate their willingness and ability to resolve those problems in the best possible way. The critical difference issue here is the importance of the human resource role in service delivery. Front-line people are a service organization's product. They make the difference between success and failure. Incompetent, uncommitted workers cannot perform front-line jobs. Service companies require employees who take personal responsibility, manage themselves, and respond effectively to customer needs. They must emphasize the selection and retention of quality people, training and support of new employees, involvement and empowerment of experiences persons, and provide rewards and incentive for superior performance.

The Successful Service Employee

Research shows that, in many organizations that deliver exemplary customer service, employees are routinely and conscientiously treated with the same respect with which they are expected to treat customers. Indeed, employees are regarded as internal customers.

Employees, particularly those on the front line, can provide insightful and accurate information about customer expectations, satisfaction, and changing needs and perspectives on the corporate culture in which they work. Neglect of internal customers seems to result not from a lack of concern for persons, but rather because management is unclear about the contributions employees can actually make. Ron Zemke, in an article in

Employee Relations Today, identified a number of areas in which employee evaluations are most valuable:

1. *Clarity of service focus.* The definition of service and service quality translated and communicated to employees at all levels of the organization.

2. *Understanding customer expectations.* Specific customer expectations must be communicated to, and be understood by, all employees. What have been the traditional practices and what needs to be changed?

3. *Ability to listen to external customers.* Front-line employees provide a wealth of information about the effectiveness of the company's attempts to listen accurately to customers. How much input does the organization seek from customers regarding expectations and needs? What communication channels exist, both formal and informal?

4. *Willingness to learn from employees.* If they believe there are open channels and meaningful ways for them to contribute to the service improvement process, employees will have a much higher opinion of the sincerity and appropriateness of that effort.

5. *Level of management commitment.* Employees tend to judge the seriousness of the organization's decision to focus on service excellence based on the visible involvement of managers who set a personal example.

6. *Standards and procedures.* Service quality is only as meaningful to employees as it is real and palpable. Setting customer satisfaction benchmarks, committing to error reduction, and providing group and individual feedback on service performance are aspects of quality service on which employees can give valuable input.

7. *Measurement of service performance.* Measurement is the proof of standards. Employees who know that their performance is being measured know just how serious the organization is about service quality for their customers.

8. *Reward and recognition of superior performance.* A key incentive for front-line and support employees is public recognition and tangible rewards for meeting and exceeding customer

needs and delivering superior quality service—celebrate success! Remember the old cliché, "The actions you reward are the actions you get."

9. *Quality of training and support.* Employees are acutely aware of how well prepared they are for a new job or how to attain new job skills. Manager participation enhances the training effort. Some aspects of manager involvement include acting as instructor, keeping employees up to date on changing customer expectations, discussing how to surpass customer expectations, working one-on-one with employees.

10. *Employees' personal commitment.* A critical aspect of the service encounter is ensuring that the employees assess their own sensitivity and commitment to providing excellent service to both internal (co-workers) and external customers.

11. *Employees' work group commitment.* A strong commitment to a work group, in terms of meeting and exceeding customer needs, may encourage a moderately committed employee to contribute more.

12. *Company-wide commitment.* The effectiveness of the organization in demonstrating its commitment to service quality among employees at all levels is influenced by the levels of commitment that employees perceive within other parts of the company. Employees demonstrate their commitment to the customer service mandate at three levels: personal, work group, and organizational. They need to know that everyone in the company plays by the same set of rules.

13. *The sales/service connection.* When non-sales employees perceive that the sales force is strong in service orientation and willing to help with problems after the sale, the likelihood that the customer will perceive the organization as service-oriented is quite high. Further, when service personnel experience a service orientation in the sales and marketing department, they tend to cooperate more with them.

14. *Policies' ability to facilitate service.* Front-line and staff support employees are only as good at helping customers, and each other, as policies and procedures allow. Organizations should know whether company rules inhibit or facilitate good

customer service. Policies and procedures should allow and support employees to use good judgment at all times; a sense of autonomy and control is very important for front-line employees who serve customers.

15. *Service recovery.* Employees must be empowered to fix service failures at the point of occurrence. They must have the freedom to act within reasonable, predetermined guidelines. John Goodman at the TARP Institute based in Washington, D.C., has found customers to be two to three times more loyal to organizations with which they have never experienced a problem. Training employees to deal with angry customers, to solve problems, and to take initiative are all equally important. The front-line service recovery activity also requires the most managerial support and organizational approval.

Accountability

Organizations and individual employees cannot flourish without structure, corporate accountability, and personal responsibility. Employees must understand that you get what you earn, that you are required to perform, and when you do perform, you will get rewarded.

Much has been written about the importance and benefits of investing in and valuing service employees. What about threats from technology, the economy, and global competition? Because people have become a greater resource than ever before, employees and managers must understand that the golden days of entitlement are gone. Dr. Judith M. Bardwick, president of her own management-consulting firm in La Jolla, CA, asserts in *Industry Week* that, "Giving people reasonably good jobs without documenting what the company gets in return can be really expensive. This attitude of entitlement results in people not working, or people thinking they are working when, in reality, they are not adding anything of value to the business." She contends that organizations have failed to educate their employees that their work is not just the jobs they perform but their ability to add value to the corporation. Dr. Bardwick cautions companies to strike a balance between entitlement and fear (of job loss.) Trevor Lukes, vice president for corporate human resources at Travelers Cos. in Hartford, CT., believes that, "Too many companies spend a lot of time worrying *about* the work that has to be done instead of what *is* the work that has to be done." Successful managers must evaluate their work regularly to determine if the work contributes to the company's bottom line. At the same time, many employees report incongruence between the actions of management and the corporate mission statement. Many employees don't understand exactly what is expected of them. In a performance survey conducted in 1992 by the Oechsli Institute in Greensboro, NC, eight out of ten managers, salespeople, and operations employees say they are not held accountable for their own daily performance.

Employees can be held accountable for their performance by identifying discrepancies that exist within the organization by the following simple techniques: 1) ask employees to describe their specific responsibilities in pro-active terms; 2) ask employees how they could be more effective and suggest three specific actions they could take every day; 3) set measurable daily goals.

The Successful Service Manager

The emerging importance of the human aspects of business means that service management requires unique and changing characteristics. Traditional top-down management paradigms tend to promote getting someone else to do the right thing, and getting things done through people, rather than expecting results from each individual. Eberhard Scheuing, professor of marketing at the Graduate School of Business Administration of St. John's University in New York and the first president of the International Service Quality Association, says that, "Overcoming 'hierarchical thinking' is essential to successful service management practices." Great service managers have good people who know what they are doing, are empowered and supported, and know precisely what it takes to keep the department running effectively.

Great service managers are masterful at promoting participative cooperation. They have constant contact with employees and customers to have a first-hand understanding of what's going on. In a service organization, front-line employees attend to their jobs but watch the personal performance and conduct of the manager to define the "real" rules. Thus, if the manager takes time to listen patiently to customers and employees, so will they. If the manager focuses time and energy on behaviors that demonstrate quality, respect, and service to the customer, so will employees. In addition to leadership by example, the manager must be able to support, guide, and direct the employees. Instead of getting someone else to change their behavior, managers should ask, "What have I, personally, done today to improve service quality in this organization?" Superior service does not happen by accident! It happens when managers think and act service, day in and day out, in obvious and subtle ways.

Successful service managers do not judge quality by quantity. Instead, they must constantly evaluate processes and attitudes. Customers judge the success of service both by the outcome (my needs were met and satisfied, or not) and by the processes leading to that outcome. Given a choice, would your customer deal with your company again? Customer choice is the essence of the service business.

In general, service managers develop processes for planning, controlling, and improving business performance to satisfy specifically defined customer requirements as follows:

1. Set performance standards.
2. Define and use procedures that best meet the standards.
3. Use measures of each work process and its outcomes to identify opportunities for improvement.

CHARACTERISTICS OF EFFECTIVE SERVICE MANAGERS

Research identifies four key characteristics commonly shared by good service managers who have developed committed, satisfied employees with a clear service focus. Also, the personal style of successful managers enhances credibility and contributes to development and retention of happy, loyal customers.

1. *Good communication.* Take time to ensure that all employees understand thoroughly what quality service is, how it is measured, and how it affects both the customers and the company's profit.

2. *Customer focus.* If the objective is customer satisfaction, then *how* it is done is less important than *that* it is done. Competent, confident people have broad repertoires. Properly trained and empowered, savvy employees will do the right thing at the right time to serve the customer.

3. *Service obsession.* Think, talk, and walk good service! Be a passionate advocate of, and preoccupied with, ensuring customer satisfaction.

4. *Role model.* Support, encourage, and teach employees. Be walking proof of your ideals.

5. *Personal style.*
> A. Calmness. Display confidence, assurance, maturity, and centeredness.
> B. Humility and curiosity. Focus on problem-solving and learning. They are approachable.
> C. Coaching. A way of life; offer suggestions, compliments and questions.
> D. Closure. Stay with the task until it is complete; nothing falls through the cracks.

COMMUNICATION

Corporate commitment to effective communication is one of the most powerful methods of including employees as valuable, contributing members of the organization. Low productivity, attrition, cost overruns, and quality problems can often be cured through the implementation and maintenance of effective communication programs. Conversely, breakdowns in communication represent the most common cause of conflict between management and labor and precipitate many other problems.

Open communication helps establish an atmosphere of trust, as employees understand they are working towards common goals. In order to satisfy a variety of needs, a comprehensive program must provide for flexibility and confidentiality. Employees will respect and participate in a program that provides prompt and complete responses and opportunities for change. Without a viable feedback component, a program can degenerate into an irrelevant vehicle for "letting off steam."

WORK GROUPS AND TEAMS

Managing work through groups or teams has become a necessity for most managers due to the restructure and downsizing of organizations. Before a work group is even assembled, the leader must prepare. The following suggests some guidelines and questions to consider:

I. *Preparation.*
   A. Type of group. Advisory; task-oriented to a specific assignment; brainstorming. The group type will determine size, structure, and membership.
   B. Communication or leadership style. How group members may perceive and interact with the leader.
   C. Member selection. Technical skills, knowledge, intelligence, motivation, personality style. Be prepared to tell each member selected why his or her particular skill, knowledge, or talents are needed.
   D. Champion for the mission. Leaders must demonstrate, through words and actions, an unshakable support of the group's mission. The leader's authority derives from an ability to motivate others to achieve the goal.
II. *Getting started.*
   A. Structure (address at the first meeting).
      1) Meeting schedule
      2) Group mission
      3) Group authority

        4) Expectations
    B. Accountability and delegation. Leader musts establish clear authority without being dictatorial.
III. *Facilitation.*
    A. Administrative logistics. Before each meeting, determine whether or not the meeting is really necessary. Draft and distribute an agenda with relevant preparation materials. The agenda should state the purpose of the meeting and differentiate among presentation, discussion, and decision items. Arrange for someone to record the meeting. During each meeting, start and end on time. State the purpose of the meeting and stick to the agenda. Summarize action or decisions related to each agenda item before adjourning. After each meeting, distribute minutes to all participants and interested parties.
    B. People issues.
        1) Leaders act as consensus-builders. Groups benefit from the combined contributions of all members. Request that each person express an opinion on each issue. The group must reach a decision that the majority will support fully.
        2) Leaders must promote mutual respect and courtesy among all members. The leader must not condone interruptions or insults; set an example of a high standard of conduct.

Motivation

Committed employees make better employees than compliant ones. They make greater contributions to the organization, are more productive and more creative, and more fun to work with. Think about someone who managed you using a dictatorial, autocratic style. You may have complied, but your performance and contributions most likely fell far short of what you could have done. So, how do managers gain commitment from employees rather than mere compliance? Numerous new sources of research and data indicate clearly that an informed employee is a more committed employee.

Because the work force of the 1950s, '60s and '70s valued security, most employees essentially managed themselves in order to retain that steady paycheck and guarantee of benefits. We now have a generation of workers who grew up knowing prosperity as opposed to the poverty of the Depression and two World Wars. Now, however, in these times of turbulent economies and global competition, employees do not embrace the same *quid pro quo* as their parents. Personal well being has become a basic requirement. Today's workers believe that, in exchange for working, they should be stimulated, challenged, and recognized for their efforts and contributions.

To make motivational efforts successful, management must focus on intrinsic factors, rewards that result directly from performing the task itself, rather than the external rewards that are given for performance. Merit pay is an accepted management practice—an extrinsic factor motivating people to work. Herbert Meyer reported in the *Harvard Business Review* that focusing attention on money often produces the exact opposite result. In fact, his research shows that, "When pay becomes the primary goal, a person's interest becomes focused on the payment rather than the performance of the task itself." Further, Meyer reports that, "To the extent that pay is connected directly to task performance, intrinsic interest in the task itself decreases."

Today's managers must find ways to energize employees with fewer levels of management, increasing areas of responsibility, and looming global competition, while opportunities for promotion remain limited. Managers often feel frustrated by their inability to reward excellent employee performance in traditional ways. Fortunately, external motivators are not the only ones that work effectively. The fact is that people are motivated by what they like to do. Learning theory psychologists have produced research that demonstrates that behavior that is intrinsically motivating is self-rewarding. So, the question of motivation becomes: "*What does one enjoy doing?*" Managers need to frame the issue in a slightly different way: "*What types of activities does this type of person enjoy doing?*" Then the focus of motivation can shift to identification and understanding of the types of employees they must motivate.

Psychologist David McClelland proposed in his "Need Theory" that there are three relevant needs in work situations that differentiate people according to what motivates them: 1) need for affiliation, 2) need for achievement, and 3) need for power. John J. Hudy, a research psychologist with Acumen International in San Rafael, CA, consolidates several motivational theories to predict what types of intrinsic activity work for particular types of persons. Hudy identifies three general categories of motivators (relationship, achievement, power), then labels five specific areas of intrinsic motivators that apply to each: 1) task preferences, 2) project preferences, 3) favored role (interactions with co-workers), 4) wants from others, and 5) skill focus.

INTRINSIC MOTIVATORS

1. *Relationship.* Need for affiliation; people/security orientation.
>   A. Prefers team tasks
>   B. Dislikes projects with high conflict and/or poor communication
>   C. Enjoys role as coach or mentor
>   D. Wants friendship and close relations
>   E. Focuses on interpersonal skills

2. *Achievement.* Need for achievement; satisfaction orientation.
>   A. Prefers moderate risk tasks
>   B. Likes personal responsibility for projects
>   C. Enjoys role as entrepreneur
>   D. Wants frequent feedback on own performance
>   D. Focuses on developing new skills/expertise

3. *Power.* Need for power; task/security orientation.
>   A. Prefers competitive tasks
>   B. Likes high-profile projects
>   C. Enjoys role as leader.

    D. Wants key information
    E. Focuses on controlling skills

Key

A. Task preferences   C. Favored role   E. Skill focus
B. Project preferences   D. Wants from others

A manager who understands an employee's intrinsic orientation can more easily identify activities that will be most stimulating and satisfying. For example, a person whose primary orientation is "power" would be assigned to a high-profile project involving competitive activity (team leader, project manager). This person could be placed in a position of authority and charged with the responsibility to develop new business contacts and gather market data (networking and key information). Thus, the employee's daily activities would closely match his or her motivational orientation and contribute to keeping motivation high.

The productive use of human resources is critical for service and engineering organizations. Classical and modern theories have thoroughly documented that effective communication between management and employees, along with opportunities for employees to develop, are still two of the most critical factors in the employer-employee relationship. Research conducted during World War II by Frederick Herzberg suggested two categories of workplace attributes: 1) satisfiers, which engendered positive attitudes and high performance, and 2) dissatisfiers, which caused negative attitudes and low performance. Satisfiers are achievement, recognition, the work itself, responsibility, and advancement. Dissatisfiers are company policies and administration, supervision, compensation, interpersonal relationships, and working conditions. These are illustrated in Figure 6-1.

Many organizations have discovered that resolving issues that cause employee dissatisfaction does not guarantee satisfaction. This phenomenon is analogous to the fact the customers now expect products that work and services that are delivered competently. Companies do not get "credit" for customer satisfaction merely because the product performs properly. This is the age of exceeding customer expectations by providing service that delights, of earning customer loyalty through problem solving, of retaining fickle customers by repeatedly delivering superior service along with perfect products, and "no-questions-asked, money-back" warranties.

Years ago, many presumed that information technology workers were motivated primarily by complex intellectual stimulation and had minimal needs for social interaction. Several psychological studies conducted in the 1970s confirmed that these workers eschewed teamwork, avoided social interaction and spoke only "computerese" and technical jargon. Technology professionals are no longer a homogeneous group. The new breed of "techies" exhibits a greater need for achievement and growth and a much higher need for social interaction in the workplace. This brings us back to the critical need for excellent communication programs throughout all levels of the organization.

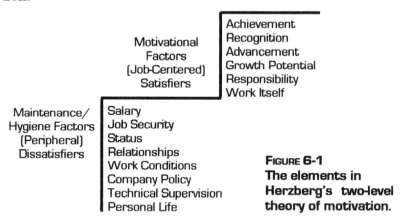

FIGURE 6-1
The elements in Herzberg's two-level theory of motivation.

MANAGING A DIFFICULT EMPLOYEE

Many managers have difficulty changing unacceptable performance of employees who do not perform up to standard or are not behaving like team players. How do managers resolve these problems without disrupting the workflow and/or negatively impacting morale? The traditional means of improving poor performance is through appraisals.

Progressive discipline typically includes verbal counseling, written warnings and sanctions, and termination if the behavior does not improve. Although this process does protect the employer from unwarranted liability and lawsuits, it usually fails to correct the problem or change the employee into a fully functioning, committed team member. Instead, it often encourages resentful compliance while failing to address the real issues. Thus, the problem with progressive discipline is that it is experienced as punitive and not constructive.

Most employees have had negative experience with performance appraisals, because they tend to be more evaluative and judgmental than constructive and developmental. Performance appraisals review past performance with little focus on future action or behavioral change. Like progressive discipline, appraisals can create compliant employees who will do whatever it takes to achieve a high rating, as opposed to being truly committed. Although many managers think that the purpose of a performance appraisal is development, most employees perceive it as a report card, a critique. A guideline for performance reviews is that nothing should be discussed or written that will surprise the employee. Since a review provides a look back, the employee should have had an opportunity to improve the behavior or situation presented in a previous performance review.

The problem that can result from the use of these two management tools is that they tend not to motivate, because employees fear the consequences rather than move towards personally responsible and empowering behaviors. The critical goal for service managers, in particular, is to have accountable employees who take full responsibility for their conduct, even when no one is monitoring them. When an employee is the company to the customer, service organizations cannot afford anything less than highly effective employees who manage themselves appropriately.

Achieving Commitment Through Coaching

Two essential ingredients for leaders are trust and respect. Trust occurs when the employee believes that the leader provides guidance and coaching for the purpose of personal development, not only as a means of getting the job done. Thus, coaching must be accomplished in a constructive manner and in a nonjudgmental context.

Motivation through effective coaching involves empowerment and support of individual employees. Virtually all employees respond to managers who take a personal interest in their welfare. However, because coaching is a process, not a event, the manager needs a plan.

Coaching sessions with employees usually take place over several weeks. The initial discussion will identify the problem behavior, elicit input from the employee, and provide specific coaching suggestions. Then, during subsequent weeks, the manager observes behavior and provides immediate feedback (positive and negative) as appropriate. Within two to three weeks, the manager should meet again with the employee and offer feedback and ask about the employee's experience, inquiring about what might be needed to assure success. If necessary, the employee should be redirected towards appropriate behaviors, and the cycle should be repeated until the behavior meets expectations.

A written coaching plan can provide a helpful reference for specific steps needed for the employee to become more effective on the job. This is not for the purpose of documentation. Coaching plans should be written in a positive, constructive manner. The initial discussion should start with the manager thanking the employee for cooperation and indicating confidence in his or her ability to successfully achieve the behavioral changes required. Next, suggestions should be made that include identification of problem behavior, and appropriate alternatives should be offered. An effective coaching plan does not include more than three to five specific suggestions for improvement; less is better.

BECOMING AN EFFECTIVE COACH

1. *Choose an appropriate time.* Before intervening, consider: Do I want to deal with this situation now? Do I have time to give my undivided attention? Will I be disturbed or interrupted? Do I have any feelings now (anger or defensiveness) that might interfere with my ability to coach effectively. Also, check with the employee: Is this an appropriate time for coaching? Would their feelings support an effective discussion

2. *Give well-intentioned, constructive critique.* Concentrate on positive feedback before delivering criticism; it will be received more readily. Provide a balance of positive and negative feedback, or the person may perceive the situation as hopeless. Be fair; listen to the employee's side of the story. Offer specific suggestions for improvement or to prevent a recurrence of similar mistakes.

3. *Communicate clearly and candidly.* Don't be afraid to tell the truth. Avoid vagueness, ambiguity, and mixed messages; speak openly and honestly. Make sure that nonverbal behavior (expression, posture, gestures) does not contradict your words.

4. *Address behavior, not personality characteristics.* Avoid pejorative adjectives to describe problem areas (lazy, slow, bad attitude). Replace "lazy" with "doesn't perform duties in a timely fashion, misses deadlines, does not respond quickly to changing priorities." Inform the employee of specific behavior that is creating the problem as opposed to stating that the employee is creating the problem. If you have difficulty differentiating behaviors from characteristics, imagine a video camera focused on the employee. What do you see through the eye of the camera?

5. *Deal with employee's emotions.* Emotions affect behavior. Be willing to invite the sharing of feelings and concerns. Create opportunity for private and informal meetings to encourage open discussions. Employees who feels defensive, helpless, frustrated, exuberant, discounted, or enthusiastic will impact the workplace through their behavior. Unexpressed feeling can fester and contaminate the work environment and often contribute to morale problems. Let the employee know that he or she is a person of value, whatever the emotion.

6. *Indicate desire for alternative behaviors.* When you say an employee has a good attitude, what exactly does that look like? An employee can't be expected to change behavior if you don't describe what is appropriate. Don't assume that employees know what to do. If they knew better, they would probably do better. Once you have identified appropriate behavior, observe, and, as Ken Blanchard says in his book, *The One Minute Manager,* "Catch them doing something right and then let them know." It is critical to assuring success to watch and guide employees as they attempt to make changes; intercede when it is clear they are proceeding on the wrong path.

7. *Listen for the purpose of understanding.* When the employee discusses problems and ideas, give your complete attention. Stay neutral, don't assume or give advice, interrupt or criticize, agree or disagree. Restate your understanding of the main points. Always maintain confidentiality.

8. *Take responsibility for your contribution to the problem.* Frequently, managers assume that the problem lies with employee's lack of capability or willingness, when, in fact, the manager may have failed to provide adequate guidance, support, information, or training. Be honest with yourself. Determine how you may have inadvertently created or perpetuated the problem. Then you can approach the employee in a very positive fashion and each can be part of the solution.

9. *Shape behavior with positive reinforcement.* There is no better way to have your expectations met than to let employees know the specific ways they have succeeded. Avoid the tendency to attach implied criticism to reinforcement, for instance, "You did a fine job on the customer contact report this week. It was much better than the last few times." You will enjoy much better results if you catch people in the act of doing something right, then reinforce, acknowledge, appreciate, and thank them.

10. *Encourage learning and experimentation.* Tolerate well-intentioned mistakes as a critical aspect of learning and growing. Follow all mistakes with a constructive conversation about what was learned. Use recognition and appreciation to encourage innovation and experimentation.

11. *Permit incremental changes.* Don't overwhelm the employee with too many changes at one time. Identify simple behavior changes, and tell only one or two at a time; begin with something that the employee can accomplish successfully. Success tends to breed more success. As self-confidence increases, employees believe they can tackle greater challenges. People enjoy being stretched and changed, provided they are treated with care and not stretched beyond their breaking points.

12. *Coach on a regular basis.* Infrequent employee interaction and feedback contributes significantly to lack of motivation and commitment. The best time to coach is "in the moment," or as close to when the behavior occurs as possible. Then employees can understand immediately and implement suggested changes. You will have new coaching opportunities as employees use new behaviors. Avoid the tendency to punish when an employee is having difficulty with something new or when things are actually falling apart.

People manage themselves, to a large extent, when they receive the feedback required to motivate and challenge them. A service manager, as coach of a departmental team, succeeds when players receive the necessary information and tools. Although not every employee will respond positively to coaching, the process allows a relationship to develop wherein both parties will know if it's time for a job change (either within or outside of the organization). The employee will have experience of the manager's good intentions and know that the manager cared enough to work to assure successful performance.

Ability and resources matter little if the employee is not motivated to apply them. However, if ability and resources are missing, a motivated employee will take steps to obtain what is needed. Thus, motivation may be regarded as the key ingredient to effective performance. A few things are certain: people need their dignity; they need recognition and support; they need fair treatment; and they need clear, direct communication about exactly what is expected.

Questions

1. Discuss the influence of human productivity on service costs.

2. Why will service management never become completely scientific?

3. Write a job description for a service manager, including primary characteristics for success.

4. Write a job description for a front-line service or support employee, and indicate desired attributes.

5. Why is it desirable for a manager to coach?

6. Discuss some techniques for effective coaching and team building.

7. What are some consequences of ineffective communication?

8. What are primary differences between service-oriented and product-oriented organizations?

9. What are the key elements of motivation?

10. What is accountability, and how can it be achieved?

7

Organizations

*A*n organization can be understood as a number of persons or groups who have specific responsibilities and are united for some purpose of work. Considered as a process, an organization includes identifying and coordinating work functions that are necessary to achieve the stated business objectives.

Legal Forms

The law requires anyone who operates a business for profit to register as a sole proprietorship, a partnership, or a corporation. Sole proprietorship, a business owned by one individual, has title to all enterprise assets and owns all the profits but must assume all losses, bear all risks, and pay all debts of the business.

It is the simplest form and is best suited to a small enterprise such as a TV repair service or an engineer who "moonlights" by repairing instruments. However, it can work for much larger operations.

A partnership is a voluntary association of two or more persons to carry on, as co-owners, a business for profit. Because of its voluntary nature, a partnership is easily set up without the legal formalities required for a corporation. It combines the talents and money of the partners and sets forth in simple terms the sharing of profits or losses. Many large organizations such as architectural firms, medical clinics, and law offices have been partnerships. However, many professionals have switched to using the corporate format since it is now permitted for individuals.

Chief Justice John Marshall defined "corporation" in the Dartmouth College Case of 1819 as "an artificial being, invisible, intangible, and existing only in contemplation of the law." A corporation is a legal person and a business entity, which can sue and be sued, hold and sell property, and engage in the business operations specified in its charter. A corporation is chartered under state laws and may be owned by any number of stockholders, ranging from one to many thousands. Its form is suited to large, complex organizations with extensive financial investments owned in shares by stockholders and managed by professionals, who may also be owners.

While sole proprietorships comprise about 69% of all business establishments, they do about 25% of sales. Partnerships represent about 5% in number and generate only 7% of sales. Corporations make up 23% of business organizations, but their sales represent 67% of the total. Other forms account for about 1% in each factor.

Most logistics and service organizations use the corporate legal form, because they are established by a parent organization that is itself a corporation. Even if the precedent were not established, the complexity, financial and legal liabilities, and ownership numbers recommend the establishment of a corporation for business purposes.

Historical Overview

The original notion of bureaucracy proposed that organizations would make decisions and have confidence that persons within the company would implement their directions efficiently and effectively. The development of a formalized structure ensures standardized procedures and functions. A bureaucratic structure derives from specialization of functions, then imposes on a hierarchy of people, each of whom has an amount of authority, a set of rules and manages a staff of personnel. Organizations also evolve their own informal structure and culture that establish traditional and customary ways of thinking and behavior.

Organization charts present a diagrammatic view of the organization, depicting the formal authority structure by job title (who reports to whom). Because the authority and scope of duties are not indicated in these charts, organizations often prepare manuals and job descriptions as an adjunct. The organizational chart designates official channels of communication and determines accountability for responsibilities to meet clear objectives (the chain of command). The chain of command should be as short as possible, because information received and passed on by many people gets distorted at each step. Authority must always be commensurate with responsibility. Anyone having responsibility for achieving a specific objective must have the authority required for implementation. Many organizations today eschew the rigid and formalized structures that can confine specialized functions, preclude interactive synergy, and inhibit cooperation. Current practices favor more flexibility to allow for rapid response times to ompetitive opportunities and threats.

Functional specialists play an important role in organizations, today and in the past. Gross confusion and inefficiencies would result if each expert within an organization reported directly to the top person. The division of functions into line and staff activity avoids some difficulty. The distinction between line and staff in business relates to the distinction between line and staff in the military. A line organization includes those persons whose work contributes directly to the achievement of a fundamental goal. Staff assists the line by providing services, developing plans, giving advice, or auditing performance. Staff handles specialized functions that require specific education, experience, or training.

Many critics of classical business theory argue that this ignores many characteristics of human nature because formalized organizational structures exist solely for the purpose of enabling people to work together effectively for a common end. Several alternative approaches to the traditional, classical organizational formats have emerged during recent years:

1. *Behavioral.* Proponents suggest that, no matter how clearly stated, orders and policies will always be interpreted subjectively because employees are motivated by many different forces. Experts suggest that management must maximize human resource potential to function effectively and achieve a high degree of interaction and performance. Some cite the need for three-way communication (up, down, and sideways between peers). Others stress the need for organizations to adapt and change relative to presenting problems.

2. *Decision Making.* This approach emphasizes that an organization's survival depends on its ability to enlist cooperation and espouses the fundamental concept of teamwork.

3. *Systems.* This perspective presents an organization as a social system in which persons constantly interact with and impact one another. The organization is not a static structure but rather is fluid, constantly seeking a state of equilibrium through feedback and interaction.

The 21st Century

Every few hundred years throughout Western history sharp transformations have occurred. In a matter of decades, society rearranges itself: its worldview, basic values, social and political structures, arts, and key institutions. We find that people born into this era can barely imagine the world in which their grandparents lived. Our age is such a period of transformation. One of the fundamental changes is that there is no longer a "Western" history or civilization; there is only world history and civilization.

Knowledge is the primary resource in this society; land, labor, and capital have been relegated to secondary positions. Specialized knowledge by itself produces nothing; it becomes meaningful only when integrated into a task. According to Peter Drucker's article, "Society of Organizations" in the *Harvard Business Review*, "That is why the knowledge society is also a society of organizations; the purpose and function of every organization, business and non-business alike, is the integration of specialized knowledge into a common task."

Mr. Drucker suggests that we already understand much about the tensions and issues that confront the society of organizations. "The tension created by the community's need for stability and the organization's need to destabilize; the relationship between individual and organization and the responsibilities of one to another, the tension that arises from the organization's need for autonomy and society's stake in the Common Good; the rising demand for socially responsible organizations; the tension between specialists with specialized knowledge and performance as a team." By definition, institutions such as society, community, and family attempt to maintain stability and prevent or constrain change. By contrast, modern organizations must be organized for constant change. They must be organized for innovation and the systematic abandonment of whatever is established, customary, familiar, and comfortable, whether that is a product, service, or process; a set of skills; human and social relationships; or the organization itself. Drucker contends that the organization's function is to put knowledge to work...on tools, products, and processes; on the design of work; on knowledge itself. In the society of organizations, we assume that anyone will have to acquire new knowledge every four to five years or become obsolete. Drucker points out that, "The changes that affect a body of knowledge most profoundly do not, as a rule, come out of its own domain." For instance, the greatest challenge to the railroad came not from changes in railroading, but from the automobile, the truck, and the airplane. The pharmaceutical industry has been profoundly changed today by knowledge derived from genetics and microbiology, disciplines that hardly existed only 40 years ago.

Social innovation, often more significant than scientific knowledge, impacts organizations such as commercial banks, the U.S. military, schools, and universities. In part, new technology such as computers, videos, and satellite telecasts will force changes in those institutions. Also, the demands of a knowledge-based society in which organized learning must become a life-long process for individuals, as well as new theories about how human beings learn, will drive change.

For managers, the dynamics of knowledge impose a clear imperative—every organization must build the management of change into its structure. Every organization must prepare to abandon everything it does every few years for every process, product, procedure, and policy rather than prolong the life of successful products, policies, and practices. Simultaneously, an organization must devote itself to creating and innovating. First it must continuously improve everything it does. Then it must learn to exploit its knowledge to develop the next generation of applications from its own successes. Finally, it must learn to innovate as a systematic process. Without these commitments, the knowledge-based organization will find itself obsolete, losing performance capacity and the ability to attract and retain skilled and knowledgeable people on whom its performance depends.

An organization is defined by its task and is effective when it concentrates on that task. Diversification tends to diminish the performance capacity of an organization. Because the modern organization is comprised of specialists, each with his or her own particular expertise, only a focused and common mission will hold it together and enable it to produce. Therefore, an organization is always in competition for its most successful resource: qualified, knowledgeable people. Because an organization consists of knowledge specialists, it must be a society of equals, colleagues, and associates. No knowledge ranks intrinsically higher than another; each is judged by its contribution to the common task. Therefore, knowledge organizations must form teams. As more and more organizations become information-based, they will transform themselves into teams in which every member acts as a decision maker and accepts responsibility for his or her own performance and for the accomplishment of the team mission. While managers in knowledge-based organizations must have considerable authority for decision making and accountability for outcomes, their mandate is not to command but rather to inspire and lead.

Pace-Setting Corporations

Looking forward to the 21st century, we see that pace-setting organizations share several common characteristics:

1. Customer-driven learning organizations will scan the market for changes and focus on satisfying customers' needs.
2. Organizations will deliver excellent quality products that add value to the life of the customer.
3. Pace-setting organizations will emphasize simplicity and speed in the delivery of products and services to customers.
4. Knowledge organizations will initiate change, innovation, and experimentation in response to changing strategic and operating environments. In these dynamic organizations, we expect:
    A. Flatter corporate structures that integrate and coordinate functions and disciplines;
    B. The disappearance of traditional functional structures with separate areas for marketing, production, finance, and information systems;
    C. The elimination of organizational boundaries and departmental constraints as individuals and teams exercise greater decision-making responsibilities (cross-functional operations will generate quicker more effective responses to internal and external environments);
    D. Increased global competition that requires a strategic orientation to diversify in both the domestic and

international arenas;

E. The formation of more strategic alliances to engage in the full range of business activities that encompasses research and development, marketing, and human resources;

F. Information technology (information systems, interactive multimedia communication, artificial intelligence, "virtual reality") that significantly alters management processes, customer relationships, and the efficacy of daily operations;

G. Increased corporate accountability from governments, minority groups, stockholders, and various other constituencies (organizations may no longer function as closed entities, cut off from the needs and demands of society);

H. The continuously changing nature of the 21st century and the requirement of organizations to adapt, analyze, educate, and learn. Transformation demands that organizations re-create and sustain learning themselves in order to foster an ongoing process of cultural, structural, and attitudinal change.

First things first! An organization must get its strategy straight, then take a long hard look at what business it wants to be in and how it intends to make money at it. Robert W. Tamasko, author of *Rethinking the Corporation*, cautions, "Don't fix stuff you shouldn't be doing in the first place." That decision dictates the organization's subsequent actions. Once a clear mission and direction are established, successful reengineering can deliver extraordinary gains in speed, productivity, and profitability.

Reengineering

Reengineering, a.k.a. process innovation and core process redesign, is the search for and implementation of radical change in business processes to achieve breakthrough results. Reengi-

neers start with the future and work backward, as if uncon-
strained by existing methods, people, or departments. In effect,
they start with a clean sheet of paper and ask, "If we were a new
company, how would we run this place?" Then, they conform
the company to their vision. However, because reengineering is
cross-functional and about operations, only strategy can determine which operations matter. Reengineering without strategy
can maim a company and lead almost inevitably to indiscrimi-
nate cost cutting.

Benchmarking provides a starting point for an organization
to understand where it stands, function by function, process by
process. The point and the power of reengineering is the clean
sheet of paper. Filling it in begins with customers. The question
is, How do they want to deal with us? Reengineers begin
designing from the outside in and make the organization wear its
customers' shoes for the entire re-thinking process.

Learning Organizations

The consistent and dominant message of this century is
change. A few wise executive leaders have recognized the link
between learning and continuous improvement and have refo-
cused their organizations accordingly. Continuous improvement
and re-invention require an unshakable commitment to real
learning. In the absence of learning, organizations and individuals simply repeat old behaviors; thus, change remains cosmetic
and improvements are either fortuitous or short-lived. Several
popular authors describe learning organizations in somewhat
idyllic and abstract terms but do not provide a framework for
effective change. In order to create an effective learning organization, a company must understand and provide: 1) simple, action-
able definitions, 2) clear guidelines, and 3) measurement tools
for assessment of learning.

David A. Garvin's article, "Building a Learning Organization" in *Harvard Business Review,* July/August, 1993, offers the
following definition: "A learning organization is an organization

skilled at creating, acquiring, and transferring knowledge, and at modifying its behavior to reflect new knowledge and insights." New ideas are essential if learning is to occur, but ideas alone cannot create a learning organization. Many organizations have been effective at creating or acquiring new knowledge but have not succeeded in applying that knowledge to their own activities. A few organizations have succeeded at translating knowledge into new ways of behaving. These companies actively manage the learning process to ensure that it occurs by design rather than by chance. By creating systems and processes that support learning activities and integrating them into the fabric of daily operations, organizations can manage their learning effectively.

Learning organizations successfully employ five essential activities:

1. *Systematic Problem Solving.* This activity derives primarily from the philosophy and methods of the quality movement and promotes several key ideas:
>   A. Rely on the scientific method for diagnosing problems (what Deming calls the "plan, do, check, act" cycle);
>   B. Insist on data, rather than assumptions, as background for decision making;
>   C. Use simple statistical tools to organize data and draw inferences. Accuracy and precision are essential for learning, so employees must discipline their thinking and attend to details. They must ask continually, "How do we know that is true?" (See Table 7-1.)

2. *Experimentation.* This activity involves the systematic searching for and testing of new knowledge using the scientific method. All forms of experimentation have a goal of moving from superficial knowledge to deep understanding. Essentially, the distinction is between knowing how things are done and knowing why they occur. Knowing how is partial knowledge and addresses norms of behavior and standards of practice. Knowing why is more fundamental, because it captures underlying cause-and-effect relationships and accommodates exceptions, adaptations, and unforeseen events.

TABLE 7-1
Xerox' problem-solving process.

Step	Question to be Answered	Expansion/ Divergence	Contraction/ Convergence	What's Needed to Go to the Next Step
1. Identify & Select Problem	What do We Want to Change?	Lots of Problems for Consideration	One Problem Statement, One "Desired State" Agreed Upon	Identification of the Gap/ "Desired State" Described in Observable Terms
2. Analyze Problem	What's Preventing Us from Reaching "Desired State?"	Lots of Potential Causes Identified	Key Cause(s) Identified & Verified	Key Cause(s) Documented & Ranked
3. Generate Potential Solutions	How Could We Make the Change?	Lots of Ideas on How to Solve the Problem	Potential Solutions Clarified	Solution List
4. Select & Plan the Change Solution	What's the Best Way to Do It?	Lots of Criteria for Evaluating Potential Solutions/ Lots of Ideas on How to Implement & Evaluate Selected Solution	Criteria to Use for Evaluating Solution Agreed Upon/Implementation & Evaluation Plans Agreed Upon	Plan for Making & Monitoring the Change/ Measurement Criteria to Evaluate Solution Effectiveness
5. Implement the Solution	Are We Following the Plan?		Implementation of Agreed-On Contingency Plans (If Necessary)	Solution in Place
6. Evaluate the Solution	How Well Did It Work?		Effectiveness of Solution Agreed Upon/ Continuing Problems (If Any) Identified	Verification that the Problem is Solved or Agreement to Address Continuing Problems

Opportunity, rather than specific current problems, tends to motivate experimentation. Experimental projects usually take two main forms—ongoing or one-of-a-kind demonstrations. Ongoing programs normally involve a continuous series of small experiments designed to produce incremental gains in knowledge and tend to generate a steady flow of new ideas.

Demonstration projects are usually larger and more complex than ongoing experiments. They tend to involve holistic, system-wide changes, often have a goal of developing new capabilities for the organization, and are usually designed from scratch.

3. *Learning from Past Experiences.* The famous philosopher George Santayana coined the phrase, "Those who cannot remember the past are condemned to repeat it." Because many managers are indifferent or contemptuous of the past, they allow valuable knowledge to escape by failing to reflect on past experiences. In fact, failure is the ultimate teacher. Knowledge organizations recognize the value of productive failure as contrasted with unproductive success. A productive failure can lead to insight and understanding and adds to the common wisdom of the organization. An unproductive success occurs when something goes well but nobody knows how or why.

4. *Learning from Others.* Some of the most powerful insights come from looking outside the immediate environment to gain a new perspective. Enthusiastic borrowing from other companies and other industries, also know as SIS (Steal Ideas Shamelessly), generates fertile ideas and provides a catalyst for creative thinking. The broader term "benchmarking" refers to the process of ongoing investigation in order to understand how work is accomplished, which ensures that best industry practices are uncovered, analyzed, adopted, and implemented. This disciplined process begins with a thorough search to identify best-practice organizations, continues with careful study of one's own practices and performance, includes systematic site visits and interviews, and concludes with an analysis of results, development of recommendations, and implementation.

Customers are another equally fertile source of ideas. Customers can provide up-to-date product information, competitive comparisons, insights into changing preferences, and immediate feedback about service and use patterns. Whatever the source of outside ideas, learning occurs only in a receptive environment.

5. *Transferring Knowledge.* For learning to be widespread, knowledge must transfer quickly and efficiently throughout the organization. Ideas carry maximum impact when they are shared broadly. A variety of mechanisms simulate this process: written, oral, and visual reports; site visits and tours; personnel rotation programs; education and training programs; and standardization programs. Because it is difficult to gain knowledge in a passive way, actively experiencing something is significantly more valuable than having it described. For maximum effectiveness, education and training must be linked explicitly to implementation. Also, when employees know that their learning will be applied, progress is far more likely.

Measurement

Managers have long known that "if you can't measure it, you can't manage it." Traditional measurement tools ("learning curves" and "manufacturing progress functions") date back to the 1920s and 1930s when studies discovered that manufacturing costs fell predictably with increases in cumulative volume. Later studies looked at total manufacturing costs and the impact of experience in other industries to determine learning rates. In the 1970s, based on the logic of learning curves, experts proposed the concept of "experience curves" and concluded that costs and prices fell by predictable amounts as industries grew and their total production increased. Both learning and experience curves still enjoy wide use in many technically oriented industries and are used to forecast industry costs and prices.

The limitation of these tools is that they focus only on a single measure of output, cost, or price and ignore learning that affects other variables such as quality, delivery, new technology, or competitive challenge. These measures reveal little about the sources of learning or the levers of change.

A more recent measure, the "half-life curve," has emerged in response to these concerns. The half-life curve, developed by Analog Devices, measures the time it takes to achieve a 50% improvement in a specified performance measure. It provides flexibility, is not confined to costs or prices, is easy to operationalize, provides a simple measuring stick, and allows for comparison among groups. The important limitation with the half-life curve is that it focuses solely on results. Some types of knowledge take a long time to digest, and some developments manifest few visible changes in performance over long periods of time. A more comprehensive framework is needed to track progress over time.

Organizational learning occurs through three overlapping stages. The first step is cognitive. People within the organization who are exposed to new ideas expand their knowledge and begin to think differently. The second step is behavioral. Employees begin to internalize new understandings and alter their behavior. The third step is performance improvement. Changes in behavior lead to measurable improvements in tangible results such as superior quality, better delivery, and increased market share. Because cognitive and behavioral changes typically precede performance improvements, a complete learning audit must include all three stages. Surveys, questionnaires, and interviews provide effective tools for each area of learning. Finally, a comprehensive learning audit also measures performance to ensure that cognitive and behavioral changes have actually produced results.

Implementation

Successful learning organizations carefully cultivate attitudes, commitments, and management processes steadily and slowly over time. The first step is to foster an environment that is conducive to learning. Provide time for reflection and analysis, to think about strategic plans, dissect customer needs, assess current work systems, and invest in new products. Training in brainstorming, problem solving, evaluating experiments and other core learning skills is essential.

Another powerful catalyst for learning is to open up boundaries and stimulate the exchange of ideas. Boundaries inhibit the flow of information, keep individuals and groups isolated, and reinforce preconceptions. Once a more supportive, open environment exists, learning forums can be created. These events define explicit learning goals and can take a variety of forms—strategic reviews, systems audits, internal benchmarking reports, study missions, and symposiums. Together these efforts help eliminate barriers that impede learning, and begin to promote learning as a commitment, a way of life.

Teams and Working Groups

Teamwork represents a set of values that encourage listening and responding constructively to views expressed by others, giving others the benefits of the doubt, providing support, and recognizing the interests and achievements of others. A team is not just any group working together. Jon Katzenbach and Douglas Smith in their article, "The Discipline of Teams" in the *Harvard Business Review,* cite performance results as the primary distinction between teams and other forms of working groups. They postulate that, "A working group's performance is a function of what its members do as individuals, whereas a team's performance includes both individual results and 'collective work products'. A collective work product reflects the joint, real contribution of team members."

Working groups are both prevalent and effective in large organizations where individual accountability has primary importance. The best working groups come together to share information, perspectives, and insights in order to make decisions that help each individual do a better job and to reinforce individual performance standards. Individual goals and accountability are always the focus of working groups. Working group members do not take responsibility for the results of others, nor do they attempt to develop incremental performance contributions that require the combined work of members.

Teams differ fundamentally from working groups in that they require both individual and mutual accountability. Teams produce discrete work products through the joint contribution of their members; a team is more than the sum of its parts. Think of a team as discrete units of performance and not just a positive set of values. Katzenbach and Smith offer the following working definition: "A team is a small number of people with complementary skills who are committed to a common purpose, a set of performance goals, and an approach for which they hold themselves mutually accountable." The essence of a team is common commitment to a purpose in which team members can believe.

Most successful teams shape their purposes in response to a demand or opportunity put in their path, usually by higher management. Management bears responsibility for clarifying the charter, rationale, and performance challenge for the team. Management must also allow enough flexibility for the team to development commitment around its own interpretation of the purpose, set of specific goals, timing, and approach. The best teams translate their common purpose into specific performance goals. The process of transforming broad directives into specific and measurable performance goals is the first critical step for a team to shape a purpose that is meaningful to its members. Teams need to identify specific goals for several reasons:

1. Specific goals help define a set of work products that are different from an organization-wide mission and from individual job directives.

2. Specificity of performance goals facilitates clear communication and constructive conflict within the team.

3. Attainability of specific goals helps teams maintain their focus on achieving results.

4. Specific objectives have a leveling effect that is conducive to team behavior. Teams that succeed evaluate what and how each individual can contribute to the team's goal and, more importantly, do so in terms of the performance goal rather than a person's status or personality.

5. Specific goals allow a team to achieve small wins as it pursues its broader purpose. The small victories build commitment and aid in overcoming inevitable obstacles that arise during the long-term process.

6. Performance goals are compelling as symbols of achievement that motivate and energize. The combination of purpose and specific goals is essential to team performance; each depends on the other to remain relevant and vital. Clear performance goals help a team keep track of progress and hold itself accountable; the broader, nobler aspirations in a team's purpose supply both meaning and emotional energy. The majority of successful teams number fewer than ten members. Small size seems more a pragmatic guide than an absolute necessity. In addition to the right size, teams must develop the right mix of skills—each of the complementary skills necessary to do the team's job. Skill requirements fall into three general categories:

A. Technical or functional expertise;
B. Problem solving and decision-making skills; and
C. Interpersonal skills. Teams are powerful vehicles for developing the skills needed to meet the performance challenge. Team member selection should be predicated as much on skill potential as on proven skills.

Effective teams develop strong commitment to a common approach—how they will work together to accomplish their purpose. Team members must agree on who will do particular jobs, how schedules will be determined and adhered to, what skills need to be developed, how continuing membership on the team will be earned, and how the group will make and modify decisions. This element of commitment is as important to team performance as is the team's commitment to its purpose and goals! Agreeing on the specifics of work and how to integrate individual skills and advance team performance is the essence of shaping a common approach. Every member of a successful team does equivalent amounts of real work. This is a very important aspect of the emotional synergy that drives team performance.

In effect, the team establishes a social contract among members that relates to their purpose and guides and obligates how they must work together. No group ever becomes a team until it can hold itself accountable as a team; mutual accountability is a rigorous test. At its core, team accountability represents the sincere promises we make to ourselves and to others. These promises lay the groundwork for two critical aspects of effective teams: commitment and trust. Mutual accountability cannot be coerced any more than people can be made to trust one another. But when a team shares a common purpose, goals, and approach, mutual respect and accountability result as a natural outgrowth. Katzenbach and Smith summarize the main differences between teams and working groups as shown in Table 7-2.

TABLE 7-2
**How to tell the difference
between a working group and a team.**

Working Group	Team
Strong, Clearly Focused Leader	Shared Leadership Roles
Individual Accountability	Individual and Mutual Accountability
The Group's Purpose is the Same as the Broader Organizational Mission	Specific Team Purpose that the Team Itself Delivers
Individual Work Products	Collective Work Products
Runs Efficient Meetings	Encourages Open-Ended Discussion and Active Problem-Solving Meetings
Measures Its Effectiveness Indirectly by Its Influence on Others (i.e., Financial Performance of the Business)	Measures Performance Directly by Assessing Collective work Products
Discusses, Decides, and Delegates	Discusses, Decides, and Does Real Work Together

TEAM FUNCTIONS VERSUS WORKING GROUP FUNCTIONS

Most teams can be classified in one of three ways: teams that recommend things, teams that make or do things, and teams that run things. Each type faces a specific set of challenges:

1. Teams that recommend things usually have predetermined completion dates. The critical issues for these teams are getting off to a fast and constructive start and achieving the handoff required to get recommendations implemented.

2. Teams that make or do things tend to have no specific completion dates because their activities are ongoing. However, management must determine the critical delivery points where team performance might have maximum impact—places in the organization where the cost and value of the products and services are most directly determined. The critical issue here is a relentless focus on the performance of each specific objective.

3. Teams that run things tend to oversee some business, ongoing program, or significant functional activity. The main issue here is to determine whether using a real team is the most effective approach. The key judgment is whether the sum of individual bests will suffice for the performance challenge or whether the group must deliver substantial incremental performance requiring real, joint work products. A second major issue is that teams that run things often confuse the broad mission of the total organization with the specific purpose of the small group at the top. Although the team option promises greater performance, it also carries more risk, because the price of taking the team approach is high: members get diverted from their individual goals and costs outweigh benefits; people resent the imposition on their time and priorities; and serious animosities can develop that undercut the potential personal bests of the working-group approach.

Working groups that run things present fewer risks than teams and have many advantages. Effective working groups need little time to shape their purpose since the leader usually establishes it. Meetings are run against well-prioritized agendas. Decisions are implemented through specific individual assignments and accountabilities. Indeed, if there is no performance need for the team approach, efforts spent to improve the effectiveness of the working group make much more sense than floundering around attempting to become a team.

Katzenbach and Smith believe that, "Teams will become the primary unit of performance in high-performance organizations." They suggest further that teams will not supplant individual opportunity or formal hierarchy and process, but rather, teams will enhance existing structures without replacing them. Organizational innovation requires preserving functional excellence through structure while eradicating functional bias through teams. Productivity requires preserving direction and guidance through hierarchy while drawing on energy and flexibility through self-managing teams. When organizations face specific performance challenges, teams can be the most practical and powerful vehicles.

Questions

1. Would a product service organization function better under an authoritarian manager or under an empowering manager? Why?

2. Describe the traditional understanding of organizations.

3. What are the challenges presented by the knowledge era? Describe the dynamics of a knowledge-based organization.

4, Describe several characteristics of pace-setting organizations in the 21st century.

5. Discuss reengineering. What is it? How does it work? Why is it effective? When is it effective?

6. What are learning organizations?

7. Describe the five essential activities employed by learning organizations.

8. What is the role of measurement in learning organizations?

9. Describe the differences between teams and working groups.

10. When should teams be used? When should working groups be used?

8

Service Training

*T*raining is critically important to a service organization. Although training can be expensive in terms of time and money, qualified people are the major asset of a service organization. Service organizations will usually be involved in three main types of training: new hire, advancement training, and management training.

Needs Identification

The first step in determining needs is to establish organizational objectives, as discussed earlier. The second step is to establish individual objectives for the employees. For example, does a person want to become the best service technician

145

around on the basic product? Does he want to get involved with state-of-the-art electronics? Does he want to assume responsibility for a total installation? And does he want to progress to management? Organizational objectives and individual objectives are matched as much as possible and training needs identified to meet the objectives of both as shown in Figure 8-1.

Once needs have been identified, the training content, methods, facilities, and resources can be identified (see Figure 8-2).

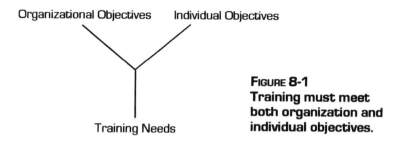

FIGURE 8-1
Training must meet both organization and individual objectives.

New-Hire Training

Even with a good recruiting and selection process, a wide variety of skills will be encountered with new hires. Affirmative action plans and equal employment opportunity requires that companies provide training necessary to qualified people even

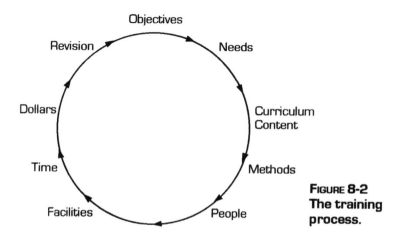

FIGURE 8-2
The training process.

though they may have had a previously low level of preparation. A typical flow of training development will be:

- Orientation to the organization
- Brief on-the-job exposure with an experienced service technician
- Formal basic training
- Product line training
- On-the-job training (OJT) with coaching

Orientation to the organization should include a formal program, either individualized or by group, covering the history, products, organizations, and overall objectives of the service organization and its parent. A tour of the facilities should be included. Complete orientation by the personnel department into all benefits and opportunities with the company, as well as company philosophy and policy on items like tuition assistance, should be included.

Individual "big brothers" should be assigned to new employees to introduce them to all members of the local service organization and orient them to the locations and people to see for office supplies, lab equipment, publications, and so on. The big brother may also be able to help with matters outside the work organization such as living accommodations and community resources, so that those concerns don't take much of the new employees' time.

After the formal orientation, the new service technician should be assigned to an experienced service technician, possibly the same big brother, for several days' orientation on the job. The length of this orientation will depend mainly on the amount of time available before the new service technician can be assigned to school. The purpose of this orientation is that new service technicians should understand the product and customer environment enough to intelligently discern the vital parts of the training program and better understand the practical applications to their job needs.

Formal basic training may require from one to many weeks,

depending on the amount of equipment included in the basic training. All personnel should receive instruction in safety precautions, reading standard schematics, and troubleshooting techniques. Formal basic training will usually be followed by specific product training. Judgment must be made on the amount of training to be given at one time, to allow new service technicians an opportunity to practice what they have learned. Figure 8-3 illustrates that the gap between present skills and the complexity of equipment and applications is growing. Reducing this gap is a challenge for product designers and program managers.

People learn best when all senses are involved—sight, hearing, touch, taste, and smell. We can give information quickest by speaking but receive it best through our eyes. No information is retained 100% at first. Depending on the importance of the information to the receiver, retention may be virtually nil or maybe 80-90%. The second time the information is received, particularly if it is presented in a different fashion, a higher percentage will be retained. This is called reinforcement. A third exposure at a later time provides additional reinforcement. However, beyond that the returns diminish in value. We learn best by doing. Motor skills, for example, that involve turning screws or measuring voltages cannot be taught from a book. They should be demonstrated, and then the student should perform the activity.

There are five major types of training new service technicians must receive: technical, people, how to train others, administration, and selling. Learning the people skills is best done by a combination of lecture, discussion, and role-play. Practical exercises, particularly using TV monitors that can play back the performance in private, are beneficial. Learning how to sell

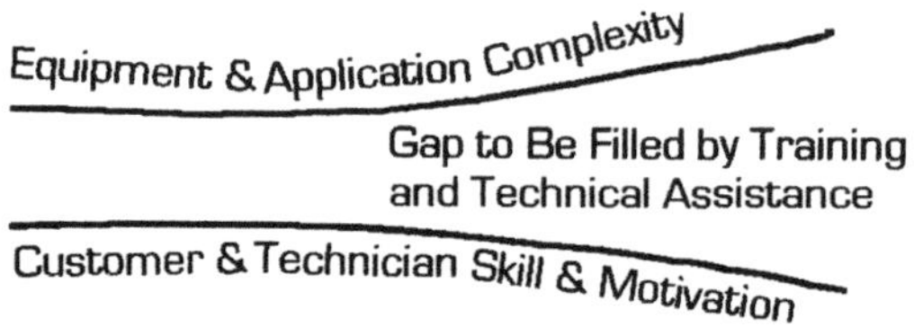

Equipment & Application Complexity

Gap to Be Filled by Training
and Technical Assistance

Customer & Technician Skill & Motivation

FIGURE 8-3
**The complexity
of equipment is
growing while
skills are fading.**

people on service and related supplies can be learned best the same way. Technicians are often "accidental salespeople" on whom the customer relies for advice. It is often a good idea to have students teach others, as teachers must refine their own knowledge and skills in order to teach them to others. It must be remembered that the typical service technician is not well oriented to people, selling, or training. These skills will require effort and practice and will not be perceived as having high priorities by the new service technician. The penalties for failure in a classroom are far less than they are in a customer's location. Figure 8-4 compares the technicians of the past who were skilled on fixing equipment but were less skilled on fixing customers, with technicians of the present and future. The qualifications of support personnel are changing so that the best technicians will usually be at headquarters where they can stimulate the design engineers to properly consider service in the product design. Super techs also support the help-desk personnel with advice on difficult issues. Field technicians of the future will follow set diagnostics, change the required parts, and be very good at pleasing the customer.

Some kinds of training can be acquired only under realistic conditions. For example, installation of equipment can best be learned by installing products in a customer's plant. Preventive maintenance—cleaning—can best be learned on a machine that has gotten dirty in a customer's operating environment. In order to learn well in a realistic condition, a newly trained person should be placed under the supervision of a team leader or field instructor to insure the learning and practicing of procedures in the field as taught in the formal schooling and desired by management.

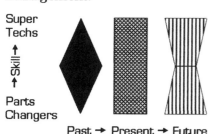

Past → Present → Future

FIGURE 8-4
Qualifications of technicians are changing.

CURRICULUM CONTENT

Figure 8-5 shows the logic for developing new product programs. Note that four skilled positions are required for developing new training programs:

- Curriculum manager
- Engineering writers
- Illustrators
- Training analysts

Two-way interactions in training allow questions to be immediately raised and answered. Information should be taught to students the way management wants, and it must be reinforced.

Which material is to be formally taught should be decided according to difficulty, frequency of occurrence, time involved, and dollar impact. For example, frequently encountered service tasks that take many expensive labor hours should be carefully established according to good time-and-motion principals. Vacuum-cleaning a machine, for example, seems like a simple mundane task, but it will consume many minutes during every preventive maintenance call. Author Joe Patton once watched an otherwise proficient service technician vacuum the same spot on a machine six times because he failed to recognize the basic principle of following a standard, efficient pattern of removing dirty assemblies first, starting at the top and working down. On that office product a minimum of five minutes, with billing value of at least $5 could be saved on every preventive maintenance call by applying good time-and-motion and training techniques.

If a difficult task has interactions that require a "feel," they should be taught on the assumption that they will be encountered often enough for the learning to be retained. Real learning comes by doing. The supervisor must make sure that a new employee is immediately put to work using new training. If not, the learning curve will never be developed. The learning curve is the speed of accomplishment and reliability with which a person performs assigned tasks. A newly trained person will not be so efficient as someone with practical experience. This rate of development can be accurately established and is very useful in determining workload and systems reliability predictions.

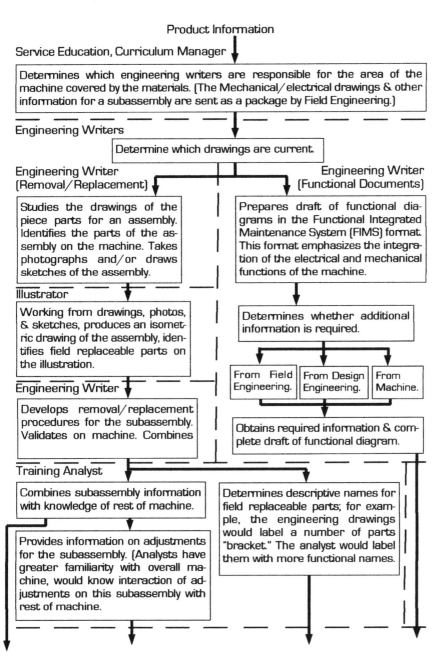

Product Information

Service Education, Curriculum Manager

Determines which engineering writers are responsible for the area of the machine covered by the materials. [The Mechanical/electrical drawings & other information for a subassembly are sent as a package by Field Engineering.]

Engineering Writers

Determine which drawings are current.

Engineering Writer (Removal/Replacement)

Engineering Writer (Functional Documents)

Studies the drawings of the piece parts for an assembly. Identifies the parts of the assembly on the machine. Takes photographs and/or draws sketches of the assembly.

Prepares draft of functional diagrams in the Functional Integrated Maintenance System (FIMS) format. This format emphasizes the integration of the electrical and mechanical functions of the machine.

Illustrator

Working from drawings, photos, & sketches, produces an isometric drawing of the assembly, identifies field replaceable parts on the illustration.

Determines whether additional information is required.

From Field Engineering. | From Design Engineering. | From Machine.

Engineering Writer

Develops removal/replacement procedures for the subassembly. Validates on machine. Combines

Obtains required information & complete draft of functional diagram.

Training Analyst

Combines subassembly information with knowledge of rest of machine.

Determines descriptive names for field replaceable parts; for example, the engineering drawings would label a number of parts "bracket." The analyst would label them with more functional names.

Provides information on adjustments for the subassembly. [Analysts have greater familiarity with overall machine, would know interaction of adjustments on this subassembly with rest of machine.

FIGURE 8-5
Developing new product training programs.

Advancement Training

Every service technician likes to be learning new things, and every company must be introducing new products if they are to survive. Most organizations have a hierarchy of advancement, both in technical proficiency and in experience pay level, through which service technicians may progress. New service technicians normally begin with the most basic products, which generally use simple technology. After they have had experience and an opportunity to learn the customer environment and practice their personnel training and sales skills as well as establish technical proficiency on the basics, the opportunity should be presented for further development. In fact, many advanced products will have service technicians trained to service them both from advanced training programs and from new hire programs. Service management must decide whether it is better to upgrade existing personnel, with the resulting void filled by a new hire, or to train a qualified new hire directly onto the advanced equipment. For example, it may be better to hire somebody with an associate degree in electronics and train him directly than to upgrade an existing person. The considerations for this decision include availability of personnel, pay required, morale of existing personnel, turnover, and timing in which the requirement must be filled. Most service organizations budget at least one formal training school and ten to 20 days of formal training per year in addition to training during normal work hours. Thus, training can be a major component of labor costs.

Management Training

When service technicians are selected for management, they must suddenly give up their tool bags and the need to accomplish everything independently and learn instead to achieve their objectives through others. New managers, who will usually understand the technology, will require major emphasis on personnel relations, communications, organization, and other supervisory techniques common to management in most organizations. Such training may be obtained through a centralized company training department that trains managers from all over the company. It may also be obtained through organizations such as the American Management Association, the Instrument Society of America, correspondence studies, or a local university. Management training provides a good opportunity for service managers to come in contact with management personnel of other functions and better understand the vital interactive role service plays. Becoming a good manager can be achieved only by actual experience. The best combination naturallyis formal study combined with experience and a knowledgeable mentor to keep a close watch and give advice and criticism as necessary.

It is a definite advantage to identify service management candidates early and begin development before they must begin acting as managers. Every organization can plan ahead and forecast management needs. Three to five candidates should be selected for every management opening, and any of those candidates who need training should be scheduled at the easiest possible opportunity. Prospective service managers will best benefit from training if it is given in short doses with time between formalized training to observe and practice. One day a week for five weeks is often better than five concentrated days, provided that eligible personnel can be so scheduled. Travel time or other reasons may necessitate concentrated training sessions, but there are advantages to less concentration with more experience and reinforcement.

Individualized Training

All people are not alike. As was mentioned earlier, it is up to the service organization to provide whatever levels of education are necessary. For this reason, individualized instruction such as programmed learning, correspondence courses, and computer-assisted instruction (CAI) can be valuable. Many service organizations use individualized instruction to bring all candidates up to a given level of achievement before attending any training. Students' motivation is high when they are new to an organization or just notified of acceptance for advancement training. Service technicians will work very hard to assure they make a good impression to undergo this training, as it is required by labor law that it be paid time for non-exempt personnel. Individualized instruction has many advantages and can permit formal classroom time to be much more effective.

Facilities

Facilities for training vary greatly. Most layouts include classrooms to hold a class of 12 to 20 persons. The rooms should have whiteboards, overhead projectors, writing tables, comfortable chairs, and good lighting and acoustics. Toilet and coffee facilities should be readily available. Laboratories will be required with all instrumentation and equipment easily set up for the service technicians' practice. You may want to have laboratories available in the evenings and on weekends so that people who want more time on the equipment may get it. Room and board should be near the training facility to minimize travel time.

Large companies such as IBM, Xerox, and NCR have international, national, or regional training centers that draw personnel from all over the world. Naturally, economies of scale and high quality of instruction are possible with these centralized facilities. Even if centralized facilities are available, much training will still take place in the local branch office. Service management should provide facilities for in-branch training at their local facility, in a parts center, or even in leased space such as a local motel. The training facility should be easily accessible to service management personnel so management can keep track of the students and the students have the opportunity to ask questions.

Contract training may also be provided through organizations such as The Association for Service Management International (AFSM International), The Compo Group, GP Strategies, Hahn Consulting, Heathkit, InterAct, Patton Consultants and the University of Wisconsin Management Institute. Manufacturers and service companies often train service representatives with their own people and usually announce schedules of classes that anyone willing to pay the price and take the time may attend.

Performance Requirements and Examinations

Every person undergoing training should take examinations frequently to assure that learning has been effective. The objectives established at the beginning of a service training program should be measurable, and every student should be required to pass them before training is considered complete. A good individualized training program will require personnel to repeat segments in which they cannot pass the test until they do pass it. Requirements should be quantitative where possible. For example, technicians can be required to isolate and correct faults in a pressure sensor within 12 minutes. Or to "locate, isolate, remove, repair, and adjust" a fluid transducer intermittent ground within five minutes. Other performances may be demonstrated less quantitatively, such as "proficiently role-play selling a service contract to a customer manager who is uncertain of the need."

A training report should be sent to the students' management at the end of the course to show how well they have done. Any remedial activities or items that should receive particular attention on the job should be identified. It's very good for student motivation to award recognition for high achievement to the top ten percent or so of a class. A course-completion certificate for the student to display is also recommended.

An adult who wants to succeed in the business of service should plan to continuously learn and upgrade his or her education. Training can make the difference between doing a task by muddling around or doing it effectively. Training is an investment in our major resource—people—that should pay off with as high or higher a return on investment as any investment in a hard product.

Questions

1. Why does training start with needs identification for the organization and the individual employee?

2. Why is some training necessary for nearly every new employee?

3. What topics should be included in an orientation program for a new employee in your organization?

4. What training for a service technician in your organization should be individualized rather than taught as a large class in a formal situation?

5. Discuss why service training requires a high proportion of "doing-it-yourself" activities.

6. Discuss whether training time should be concentrated on techniques that are difficult to learn or on items that will consume the most time,

7. Should every service technician be taught to solve all potential problems? Why or why not?

8. What opportunities exist for individualized instruction such as CAI, web-based, and programmed learning in your organization?

9. What conditions make individualized training preferable to centralized group instruction?

10. What items would you as a manager like to see included on training reports about your employees?

9

Maintenance Technology

*E*very product will fail sometime. When given a choice between no failures and fast fixes, rational managers should emphasize avoiding any need for maintenance. No need is better than fast fix!

Maintenance means all actions necessary to retain an item in, or restore it to, a specified condition. Because people to whom perceptions are more important than facts often determine the need for maintenance, we use the term "service" to include both maintenance of equipment and good customer relations. The goal of good maintenance service should be to maximize operational availability at reasonable cost. Operational availability A_i is the probability that a system will operate satisfactorily when called upon in an operating environment. It is normally expressed by the formula:

$$\frac{\text{MTBM}}{\text{MTBM} + \text{MDT}}$$

where MTBM is mean time between maintenance and MDT is mean down time, including administrative and logistics supply times. MTBM includes both MTBF (mean time between failures), a measure of equipment reliability, and PM (preventive maintenance). Maintenance is generally divided into two main groups, corrective maintenance (CM) and preventive maintenance (PM) (see Figure 9-1). Total quality management (TQM) and related strategies for just-in-time (JIT) production place heavy emphasis on effective support that results in low down time and high availability. As shown in Figure 9-1, several additional names are attached to each type of maintenance. Corrective maintenance is also called unscheduled maintenance (UM), referring to actions that are performed as a result of failure to restore an item to a specified condition, as well as emergency maintenance (EM) or repairs.

We are often so busy trying to do maintenance faster that we forget about the opportunity to plan ahead and eliminate the cause of the failures. This is another example of proaction (eliminating the need) being much better than reaction (fixing the failure faster or cheaper). In modern automobiles, for example, electronic ignition has eliminated the need for frequent replacement of distributor points and the problems they previously caused. If a choice must be made between allocating resources to reliability or to maintainability, emphasis should be placed on reliability. But remember, everything will fail sometime, so at least minimum maintainability must be implemented.

There are three main types of maintenance, and three major divisions of preventive maintenance, as shown in Figure 9-1.

Think of the maintenance relationships as the fingers on your hand. The thumb represents the critical improvement branch. The middle three fingers (like the Boy Scout sign and the motto "Be Prepared") are the branches of preventive maintenance, which are central to good equipment performance. The little finger, which represents failures that must be repaired,

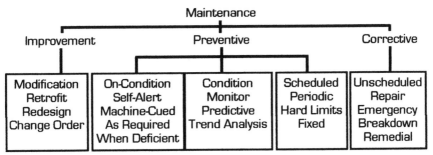

FIGURE 9-1
Maintenance relationships.

should be the smallest component of the maintenance system.

The authors classify predictive maintenance as a subset of preventive maintenance. Before going further with preventive maintenance, let's look at the typical reliability bathtub curve shown in Figure 9-2.

Early infant mortality failures, often the result of poor quality manufacturing or defects introduced during service, are minimized by a "burn-in." Some equipment, such as a piston aircraft engine, is broken in for several hours at "slow time" in order to set the moving parts properly. For aircraft, such tests are usually performed near an airport to let the aircraft glide to a landing if the engine fails during the critical first hours.

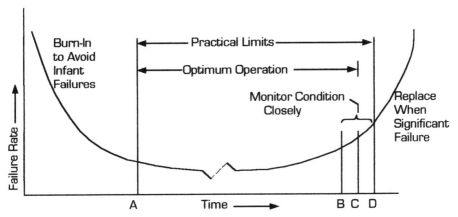

FIGURE 9-2
Typical reliability curve.

The middle part of the bathtub curve is commonly called "random failures" or constant-failure-rate failures. The midsection of the bathtub curve is generalized as composed of many possible causes of failure, with the probability of any one being quite small. Then, if wearout contributes to failures, the failure rate will increase, as shown in the last part of the curve. Failures here are caused by metal fatigue, erosion, decreased elasticity, increased resistance, fluctuating dielectric constants, weakening cathode electron emission, and other physical characteristics that change with environment, time, cycles, and operation.

Why don't we run all equipment to failure and then just fix it? Because the failure may occur at a very inopportune time, may be highly aggravating, can result in reduced production, and can cause excessively high cost. On the other hand, it is possible to do too much scheduled maintenance and thereby induce problems and incur excessively high costs. A total systems approach is necessary to determine the best combination of these factors.

Why don't we fix a PM point and do preventive maintenance on everything then? Figure 9-3 shows the effect fixed PM has on use.

Note that the reliability bathtub curve is a composite of several other curve forms and actually fits only a few components, such as motors that have both electrical, electronic, and mechanical parts. Most digital electronic parts have early failures and then a stable life. Other parts have a virtually flat or steady, slowly increasing failure rate. Some, where user-induced failures

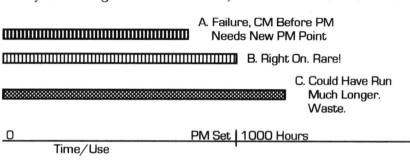

A. Failure, CM Before PM
Needs New PM Point

B. Right On. Rare!

C. Could Have Run
Much Longer.
Waste.

0   PM Set | 1000 Hours
     Time/Use

FIGURE 9-3
Fixed PM effect on use.

are prominent, have few initial failures and then more failures as more new operators try to use the equipment. The rate of user-caused failures will usually start low because the early adapters are generally more knowledgeable and often actually read the instructions before trying to operate their new gizmo. As more people acquire the product, more operator-caused problems will appear because of both more people involved and those people tend to be less qualified in operation. About 90% of potential conditions can best be maintained by inspection, lubrication, and monitoring to track operating conditions and predict when direct maintenance is required to prevent failures.

Sensing an Impending Failure

A functional test that indicates go/no go gives the operator or maintenance person a clear indication of need. If a clear threshold exists such that the equipment will operate well on one side of the threshold and not operate on the other side, devices may be used to clearly indicate equipment status. The human body contains many sensors. While operating a car, we hear the smoothness of starter operation, gears, valves, and exhaust sounds. We feel the car lurch as the clutch engages, sense vibration on rough roads, and notice the temperature. We smell an odor if oil or electrical connections are hot, and see the condition of the body, spark plug corrosion, and exhaust smoke. Unfortunately, human sensing is not always reliable, and perceptions are frequently invalid. A rapid deviation from normal is naturally easier for us to sense than is a slowly changing condition. For most items we need sensitive instruments to assist us in detecting trends. Thus, continuous-reading gauges in automobiles have been generally replaced with "idiot lights" that turn yellow for caution and red for catastrophic malfunctions

Inspection to detect impending failures has a good payoff if there are parameters that give an accurate indication of impending failure and if there is a long enough period after inspection to allow for preventive maintenance to prevent failure. Figure 9-4 shows how the failure speed affects inspection payoff. To be effective, condition-monitoring maintenance requires a threshold value of some parameter beyond which failure is probable and appreciable operating time between the occurrence of the threshold value and failure.

Inspections are generally ineffective for constant failure rate failures because the time interval between the attainment of the threshold value of the parameter and the occurrence of the failure is small. Therefore, constant failure rate failures can rarely be anticipated by inspections or voided by scheduled maintenance. Scheduled maintenance does not always improve inherent reliability. For example, inspecting your automobile tires will determine whether alignment is good and they are wearing evenly and will allow you to have a defect corrected if appearance indicates a problem. But it will not prevent your tire from going flat if a nail punctures it a few miles down the road.

Detection Aids

Test methods for determining whether service is required can be relatively precise. However, human beings have to determine the objectives, goals, and specifications required to

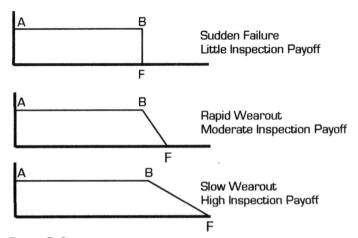

FIGURE 9-4
Failure speed versus inspection payoff

measure parameters against those standards. The test methods may be categorized as manual, semi-automatic, automatic, and integrated. The cost relationships of these maintenance detection methods are shown in Figure 9-5.

Manual checkout usually requires personal manipulation of standard instruments such as voltmeters and oscilloscopes to detect malfunctions or impending failures. It is slow, labor-intensive, and generally reliable. Semi-automatic checkout refers to test methods that utilize both manual and automatic equipment. The checkout is considered semi-automatic when more than 2% but less than 50% of the test time involves operator participation. When several similar systems are to be tested, it becomes feasible to go beyond manual checkout and use semi-automatic. This feasibility usually occurs when six or more identical systems are to be used. Semi-automatic checkout equipment is largely a compromise. Initially it costs more than manual testing equipment but less than automatic. It is much faster than manual but slower than automatic equipment in performing tests. Semi-automatic checkout equipment is more complicated than manual test equipment but much less so than automatic. Semiautomatic test equipment finds particularly good application where:

- Manual test equipment cannot perform the required testing fast enough,
- A high degree of repeatability between readings or settings is necessary,
- Frequency of use is low to moderate,
- There isn't enough time to wait or enough money to purchase an automatic test set, or
- Increased size and weight can be tolerated.

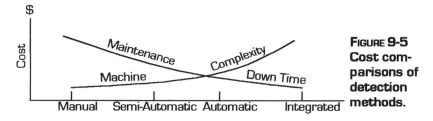

FIGURE 9-5
Cost comparisons of detection methods.

Automatic checkout equipment (ACE) may be either ground support equipment (GSE), built-in test equipment (BITE), or special technician test equipment. Automatic checkout equipment is normally a collection of test instruments that are designed to minimize the duties of human operators. Computer software is often used to run the tests and analyze results. Many field service organizations equip their technicians with laptop computers that can run diagnostics on the equipment. Even automobiles produced in recent years have connectors into which computerized equipment is plugged to run diagnostics evaluations on the engine and operating components. The computer can take many measurements each second and can analyze operating conditions far better than a human could with manual instruments. In fact, the real advantage of computerized instrumentation is that it can adjust ignition timing, duration, advance, and other parameters during normal operation to enhance performance as well as reduce failures.

From a service maintenance point of view, one of the goals of ACE is to allow the operator to thoroughly check out the equipment and then, if a malfunction is detected, notify the technician with details to enable the technician to arrive with proper documentation, tools, and parts. Remote diagnostics that can be performed via telephone lines or other communications links bring the major advantage that needed parts can be identified and acquired before the technician goes to the site.

There are often customer concerns about allowing constant electronic access to equipment. Customer management often decides in favor of allowing the ability for service to continually analyze equipment. Other sensitive installations protect equipment with a firewall or keep the service modem unplugged until it is needed for analysis. Remote diagnostics help to keep good parts in the field and reduce the level of CND (could not determine) / NTF (no trouble found) parts returned for repair.

The automatic checkout equipment hardware and software are given the task of selecting tests, recording results, correcting and analyzing data, and making decisions based on test results. Normally, a checkout is considered to be automatic when a human operator is involved less than 2% of the checkout time. Automatic checkout equipment may be called upon to perform several management functions:

1. Confidence testing or malfunction testing to verify system readiness and assure a high probability of mission success

2. Maintenance testing for malfunction isolation to speed repair and thus extend the useful system life

3. Failure prediction to detect and advise of drifts or trends that may lead to failures

Automatic checkout equipment adds complexity to a system, and the complexity often leads to lengthy down time and high cost. Properly designed automatic checkout equipment requires considerable time for development, production, and debugging. Unless a large number of tests and diagnostic routines are required, the full capabilities of internally programmed checkout equipment will be wasted. Automatic checkout does not constitute a cure-all. It is a challenge in systems design. Designed-in diagnostics must also be flexible and reprogramable to accommodate future changes.

Integrated checkout uses equipment, normally electronic, that is designed into and becomes an integral part of major equipment. The measurement of many different types of signals, such as voltage levels, frequencies, pulses, and operational or sequential time relationships, may be accomplished by design integration of small electronic assemblies into the equipment. Condition indication measurements would be made at the input and output of each replaceable assembly. The test result signals may be communicated to onboard devices or may be accessed only when the equipment is connected to a diagnostic device.

Examples of integrated checkout and operational control are found in automobiles. Sensors continually monitor critical parameters and send signals to microprocessors that evaluate them many times a second and apply corrective action when necessary. Fuel and air adjustments to gasoline engines, ignition timing changes, and anti-lock brakes are examples. On the other hand, high cost and complexity will keep foot-actuated brake systems in use for a long time. In future years, on-car devices will provide corrective action as possible and then alert the driver to the need for specific shop maintenance actions. This exemplifies fault-tolerant equipment and predictive/preventive maintenance.

Whenever possible work with program management, design, and production to help them build serviceability into products. Show them how investment now will pay off later in fewer failures, faster repairs, higher customer satisfaction, and reduced costs. Engineering and Manufacturing usually have major targets of time and cost, so need top management to goal them also to future service costs.

Essentiality and Priority

The concept of essentiality was developed to enable Polaris and Trident submarines, which would be under the sea for long periods of time, to recognize the potential failure of items having a major impact on mission requirements that should have redundant components or stock replacements. Conversely, items of little consequence could be almost disregarded. For example, the critical inertial guidance system had to have adequate backup, but a radio for listening to commercial stations was not critical.

This concept has been transferred to commercial business, typically using a four-point rating of importance such as the following NUCREC classifications for need urgency:

1. Safety and extensive critical damage
2. Not operable and not producing revenue
3. Operating at substandard levels
4. Minor cosmetic problems

The NUCREC scheme helps to prioritize efforts. The acronym comes from Need Urgency x Customer Rank x Equipment Criticality. Obviously, need urgency levels 1 and 2 require corrective actions, whereas level 3 might be fixed when a service technician is next scheduled at the account, and level 4 may be corrected as convenient. Typically, each customer has a rank assigned on the customer record as a joint decision between sales and service. Each piece of equipment should also have a criticality assigned: 1, 2, 3, or 4. When a request for service is received, the call receiver decides the need urgency based on the caller's information. A computer program or mental logic can multiply Need Urgency x Customer Rank x Equipment Critical-ity. For example, a 1 x 1 x 1 = 1 situation would probably have everyone following the disaster squad to the customer's site. At the other extreme, 4 x 4 x 4 = 64 and would be on the bottom of the list until raised either by automatic progression over time or by a human overriding the mathematics. Service calls should also be prioritized by response time, target start time, or target completion time. Failure detection logic, shown in Figure 9-6, aids in deciding what kind of detection system should be used.

The first question to be asked is whether the failure is critical. If the answer is no, then all items should be itemized by their class order.

If the failure is critical, ask whether the function is hidden or not. If the answer is no, the operator should visually inspect that item.

If it is hidden, the next question is whether the impending failure can be effectively detected by integrated checkout. If yes, then an integrated or semi-automatic detection system should be used.

If no, a human checkout plan should be considered. Special maintenance checks that would detect impending failure should also be used. Finally, if all else fails, then "hard" time limits should be established. Recognize that there may be advantages to setting "hard" time limits to help undisciplined operators identify needs for maintenance. With automobiles, for example, a 3,500-mile oil change is certainly not correct for all cars (see Figure 9-3), but it is much less expensive than including built-in test equipment and establishes a maintenance point to which most operators will adhere.

The major tasks required during service maintenance are:

- Detection
- Diagnosis
- Isolation
- Remove and reinstall
- Remove and replace
- Repair
- Adjust / align

- Calibrate
- Certification
- Change/modify
- Inspection
- Refurbish
- Recondition

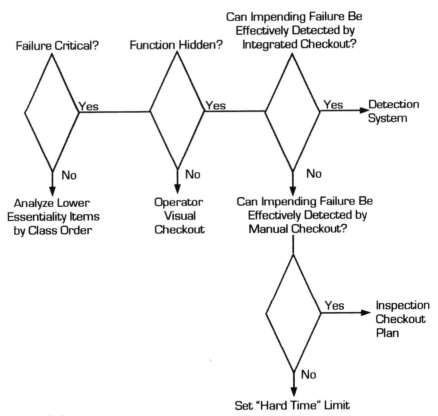

FIGURE 9-6
The logic of failure detection.

Task Analysis

The maintenance system is typically organized as shown in Figure 9-7. It is often difficult to segregate detection from isolation, and the two may be combined for some equipment. For example, we may detect that a car is not starting properly but must then isolate the trouble to the electrical system or the fuel system and then further search for the specific component of the faulty system. Decision-tree logic is very useful for this purpose, as it leads a technician through the decisions by a series of questions and yes or no answers.

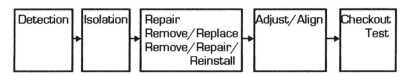

FIGURE 9-7
Maintenance logic flow.

Maintenance Standards

Standards for cost and the use of replacement parts may be set for all maintenance activities. As fault diagnosis and isolation will be by far the most expensive items in terms of both time and cost, good technical documentation is very important. Once a technician determines where the problem lies, he can usually correct it quickly, but he often corrects it at too high a cost. For example, many high-tech companies typically find that 30-45% of the electronic modules returned as "defective" are in fact "good." Reasons can be proposed. If the diagnostics were faulty, it was easier for the service technician to replace the entire group of suspect parts rather than find the single true problem. If the fault were intermittent, the service technician replaced the "most likely" source of failure in the absence of any better knowledge. If the service technician felt a need to show the customer that something was really wrong, he pulled the part that was easiest to remove. As pressure increases toward fast restoration times, parts replaced to fix a problem that do not fix the problem are rarely replaced. That often leaves technicians with parts of questionable quality in their stocks, or results in NTF (no trouble found) returns. These solutions are all wasteful!

Standards for maintenance activities are difficult to establish accurately for every situation since environments, equipment, people, and the problem/cause/action requirements vary. Time and motion study is useful for initial estimates. Good reporting systems will gather data on every service call and then permit analysis of standard activities, work elements, and delays. One successful approach, called work force management, starts with the premise that present conditions and times are generally accepted by everyone involved. Without worrying whether the absolute times are "good" or "bad," work force management points out to management and employees alike where time is being spent and what delays are impeding satisfactory service. Active participation of everyone involved usually results in rapid and sustained improvement. Total quality maintenance (TQM) and similar continuous improvement efforts help both quality and quantity of service.

One cannot easily control technicians or their performance in the field, and different customers want different things. Yet, once conditions in the field get the same kind of attention that conditions inside a factory generally get, many new opportunities become possible. Discretion is the enemy of orderly standards and quality. Many variations and frequent changes can reap havoc with service in the field just as with any manufacturing operation.

If customer service is consciously treated as "manufacturing in the field," it will get the same kind of detailed attention that manufacturing does. Service should be carefully planned, controlled, automated, audited for quality, and reviewed for performance improvement and customer reaction. Moreover, the same kinds of technological labor-saving and systems approaches that now thrive in manufacturing operations can be extended to help improve service.

Throwaway Maintenance

Many products ranging from television sets to military weapons are designed with replaceable modules that are to be thrown away when they fail, rather than repaired. As electronics replace electro-mechanical equipment, products become smaller, robotic assembly provides the advantage of low cost production, increasing repair costs, and availability of products for demanufacture all promote throwaway.

Many considerations go into this decision, including:

- Capability for repair
- Competition
- Diagnostic equipment
- Documentation
- Ecology
- Facilities
- Material availability
- Parts costs

- Personnel and training
- Physical distribution
- Pipeline quantities
- Test equipment
- Transportation
- True failure rate
- Usage rate

The typical service technician does not like to throw anything away, especially if costs are under pressure and will appear less if it is fixed instead of a new part being ordered, or an immediate need arises and a replacement part cannot be obtained right away. Then the technician will try to fix it, and all the detailed analysis in favor of throwaway is disregarded. If the supply system does not provide adequate replacement when they are needed, then repairs become practically mandatory if they are technically possible.

A 100% throwaway maintenance program is possible for low value parts. Many companies use a base line and in the field will scrap any part that costs less than $125. This is a typical break-even point for the direct costs and human efforts that are necessary to return and repair parts. The point of no return is increasing when you add all costs of tagging the part, repackaging, labeling, arranging transportation, receiving, screening, repairing, and retesting a part.

Realistic analysis backed up with adequate spare parts, documentation, training, and discipline is vital so management can assure that the concept of throwaway maintenance is followed in fact. New electronic technologies for microcircuits and large-scale integration will relieve the problem. They are, fortunately, very reliable and lower in cost but require very sophisticated repair facilities. Naturally, it will become increasingly more important to do realistic analysis during the concept and design stages to ensure that throwaway maintenance is advantageous, but success will yield huge logistics savings and more useful products that are easier to service. Do note that if components are designed for service replacement and repair, they also include the discard option. The reverse is not true. If components are designed for throwaway, then they can probably not be repaired.

PCB Repairs

Printed circuit boards (PCBs) are used in many products and must often be repaired. They are treated here as a special case, since 20 to 60% of boards returned from the field are apparently good when tested. Testing of misdiagnosed boards that are actually good costs more than does testing and repair of bad boards where the fault can be quickly found. The question is, why was the board returned? Did it actually not work in a specific equipment, or was it replaced through faulty troubleshooting or to placate a customer? Several companies have the policy of repairing bad boards, but scrapping boards that test as good. This is, however, excessively expensive. Most repair houses serial number boards so they can determine if a board was ever in before for repair. The third time that a board comes for repair with no trouble found, that board is destroyed. Experience shows that scrapping a possibly good board is lower cost than returning a board with undetected problems to the field. Remember that costs are at least ten times higher in the field than in the shop. Angry customers, technicians lacking confidence, and high expediting costs cause the multiple.

A preferable method is to diagnose all returned boards and, if a faulty component is identified, to engrave it and carefully mark the position. The component is removed and tested separately. If it is defective, it is replaced with a good component. If it is not defective, it is put back in the board and the PCB retested for design effects. Obviously this takes time, so is concentrated in the early stages of product life when a found flaw can be quickly fixed before many products are built. Most board repair processes that have engineering change orders (ECOs) to accomplish will make those changes first and then test the board. The ECOs often fix the problem for which the board was returned.

All repaired boards and those on which a defect could not be found should be subjected to "shake and bake." This means rapidly taking a board from ambient temperature down to -20° C and holding it there for about 20 minutes, then heating it rapidly to 65° C and holding it there for 20 minutes before rapidly returning it to ambient for test. Vibration may be added, if typical of the part's operating environment, to help catch faulty connections. This procedure will weed out an additional 15% defective normally due to mechanical failures from inadequate strain relief and poor production quality. Component selection is a minor part of unreliability. Production quality causes most problems, with design deficiencies next. Information to date indicates that the failure rate of the first year is about three times higher than in following years. Indications are that the failure rate then remains flat for many years before wearout sets in. Even then, the wearout is due mostly to problems caused by initially poor production design or technique. Heat is a major enemy of both electronic and mechanical components. Microcircuits can generate enough heat, and even internal friction, that wearout may become a future problem. It is interesting that complex components and boards generally cause few problems because more attention is given to them.

If a defect is found and corrected, the repaired board will probably be more reliable than a brand new production one since early failures have been weeded out. A good rule of thumb for pricing PCB repairs is 20-30% of the new parts cost. Obviously this means that for expensive parts, repair is a much better option than new procurement. Note, however, that limited available parts may mean that repair is necessary at any cost.

Do-It-Yourself

Many customers are interested in doing as much as possible themselves before they succumb to an expensive service call. This should be encouraged so long as it does not present a safety hazard or potential equipment damage, since it gets the product back into service quickly and satisfies the customer. A product small enough to be easily transported by the customer may well be brought to a central service center by the customer or by a pickup and delivery service. This means that expensive customer engineers need not waste their time travelling and can do repairs where test equipment and spare parts are readily available. Automatic diagnostic equipment, which is too expensive to give to each individual customer engineer, can be used at such a repair center.

The ideal situation is that any customer service should need no tool other than a thin coin, and all customer education should be through self-guiding features of the equipment. Built-in diagnostic and/or warning capability is possible if it can be economically justified. Hot-swap parts means that parts can be replaced without turning the power off or having to reboot a computer. This can save considerable time. In some cases hot-swap enables replacement by a trained courier at lower cost than a technician would charge. If the equipment is portable and shipped ready to use, the customer can then install and remove his own equipment, which has many advantages. Consideration should also be given to like-for-like exchange of equipment if it is necessary for the customer to bring it to the repair center. At least, "loaner" equipment should be available if the customer's machine will be in repair for a significant length of time.

Telephone help desks and technical assistance centers should be staffed with qualified customer service personnel to answer queries, guide customers in performing minor maintenance, and order any parts the customer may require. With Internet and web technology it is possible to allow users direct access to frequently asked questions (FAQs), technical bulletins, previously solved problems that enable the customer to solve the problem fast and without needing direct human help. In order for the do-it-yourself strategy to succeed, the operation must be simple. Technology in concept and design may be very complex, but the customer's responsibilities must be simple.

Maintenance Technology

Modern in-service reliability analysis shows that the real incidence of an adverse age-reliability relationship is much lower than intuition had implied. Far more problems have been encountered by using low-reliability people to service high-reliability products. A good rule for maintenance to follow is "fix anything that is defective; check condition of critical items; and if it is working right, don't touch it!" While this is an arguable statement to persons who say that better performance may be possible, experience shows that touching something that is working well has the potential for causing problems that were not originally present.

Predictive Maintenance Data

When to service equipment can be a technically driven decision once people provide the objectives and standards. Many pieces of equipment, however, cannot afford the high cost of sensors and detection devices to self-alert for the need to maintain. For those situations, we switch to statistics, probabilities, and the management science tools of system analysis and decision theory. The key is effective measurement of performance, service, and costs. Table 9-1 shows a small section of an operating report for school buses. The main source of information for this report is the driver of each bus, who completes a report each time the gas tank is filled and oil is put into the vehicle. The maintenance supervisor reports any repairs and records the odometer reading at the end of every month so the report can be run for a one-month period. Targets have been established for each item so that significant variance from the target can be indicated. The report flags any bus that is operating significantly worse than target. Any bus that has a significant change will be checked carefully to determine whether it is having problems that require maintenance action or, perhaps, disposal.

TABLE 9-1
School bus maintenance report.

VEHICLE	ODOMETER		GASOLINE		OIL	
#	Mo Mi	VFT Mi	MPG	VFT Mi	Qt/K	VFT
10	719	-281	4.0	-0.6	1.4	-2.0
15	548	-452	3.3	-0.3	14.0	11.7
20	976	-24	3.8	-1.1	1.0	-1.1
25	1250	250	5.1	0.2	0.0	0.0
30	1065	65	5.4	0.3	0.0	-1.8

VEHICLE	REPAIRS		OPERATING COSTS	
#	MTD$	VFT$	Mo	Avg
10	260.86	379.14	0.111	0.132
15	201.05	438.95	0.187	0.166
20	236.19	403.81	0.132	0.114
25	259.03	380.97	0.095	0.112
30	187.82	452.18	0.094	0.111

One of the big advantages of this type of report is in the control that attention brings to parts and consumables. In the past, gasoline, oil, and spark plugs occasionally found their way into private automobiles instead of the buses for which they were intended. Interesting improvements have been noted in bus mileage per gallon where buses allegedly getting only three miles per gallon suddenly get five because all the gasoline recorded against the bus is now going into the bus's gas tank! A bus that requires 14 quarts of oil per thousand miles certainly needs maintenance. Radical changes or large deviations from standard in repairs and operating costs are certainly cause for further investigation. A report such as this is not in itself the answer, but it provides information that can indicate significant changes to maintenance and business management.

Premium-class modern automobiles often have built-in instruments that display instantaneous and average miles per gallon. That is helpful to drivers, but it does not show variations over time that could indicate a problem. And, of course, many cars do not have some gadgetry. A simple record every driver should keep is shown in Table 9-2.

A 3 X 5 card or notebook with columns for mileage and gallons of gasoline allows a motorist to determine the mileage that has been driven and the gasoline consumption in miles per gallon. The records kept by the author read from the bottom up, to make addition easier, and include date and cost for tax records. These actual data from an actual small car illustrate the variability in data due to driving conditions and the level to which the gas tank is filled each time. As the tank is usually filled at a self-service station, that variable is under better control than it would be if random gas station operators filled the tank to

TABLE 9-2
Small car miles per gallon (MPG) calculations.

MILEAGE	MILES THIS FILL-UP	GALLONS OF GAS	MPG	DATE	$COST
			Mean		102.05
Total	2,379	84.1	28.29	σ 0.86	($0.042/mi)
58,543	281	9.6	29.27	4/20	11.71
58,262	241	8.8	27.38	4/13	10.74
58,021	232	8.3	27.95	4/07	10.13
57,789	266	9.4	28.29	3/29	11.56
57,523	153	5.3	28.91	3/17	6.52
57,370	250	8.8	28.41	3/14	10.56
57,120	266	9.1	29.23	3/08	11.10
56,854	209	7.8	26.79	3/02	9.44
56,645	234	8.5	27.53	2/25	10.29
56,411	247	8.5	29.06	2/18	10.20*
56,164		Full		2/11	*tune-up

varying heights. In this case, the author felt the car was not performing as well as it might, as over a year had passed since a major tune-up had been performed. In spite of mileage data within control limits, the engine was tuned on 4/20, resulting in a $90 cost and no significant improvement in performance. The data should have been believed! It is interesting to note that the standard deviation for all data to date is a very tight 1.6 around the mean 28.4. The largest excursions from the mean during this data period are deviations of -1.50 and +0.98. Remember that we are much more interested in the negative variation than the positive, as the negative will indicate a need for maintenance.

Conclusions

To summarize service technology, the following conclusions can be made:

1. Quantitative facts are better than qualitative intuition.
2. Maintenance need often varies from the norm.
3. Reliability-based maintenance can be individually determined.
4. Technology aids detection of needs.
5. People must establish criteria and limits.
6. Safety is paramount.
7. Inherent improvements come only by design.
8. If it works well, don't touch it.

Questions

1. Select a product and list the items of preventive maintenance that should be accomplished on it.

2. On the same product, what are the most common failures and their causes?

3. What inspections on your sample product would be desirable and effective to give an accurate indication of impending failures?

4. Why is automatic checkout equipment not a solution to all maintenance problems?

5. For the major failures of your product previously listed, which are essentially 1? 2? 3? 4?

6. Why do service technicians often replace parts that are later found to be good?

7. Discuss the validity of a production-line approach to service in your organization.

8. What new technologies applicable to your products would indicate throwaway maintenance instead of repair?

9. Are there reasons that products should not be designed for "do-it-yourself" maintenance?

10. Discuss why equipment should not be touched if it is working to specifications.

10

Inventory Management

Management Objectives and Goals

*T*he objectives of inventory activities usually are matters of customer service as measured by product operational availability, service response time, support level, and cost. Customer service to a retail operation usually means having the items the customer wants to buy. If a desired item isn't in stock, the customer may have to go somewhere else, and the sale is lost. To a product support manager, service may mean having enough "spare" parts available to fix an inoperative machine, get an aircraft flying again, or fix a car for the irate customer.

Operational availability (Ao) is a popular topic mainly because it is often too low. In many instances it is too low because the mean logistics delay time (MLDT) is too high. MLDT is often the down time while a service technician is waiting for necessary replacement parts. Customer-oriented measures of product availability focus on service as perceived by the customer. These measures include the percent of service calls for which necessary parts are on hand, the reverse condition which is often termed 'broken calls' where necessary parts are not immediately available, percent of orders completely filled, percent back-ordered, percent shipped on time, and percent shipped within specified time periods.

The first management objective to be determined is what percent of all line-item orders should be filled within what time limit. Isn't management going to say, "We want to satisfy 100% of our demands immediately?" Not if they are intelligent, knowledgeable management! They should understand that the only way to satisfy all demands is to stock an infinite supply of parts. As an infinite supply of spare parts would cost an infinite amount of money, this solution is obviously unacceptable. On the other hand, having no spares will produce a low assurance against stock-outs, but rarely 0%, for even with no spares, the possibility exists that no spares will be demanded. Thus, we can have neither 0% assurance nor 100% assurance, but we can obtain some level of assurance between 0% and 100% by varying the number of spares stocked. Increasing the number of spares increases the assurance against stock-outs and decreasing the number of spares decreases the assurance. Thus we can set our goal as meeting demands 95% of the time from immediate stock, with the remaining 5% to be met within 24 hours. The time can usually be reduced by expeditious ordering, production, transportation, and special handling—all of which cost money. Because we realize that a high probability of parts support costs a large amount of money, we must continually determine sensitivity, optimum levels, and cost constraints in order to get the most for our money. Management will usually have an objective of performing within the budget, which translates into a specific goal of providing the service parts inventory for a certain price

When you need one widget from inventory, you are really interested only in whether there is one widget or no widgets in the stock room. If there is one item, you are satisfied. If there are no items, you are dissatisfied. However, additional items in the stock room do incur carrying costs. This cost often amounts to about 30% of an item's value per year, because of the cost of handling, information, storage space, security, insurance, taxes, and the cost of capital. The cost of capital is the charge for borrowing the money or what your company can make in profit from alternate uses of the funds. If your demand is fulfilled, you are happy. If you are on the supply end of the supply-demand function, you have other concerns: Can I fill the next order promptly? What is my safety stock? Have I reached my reorder point? What is the economic order quantity? Is demand changing? It is up to the inventory manager to advise management of sensitivities to cost, time, and support so that management can decide what balance they desire.

Demand

What causes demand? Demand is usually synonymous with usage. For a new item it is probably the sum of sales to customers plus defective or damaged items that cannot be sold. For spares support, usage will be the failure rate plus replacements due to incorrect diagnosis or damage by faulty repair efforts, parts received defective, and quantities necessary to fill the "pipeline." Obviously the usage is above and beyond the technical failure rate and requires the prediction assistance of experienced personnel. Demand will be higher than usage if additional parts are being requested to fill pipelines or safety stocks. Note also that demands will equal or exceed issues, since parts are not always available for issue to meet all demands.

Order Quantity

The usage rate that we have just determined, based on failures plus modification factors, must be further expanded to consider the replacement level, other suitable parts, repair or scrap, level of repair, location, and essentiality.

The use of other substitutable parts is of course enhanced

through standardized design and support. The more common parts there are in a system or product family, the more chance there will be of filling a part need from any of several sources. The next higher assembly may of course provide replacement parts. That next higher assembly may be a very acceptable level of replacement. Inventory carrying charges will be greater, but mean down time will be reduced. The time could be particularly significant if there are interactions between parts in the assembly that require time-consuming checks and adjustments or special documentation and tools. Knowledge of the next higher replacement level is also valuable for contingency planning.

Determination of whether a part should be scrapped or repaired has a major influence on the number of spares required. If a part is scrapped, an additional part is necessary to replace every one used. If a replaced part is returned for repair, then the return and repair pipeline recycle time determines the quantity needed to fill needs during the part down time. High-volume, high-cost assemblies will normally be repaired, but low-volume, low-cost parts should be designed as expendable for throwaway maintenance.

Spares location also interacts with operational organization, as well as facility planning, selection, and operation, because the more places there are to stock parts, the more parts are required.

It does not make sense to stock all parts at every level. An important consideration is the ability to have accurate information on where a part is quickly available. Needs may then be satisfied from several possible locations within the system. For example, every generator set may have its own spare fuses and fan belt. The service technician who services many generators may not need to carry those items because he can borrow from another generator for later replacement. The technician may then be able to go to a team stockroom and replace the supply. That stockroom may be directly supported from a central distribution center.

LOCATION

Time to resupply is a function of the source location, with

expected time based on actual field data for existing products. This is illustrated in Table 10-1.

TABLE **10-1**
Resupply time by location type.

Stock Location	Typical Time to Supply to Machine
At Equipment Site	10 Minutes
Service Technician	15 Minutes
Strategic Courier	1.5 Hours
Service Branch	2 Hours
Central Depot	Overnight
Factory	2+ Days

TURNOVER

Inventory turnover is an important function since no item should lie dormant at any location. It is necessary, however, to realize that response time, support level, and costs are much more vital service measures than is turns. The service parts supply of a home appliance repairman, aircraft mechanic, or computer customer engineer can be scientifically modeled for optimum results from the total system. As a rule of thumb, a traveling technician should carry low to moderate priced parts that he will use at least every three months or four times per year. If the parts are not being used at that rate, they should be dropped from the authorized stock list (ASL) and moved to the next higher stocking point for consolidation. The evaluation of what parts should be held where and in what quantities should undergo continual revision, as much time can be lost (but not reported in typical reporting systems) while getting necessary replacement parts.

STOCKS

Stock-keeping units (SKUs) are a handy reference because each SKU described separately differs from others in shape, size, color, fragrance, strength, reliability, or other characteristics. These differences are termed as *Form, Fit, or Function.* A unique part number designates a SKU. The parts unique to service are termed field replaceable units (FRUs). These parts are usually a sub-set of the manufacturing parts used to build the equipment. FRUs are designated as the only parts to ever be carried since they embody the one best way to fix any field problem. Probably only ten to 20 percent of the FRUs will be high-use parts, usually termed *active*. The authorized stock list for each technician should be determined from the active FRUs, based on the products to be supported with related restore times and cost requirements. This Logistics Business Model can be effectively determined using scientific statistical modeling.

Inventories may be classed as basic demand, in-transit, safety, or dead depending on the reason for which they are held. Basic demand stocks are those required for filling orders under conditions of certainty where we can accurately predict demand and replenishment time.

In-transit stocks are those parts enroute from one inventory location to another. They may be considered as a part of basic stock even though they are not available for use until they arrive at their destination. Many modern transportation functions include in-transit as a means of warehousing the supplies where arrival time may be accurately predicted. Many service organizations use FedEx, UPS, or another overnight service for outbound shipments and two-day service for return of defective and excess parts. Those transportation services with tracking capability are very consistent and reliable for delivering service parts.

Safety stocks are those held in excess of the basic inventory because of uncertainties in either demand for the SKU or replenishment time, or for disaster or security reasons.

Dead stocks are those for which no demand has occurred over a specified period of time. If no further demand is anticipated these excess and obsolete parts should be scrapped and their value expensed off the financial balance sheet.

FIFO and LIFO are common terms to inventory, meaning *First In-First Out* and *Last In-First Out*. Normally FIFO is used for physical movement of parts to assure regular use of items in inventory and avoid obsolescence, excessive shelf life, and deterioration. However, accounting policies usually use LIFO for improved financial reporting to accommodate inflation. The monetary LIFO valuation may be different from the physical movement LIFO unless there is identification of specific inventoried items such as serially numbered equipment, in which case both must be LIFO or both FIFO. Avoid FISH, which humorously stands for *First In - Still Here.*

The term "ABC Inventory Policy" refers to a collection of prioritizing practices to give varied levels of attention to different types of inventories. Note that ABC for service parts is different than ABC for production parts since service priorities may depend not only on unit cost of inventory items and usage rate, but also on essentiality, strategic value, seasonal effects, customers served, shelf life, and ease of storage.

Inventory Management Under Uncertainty

Inventory policy decisions would be relatively simple if customers organized their requirements for an equal number of all items every day of the week, and further if the time required to schedule, produce, and transport replenishment stocks were known and constant. While these conditions rarely happen, the model that describes such an ideal situation should be understood so that real world variations can be applied. The two major influences on the quantity of a product to order are 1) the cost of placing an order and 2) the cost of carrying inventory. As the cost of placing an order or setting up a manufacturing run is assumed to be constant for any size of order run, the cost per unit will decrease as order size increases. However, as order size increases, it will take longer to deplete the quantity ordered and the average inventory level will be higher; therefore carrying charges will cost more, as illustrated in Figure 10-1.

With fixed, known demand the average level of inventory fluctuates half as much as the change in reorder quantities. We can see that the more we order each time, the higher will be the average amount on hand and the higher our carrying charges will be for interest, warehousing, insurance, storage space, taxes, obsolescence, and damage. However, the relative costs of carrying and ordering inventory vary inversely as in Figure 10-2.

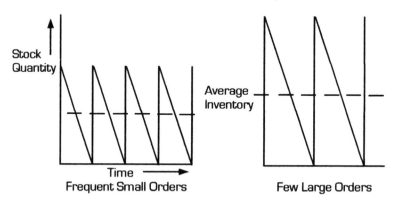

FIGURE 10-1
Order size versus average quantity on hand.

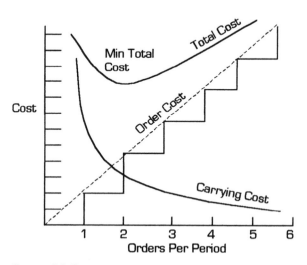

FIGURE 10-2
Minimum cost is the lowest combination of order and carrying costs.

The problem can be represented mathematically by stating total costs as

$$C = \frac{QUR}{2} + \frac{AD}{Q}$$

where C = total inventory cost
   Q = quantity ordered
   U = average cost per unit
   R = annual inventory carrying rate as a percent of product cost
   A = the set-up or ordering cost
   D = demand during the period

This simply says that $QUR/2$ is the annual carrying cost of one half the quantity ordered, $(Q/2)$ times the unit cost (U) times the annual inventory carrying charges (R). It also says that AD/Q is the annual ordering or set-up cost in terms of the number of orders per year (D/Q) times the cost per set-up order (A).

The optimum value for Q is found by setting C equal to the minimum value and taking the first derivative of a cost equation that solves for Q = *Square Root of* $2AD/RU$. This formula for optimum quantity is most commonly known as the economic order quantity (EOQ) formula.

For example, if the set-up cost for a small production line is $500 and annual unit demand is 225 units, which cost $40 each and have carrying charges of 30% per year, how many should be ordered at one time?

$$EOQ = \text{Square Root of } (2AD / RU)$$
$$= \text{Sq Rt } [(2 \times 500 \times 225) / (0.30 \times 40)] = 137$$

Thus, the line would be set up and 137 units produced each time.

REORDER POINT DETERMINATION

Ideally, we would like to have the first of the new units available just as the next order is received following stock-out of the earlier supply. The question is, "How many parts will we use during the reorder cycle?" If our sample demand was a normal 2,000 over 365 days per year, that would be 5.5 units per day. Working backward, if we had a perfect transportation time of seven days, a production time of three days, and an order-processing time of four days, we calculate a reorder cycle of 14 days, so we would place the order when the bin quantity reaches 77 items (5.5 x 14). This process is shown in Figure 10-3.

INVENTORY MANAGEMENT UNDER UNCERTAINTY

Theory is fine, but reality does not always follow theoretical guidelines. Unlike manufacturing, service doesn't usually know what demands will occur for parts, how much reorder time will be needed, what breakdowns and delays will occur in transportation, and whether the handling will be affected by the fact the order comes through late on a Friday afternoon. There may be great variability on all these factors. We can adjust two parameters: order quantity and order timing. As the initial impact comes from the demand, the order timing is more important. Order

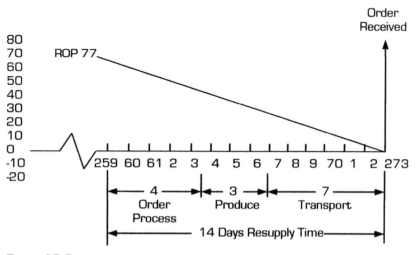

FIGURE 10-3
Reorder point (ROP) considerations.

quantity, of course, determines the frequency with which we expose ourselves to potential stock-out conditions as well as the average items in inventory, but in terms of units left on hand it is the point at which we place our order that will determine our ability to fulfill demands. Herein lies the need for our understanding of the distributions, means, and variance.

Geneseo Instrument Gizmos (GIG) makes parts for process controls and instruments. One of their most popular items is a "Multigiz." In order to determine demand, the president (who is also the sales manager and production manager) tabulates orders for Multigiz over the past year. He notices a seasonal trend, which reaches its peak in September. He also notices minor patterns based on days of the week and the end of the month, but he decides to disregard these in figuring demand for the last year (consisting of 250 operating days). He plots the demand data as shown in Table 10-2.

From the data in the table, the president can see that he can fill 81.6% of the orders immediately by having three Multigiz in stock during any day. Having four units gives 10% more, or 91.6%. Doubling that quantity to eight units adds 7% better service, and having five times that many adds the remaining 8.4% necessary to give 100% immediate delivery. Figure 10-4 is a histogram of the same data.

TABLE 10-2
Demand data.

Demand	Number of Days	Total Units	Frequency %	Cumulative Frequency %
0	50	0	20.0	20.0
1	57	57	22.8	42.8
2	65	130	26.0	68.8
3	32	96	12.8	81.6<
4	25	100	10.0	91.6
5	4	20	1.6	93.2
8	13	104	5.2	98.4
16	1	16	0.4	98.8
20	3	60	1.2	100.0
	250	583		

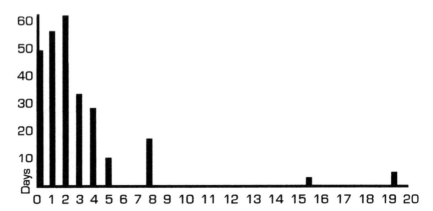

FIGURE 10-4
Graphic display helps make the demand numbers
easier to understand.

The replenishment cycle also varies in length, mainly because of sporadic delivery schedules of components, as the actual deliveries are shown in Table 10-3.

$$\text{Mean } \mu = \frac{\Sigma X}{N} = \frac{144}{20} = 7.2 \text{ days}$$

$$\text{Standard deviation } \sigma = \sqrt{\frac{\Sigma(\overline{X} - x)^2}{\Sigma N}} = \sqrt{\frac{\Sigma D^2 N}{\Sigma N}} = \sqrt{\frac{99.20}{20}} = \sqrt{4.96} \cong 2.23$$

We can now see that the range of deliveries is between five
and 15 days with a mean of 7.2 days and a standard deviation of
2.23 days. Seeing the data in graphical form helps people
comprehend that most deliveries are between five and ten days
with a preponderance at seven days, but occasionally a delivery
goes astray and takes 15 days to arrive. The concept of using
standard deviations to measure the spread of data is very useful
in many aspects of the service business. For example, part
returns are seen to average one week in a typical organization,
but some technicians just don't get their parts back on time.
Three standard deviations, which will account for about 98% of
all events on one tail, often amount to four weeks or more. Thus
we know that while half of our returns are back in a week, the

TABLE 10-3
Resupply data.

Days (A)	Number of Deliveries (N)	Cumulative Delivery Days (C)=a x N	Deviation per Delivery (D) [∞C/∞N] - A	D^2	D^2N
5	4	20	2.2	4.84	19.36
6	4	24	1.2	1.44	5.76
7	6	42	.2	.04	.24
8	3	24	.8	.64	1.92
9	1	9	1.8	3.24	3.24
10	1	10	2.8	7.84	7.84
15	1	15	7.8	60.84	60.84
	20	144			99.20

rest straggle in over the following month. We only addressed one tail of the distribution because only the late arrivals concern us. Early arrivals are good. This data also enables us to pinpoint the technicians who are late returning parts, so they can be reminded to get the parts back fast.

For simple management information, the arrival time is plotted against deliveries as shown in Figure 10-5. Each time a delivery is received the data should be automatically recorded

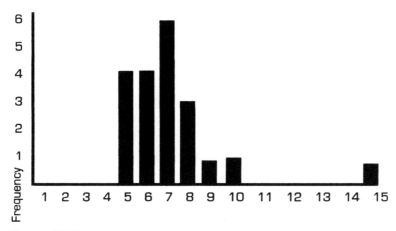

FIGURE 10-5
Resupply histogram.

and added to the chart, keeping the information continually updated. It helps also to have charts prepared for each supplier, factory, distribution center, or other useful group. Information in this graphic form helps management to recognize trends and potential problems, motivates the organizations involved to do better because they are on display, and stimulates the continual attention necessary to assure adequate arrival times.

Taking the reorder quantity as set at 30 units, because of the capacity of the delivery trucks, how often should we place a reorder? The point to reorder is triggered by the quantity of parts remaining.

The probability of demands can be read off the frequency demand chart, Table 10-2. GIG management has established a goal of being able to fill 90% of the orders from stock on hand. Looking at the demand table, this requires four units on hand at any time, which would give a cumulative frequency of 91.6%. What is the chance of encountering a certain level of usage during the order cycle? The rules of computing probability give us a basis for computing the chance. For example, what is the chance of having a demand for four units every day during the seven-day average order cycle? The extremely small probability of about five per 100 million is only part of the situation, as we are interested in the cumulative probability of having a demand greater than the supply.

The question we must ask is, "What is the probability of stocking-out before the new units arrive?" From our earlier work, we can calculate that the average demand was 2.33 units per day over the last year (583 total units/250 operating days). Each delivery gives enough components for 30 units. That means we should reorder about every 13 days (30 / 2.33 = 12.88 days). Since our average delivery time, which is also the median or typical delivery time, is seven days, the first order should be placed seven days before we expect to need the units, which is about six days after the arrival of the last order. Seven days at the average 2.33 parts used per day equals 16.3 parts. We round the reorder point up to 17 since we can't order a fraction of a part. To be safe we round up instead of to the closer whole number.

If demand should suddenly increase during the time prior to placing the order, the order could be made up only at the cost of very high expediting expenses. If demand is known to be certainly predictable then we can see from Table 10-3 that ten days delivery time will account for about 95% of the situations (19 of 20). Therefore, if we want a 95% service level, we must order ten days in advance of expected need, which is at a reorder point of 23 units (demand of 2.33 per day times ten days). It can thus be seen that an additional stock of six units (23 minus 17) is necessary to provide the difference between a 50% service level and a 95% service level. That additional safety stock of parts is insurance against stock-out, but those added parts cost money. A service manager must weigh the cost against the possible benefit, just as for most business investments.

The quantities of parts that field people stock are inversely related to their confidence in our ability to manage service parts. Parts inventory quantities will be low if field personnel believe that the authorized parts stock is correct, those forecasts are accurate, and that when they order parts the demanded item will be rapidly supplied. Stocks will be high if there is low trust in rapid resupply.

Top Ten Techniques

Many years of experience have identified ten techniques that are considered most important for managing service parts:

1. Gain management support
2. Emphasize customer satisfaction
3. Establish goals
4. Use life cycle cost and profit analysis
5. Minimize personnel delays
6. Centralize
7. Concentrate on the critical few
8. Control provisioning, forecasting, and excess
9. Promote quality
10. Use computers to expand on human capabilities

GAIN MANAGEMENT SUPPORT

The best ideas in the world backed by the soundest of logic and econometrics will fail unless they are championed by the persons in charge and supported by upper management. A major challenge in managing service parts is that logistics has been regarded as a mundane, but necessary, function that only needs attention when severe problems arise. Now is the time for good men and women to speak out about the virtues and profits of sound inventory management.

People always support projects best if they understand that the results have positive advantages to them. "What's in it for me?" is a common, if frequently unspoken, question. Make sure that management understands the benefits of effective parts management in terms that they can feel emotionally, beyond the black ink on a financial report. A bit of showmanship and desk pounding about the angry customer who was going to throw the product out and was made friendly by the critical part arriving in time to help him meet the deadline can go a long way toward arousing management enthusiasm!

EMPHASIZE CUSTOMER SATISFACTION

Customer satisfaction is the end measure of success. Too often, service performance is measured by "bitch level." If there are no complaints, then everything must be running right. Survey your customers. Rank customers according to the amount of business they do with your company. The marketing costs of doing repeat business with satisfied, existing customers are a small fraction of the costs for gaining new customers.

GOALS

Every organization should have goals that are written, measurable, understandable, challenging, and achievable. For example, "At least 85 percent of all parts that could cause equipment down time shall be available with the field engineer, 95 percent will be on site within four hours, and 99 percent of the parts will be delivered within 24 hours." By measuring ourselves against such written goals, we can know immediately if we are successful or not. A useful technique in goal setting is to have the people who must meet the goals participate in the goal setting. With proper leadership, most organizations will set goals for themselves that are much higher than management might dictate. The added advantage of participation is that people will work harder to achieve the target they set for themselves. It also helps to use scoreboards and frequent reporting on what actual results are as compared to those goals.

Use Life Cycle Cost and Profit Analysis

Business strategy and planning should evaluate the complete "womb to tomb" life cycle of products and parts. Design sets the stage for the following production and service efforts. A product is designed and built once, but must be serviced many times. Since service revenues will exceed the original hardware and software sales revenues for many products and bring higher profit margins, the influence of service must be carefully evaluated.

Revenues tend to be fixed. Therefore, in the basic equation (Revenues -Expenses = Profits), expense reduction is an effective tool to improve profits. There are also techniques such as parts contracts, leasing parts, shared inventories, and confidence kits that can stimulate parts revenues.

Make sure that the expected benefit of carrying a part is greater than the expected cost of carrying that same part. The decision is simple: If the benefit is greater, then stock it; if the cost is greater, do not stock it. Holding parts in inventory waiting for a need costs about 30% a year. That means if a module costs you $1,000, it consumes about $300 each year in facilities, labor, information, obsolescence, insurance, taxes, and money tied up that could be better used elsewhere. Capital parts often claim investment taxes credits and are typically depreciated a fraction each month. For example. A $3,000 personal computer might be depreciated over three years (it could be as few 18 months), so 1 / 36 ($83.33) could be expensed as depreciation each month. Long-lived equipment such as X-ray machines or power plant turbines might be depreciated over seven or more years. Some people assume that the carrying costs are being recovered. That depreciation expense is correct only for the acquisition costs, and even their recovery as a depreciation expense is regained only over a long time period. The carrying costs on completely depreciated parts are still typically over 18%.

On the value side of this equation is the probability of needing the part and the value that will be received (or the cost that will be avoided) by having it on hand. If you sell parts direct to customers, dealers, or distributors, then there is profit to be made if you have the part. But if you don't have the part and customers can go elsewhere, then they may go to another vendor. In the future they will probably go there first. Contracted service, which is a large percentage of most organizations' revenues and expenses, is a different situation. If you have contracted to support a customer, then parts must be made available regardless of how much effort and expense are required.

Contract revenues are fixed, and the expenses vary according to the effort and expediting required. Thus, if parts expenses can be kept low, then profits will be high. If extra effort is required to get people out of bed at overtime rates, make emergency shipments, and have field engineers traveling to get parts, then expenses will be high and profits will be low. Just the direct costs of expediting are usually $40 to $250 and up. Many expediting costs are not quantified as easily in monetary terms as they are in mental anguish.

MINIMIZE PERSONNEL DELAYS

If at all possible, avoid having field technical personnel travel to get parts. Parts-chasing time is expensive in both lost revenue and personnel frustration. Part of the solution is an Authorized Stock List (ASL) that accommodates about 85% of all parts needs. The optimum ASL should be calculated and may exceed 95% of needs for a specialist field engineer. Supply the remaining parts, which are hopefully of low essentiality, when next convenient. Or, if the parts are required for a down machine, have them delivered to the field engineer by a less expensive person. Roving parts vans, taxis, and even courier services are generally less expensive than diverting an expensive, technically competent person to transporting parts.

Recognize and use the distinction between a demand-based and an issue-based parts management system. If a part is requested (a demand) but is not available for issue, often no record is kept and the engineer spends time finding an alternative solution. We need to know if the requested part was on the stock list or not. Often, parts that should be stocked are not for financial, space, or other dubious reasons. Another situation is requests for parts that are not stocked and possibly not even identified in the service parts system. We need to log the demands for every part so we can periodically evaluate if we are stocking the right parts.

In the future, fault-tolerant hardware with remote diagnostic capability may be largely maintained by a parts courier who will be able to locate the defective equipment, safely open the electrical panel, remove the module with the lit red LED, install a good module, and politely inform the customer that the equipment is again working at full capacity. The technical talent will be at the Headquarters Technical Assistance Center and most of the on-site work will be done by these "Customer Service Technicians" who are qualified to a higher level in customer relations than in technical skills.

CENTRALIZE

Information should be centrally known on parts availability at every level of an organization. Parts stocks to meet service levels should be located at the point of need, but any additional quantities should be centralized. If you consolidate parts to a central location where they can be found in a hurry, then transportation means exist to get them quickly to where they are needed. The key is rapidly getting your hands on the parts.

One company that produces and services products for the banking industry had three regional distribution centers across the United States as well as the headquarters central stock. By gradually eliminating the regional centers and consolidating inventories, they saved over $1.5 million and are actually providing a higher level of customer service. Inventory shrinkage that was $300,000 two years ago is now reported to be only $6,000. A major computer company with thousands of installations has consolidated inventories into about 75 clusters across the United States and reports significantly better performance than with the previous large numbers of parts at sites and riding with field engineers. Another company with fewer sites finds 13 depots to be optimum. Centralization is a matter of balance.

These issues go back to the topic of confidence. If people in the field have confidence that they can get the parts quickly from the central location, then they won't try to keep so many caches of parts in their own possession.

CONCENTRATE ON THE CRITICAL FEW

Pareto's Principle, which is known to many people as the 80/20 rule, points out that there are a few critical items in most things we do that make the major difference, and most of the items around us are relatively insignificant. For example, most parts demands are for a relatively few items that turn over very fast, but many items sit in our inventory with just one or two uses a year. On the other hand, problems in defective components will come from just a few of the total parts. This "principle of the critical few" also relates to the authorized stocking list of parts that should be kept in a field engineer's car trunk or on site. Many service organizations can fill at least 90 percent of demands for parts with only five to ten percent of all the stockkeeping units in their inventory.

The critical few will often be high turnover parts. They may also be high dollar, long lead time, most essential, or even those parts that are prone to disappearance. These various factors may be lumped together into a single classification referred to as A, B, or C, or if you prefer, 1, 2, or 3. This is a more sophisticated evaluation than manufacturing uses in their ABC system, which is normally based on the high extended value parts being A, the midrange being B, and low values being C. Classifications may be much more complex with different actions tied to the individual parameters. However, experience shows that most humans are unable or unwilling to apply the effort necessary to manage detailed criteria. The results are much more effective when all the criteria are combined into a single class rating. Preferably, no more than 10 percent will be Class A items; perhaps the next 20 percent should be termed Class B, etc. Then you can manage by class for cycle counting, control attention, and stockroom locaion, with the most effort given to the As where we get the most benefit for the effort.

When the very first product goes out the door, a kit of parts to meet expected needs should accompany it. As needs are more accurately identified, kits should be eliminated. There are several schools of thought on this issue of authorized spares. One extreme says that headquarters knows best and should direct precisely the parts and quantities to be carried. The other extreme insists that only the field engineer responsible for that site and products knows what parts are required and that she should be allowed to carry anything she wants. The best solution is a balance between the extremes. There should be an authorized stock list (ASL) determined by headquarters' technical and financial expertise. Quantities should be determined based on the product populations to be supported, geography, fill rate requirements, and the cost of carrying the parts versus the expected benefit. Management Metrics Services, Inc. (MMSI) provides this capability as an outsource partner.

Keep parts as central as possible and manage strongly from that level. A good information system will assure that field needs are accurately reported to headquarters so the information can be refined into a statistically accurate recommended stock list. The field engineer and her manager should have the final say because there are territory changes, unique environmental situations, and other factors that headquarters cannot possibly foresee as accurately as field personnel can. If a field engineer says, "I must have that part," then let her have it, but track how often it is used. If the part is not used for the next three months, remove it from her stock and put it at the next higher level. If the part is not used from that level in the next six months, then consolidate it to the central facility. Some parts will be kept only at the World Distribution Center. Today, if we can get our hands on the part, we can transport it rapidly to wherever it might be needed. Yes, customs inspectors may cause some delay, so a few parts may be kept in specific country distribution centers. The important thing is to get your hands quickly on the part. That is much easier to do if they are centralized than if parts are scattered all over the country.

CONTROL PROVISIONING, FORECASTING, AND EXCESS

The best way of reducing investment in service parts is to avoid ever getting those parts into inventory. Most stock rooms today have excess parts that can and should be eliminated. But, when we try to sell those parts to recover some of our invest-ment, we typically find that they are obsolete, defective, and worth very little. That reality should feed back to the beginning of our parts acquisition cycle. Stimulate accurate provisioning decisions on what parts should be stocked and how many. The best strategy is to have on hand a small quantity of the parts that will probably be needed, with flexible arrangements in place to rapidly acquire parts to meet additional needs. Initial provision-ing based on handbook, laboratory, and "similar to" information can be reasonably accurate. However, there will always be a few parts that were never expected to fail but somehow do; and some parts expected to fail that don't.

Watch out for two common problems from manufacturing. The first is, "Don't worry about ordering your spare parts, I've ordered ten percent extra of everything for you." That approach is naive because every component does not fail routinely, and those few things that do fail will need frequent replacement. The second problem comes at end of production when the manufac-turing manager says, "We have a million dollars worth of transports left over at the end of our production. I am going to transfer them to Service." That is a gift horse whose mouth should be shut before it bites you. Forecasting of needs for service parts requires knowledge of demands from the past and also what supply and demand factors are expected to change in the future. Use of parts can be forecast with the aid of regression analysis, exponential smoothing, and other techniques to fit the particular situation. Most service parts are low usage and are best forecast by humans with computerized historical data and information on expected market demand and technical supply. This is the business of $i2$, LPA software, MMSI, and Servigistics.

Elimination of excess is one of the most difficult tasks of any parts manager. You know, by the laws of probability and statistics and Murphy, that as soon as you let the parts go you are going to need them. Service is a probability business, unlike manufacturing, which is based on deterministic one-to-one direct ratios. Rather, we know that even with a 98% delivery rate, 2% of the time that part can not be delivered. We must learn to live with probabilities and manage by them.

Elimination of excess means you must get the value out of those parts as quickly as you can. If you can get them back to the vendor while the parts are still useful in manufacturing, then do so. Or, perhaps you can contribute them to a hospital or an educational institution and at least write off the contribution. Put money in your annual budget so those funds are routinely available to write off those parts from your reserve account. The important thing is to get rid of excess parts so they no longer take up space, people's energy, data collection, taxes, and other resources that are better focused on the critical few.

PROMOTE QUALITY

Quality in service parts means more than just conforming to specifications; it means meeting the customers' needs. This then requires starting with an accurate identification of what the customer perceives he wants. For example, if the customer wants an off/on switch, but the description or drawing or identification numbers are vague...or the wrong part is pulled from the shelf...or the wrong part is packed in the right box...or for whatever reason the part is not correct...then the customer is angry. Add the problem of dead-on-arrival (DOA) parts! A very bad situation is created when the field engineer responds, diagnoses the problem, and tells the customer that the part is special ordered and will arrive tomorrow morning at 8:00 AM, but when the part is installed, it does not work! Again, whether the part is new, rebuilt, damaged in shipment, misordered, or whatever, makes no difference to the irate customer, the frustrated field engineer, or to the manager whose expenses must reflect the additional service calls and expediting charges. For those of us who measure (and we all should), 100% is often an elusive target. But anything less than perfect needs to be improved.

USE COMPUTERS TO EXPAND ON HUMAN CAPABILITIES

Use a computer to keep your parts records, no matter how few parts you manage. A PC (personal computer) can keep the records, do the calculations, and alert you to special needs far better than any human can. A spreadsheet program can easily calculate average pricing, reorder points, and economic order quantities. A database program should be used if the number of SKUs exceeds 200.

The reorder point (ROP) should trigger when we order replacement parts to our stocking facilities. Individual field engineers should operate on a weekly replenishment for normal use parts stock. A system that reports parts used on each service call can initiate automatic one-for-one resupply of authorized parts. At higher levels, however, the ROP should be automated as one tool for optimizing inventory on hand. Remember that the computer is operating in the past and must have human inputs concerning pending design changes, supply alterations, and changing demands.

Consider not only the parts that are on hand, but also parts in repair and parts already on order. One organization foolishly designed their new computer system to consider only the on-hand quantities. When that ROP was reached, an order was automatically placed to the vendor. The next day, because the part count was still below the reorder point, another order was generated. This happened for several days until the vendor called to ask if they really needed so many parts, since the quantity was more than they had ordered in the past three years. They quickly revised the program to net out the orders already placed, and also put the needed human attention onto the situation rather than placing blind faith in the computer. Repairable parts offer an opportunity for rapid turnaround and reduction of both inventory and costs. The points to be made for repairables influencing the reorder point are that their lead time is generally under internal control, they can be managed much more directly, and they provide a great opportunity for better turnover and use of assets through rapid repair lead-time cycles.

If you concentrate on these top ten items, you will achieve success with service parts.

Questions

1. How does logistics delay time for getting replacement parts affect service on your products?

2. What percentage of service parts support do you recommend that an automotive dealership carry in its own inventory?

3. Assume that you manage the automobile service center. What items make up the carrying costs for your spare parts?

4. Should every part in a system receive equal treatment?

5. What are the benefits of standardized design and components to inventory control?

6. What factors influence the location of spare parts?

7. What are the advantages and disadvantages of *FIFO* versus *LIFO* for inventory physical control and accounting in your service organization?

8. If items are delivered to inventory in batches of 500 and are used at a rate of four per day, how many deliveries are required every 250-operating-day year?

9. Given these historical demands, which are expected to hold steady, how many units should be on hand to give a 90% service level?

Units	Frequency	Frequency %
0	0	0
1	3	8
2	10	27
3	20	54
4	3	8
5	1	3
		100

10. From questions 8 and 9, this part costs $175. What is the total cost per year to carry and replenish the designated inventory if ordering cost is $150 per order and carrying cost is 30%?

11

Physical Distribution

*W*arehousing, order entry, pack, pick, ship, physical counting, and transportation are all important elements to hardware service. Physical distribution is defined by the American Management Association as "the movement and handling of goods from the point of production to the point of consumption or use."

Large amounts of valuable service efforts are spent in getting items to the right place at the right time. The effects of physical distribution show in both labor and materials expense for service.

Responsibilities given to physical distribution departments include:

- Customer service
- Exporting
- Financial control
- Forecasting and planning
- Inventory control
- Invoicing
- Management information
- Material handling
- Methods & processes
- Order taking
- Picking
- Packaging
- Personnel
- Pricing
- Production planning and scheduling
- Purchasing
- Research and analysis
- Shipping and receiving
- Traffic and transportation
- Warehousing

An old adage says, "You can't sell what you can't provide, and there is no use providing what you can't sell." A product must have four utilities: form, time, place, and possession. Product planning, design, and production create the form; marketing creates the possession; physical distribution creates time and place, and all integrate to provide quality—that is, the right thing in the right place at the right time at the right quality at the right cost. Profits result only if all utilities are integrated and satisfy the customer.

Physical distribution (PD) may be organized in structures and still be guided by the marketing concept. It is, however, by direction that distribution is often organized in a logistics department to handle both finished goods and parts, including consumables. Physical distribution may also be found under marketing, along with sales and service, in an organization all its own, or under production, depending on its prime activities and importance within the firm.

Delivery Response Time

If you can provide the right item at the right place at the right time in the right quality, then price is the last consideration. One of modern service's major challenges is to provide parts on same-day response times. A typical service level agreement (SLA) on a customer network server requires four-hour response time and six-hour restore time. Effective service requires remote diagnostics to identify the part that the technician needs at the service call. The technician may routinely carry some of those parts in his authorized stock list (ASL). Other parts—probably low use, expensive components—must be rapidly delivered to meet the technician in time to restore the equipment to operating condition. Table 11-1 shows the approximate number of locations required in North America.

Obviously the cost of support will increase significantly when response time is short and the service level must be high. This is an effect that service managers need to impress on sales people who may not realize the high costs of same-day service. Note that fast response requires additional technicians similar to additional parts, in order to have a person available to arrive quickly at the troubled site. Most service organizations charge 25% to 100% additional for four-hour response compared to next-day response.

Channels of Distribution

The distribution function has two components: the transaction creators and the physical movers. Some large companies, particularly in the industrial durables segment, control all channels from production through to the end user. Most firms, however, use intermediaries to sell and move their goods or services. These middlemen are involved in both movement and legal exchange of title. Middlemen are the wholesalers, retailers, distributors, jobbers, and drop shippers who buy and sell on

TABLE 11-1
Faster delivery needs more, closer stock locations.

Required Delivery	Number of Stocks
Overnight for Next AM Delivery	1
8 Hour	9
4 Hour	20
2 Hour	120
1 Hour	Local

their own initiative and deal with the risks of ownership.

Industrial goods differ from consumer goods in that they are typically durable items of strength and long life used in the production of further goods. Industrial distributors deal mostly with manufacturers, utilities, transportation firms, repair shops, and specific industry segments such as paper mills and food processors. Figures 11-1 and 11-2 show the typical middlemen in the channels of distribution.

Order and Information Systems

The computer has revolutionized information processing in the modern distribution center. Companies with many warehouses often have central data processing with terminals on line to every inventory location; orders can be quickly input, stock confirmed, shipping documents prepared, inventory debited,

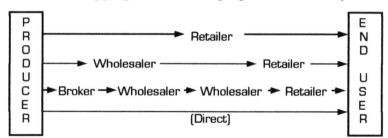

FIGURE 11-1
Channels of distribution for commercial goods.

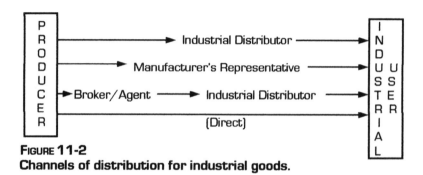

FIGURE 11-2
Channels of distribution for industrial goods.

and movement directed. The elements of the order-processing system are shown in Figure 11-3.

A complete system will update inventory, process back-order reports, prepare purchase orders, query other sources for items not in stock, and provide management reports as desired.

A distribution system functions best on a planned basis with the work detailed at least a day in advance of the action, but there will always be a critical few who need an item fast. Emergency situations will inevitably arise, in which the normal order and delivery system is not fast enough. Procedures should be established for such events to allow the special preparation of paperwork (paper labels, airbills, and packing lists must still be on paper even if must of the rest is electronic) and picking of emergency parts for rapid shipment or pickup. Strict accounting should be kept of those expensive expediting actions and controls established to keep the rate under 15% of the total. Since the cost of the physical distribution often amounts to from 10% to 35% of sales, considerable attention must be paid to cost

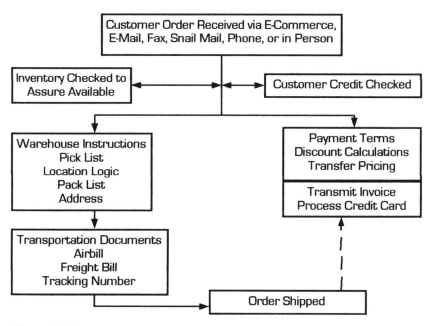

FIGURE 11-3
Elements of an order processing system.

control. After all, the leverage at a 20% level is such that reducing expenses $2 is at least equivalent to a sales increase of $10!

Inputs Required by Physical Distribution for Durable Goods

The development of practical and cost-effective distribution plans requires a continual dialogue between PD personnel and the technical and marketing organizations. Factors significantly affecting PD plans are as follows:

1. *Physical characteristics of the product/accessories/parts/ modifications/support equipment.*
- Physical size (dimensions, weight, etc.)
- Product modularity (subsystem physical breakdown)
- Transportation specifications (humidity, temperature, vibration, etc.)
- Storage specifications
- Handling requirements
- Packaging specifications
- Dangerous article identification

2. *Physical characteristics of consumables.*
- Shelf life
- Temperature
- Humidity
- Special handling requirements or hazards

3. *Demand levels forecast.*
- Parts identification
- Documentation
- Manufacturing schedule
- Machine level demands
- Field start-up requirements
- Off-lease and trade-in returns

4. *Installation/removal concept.*
- Single person or team
- Rigger
- Timing
- Special handling techniques

5. *Rehabilitation.*
- ✓ Defective product and parts repair/replace/scrap/return
- ✓ Procedures
- ✓ Minor refurbishing criteria and goals
- ✓ Major rebuild criteria and goals

6. *Related business strategies.*
- Effects on other products
- Price lists
- Time schedules

Packaging and Handling

Costs of packaging are currently above $25 billion annually for materials, equipment, and labor. Material-handling activities easily exceed $45 billion annually. These two areas of logistics, along with computer technology, have seen the greatest technological advances in recent years through the use of bar coding, robotics, and computer automation.

Packaging must consider four concerns: protection, ease of use, promotional value, and economy. Packaging must protect the product on its trip to the customer. It should keep an electronic board from encountering electrostatic shock as well as physical damage. The package should be easy to open, but at the same time secure its contents from pilferage and environmental harm. Reverse logistics should also be considered. Expensive packaging should be easily returned to the supplier and throwaway items should be easily disposed of. Packaging can be an effective advertisement. Think of the Gateway 2000® black-and-white cow boxes. What company would send a box labeled "From Mr. Goodwrench®?" When Hewlett-Packard includes a return self-mailer envelope with inkjet cartridges they are getting the cartridges away from refilllers (competition) and also helping to keep the plastic out of landfills (ecology). At the same time, packaging costs must be kept low and if the weight of the package is low, then transportation costs will be low.

Consumers today are willing to spend a little more money for convenience, appearance, dependability, and prestige. Packaging is an important vehicle for projecting these qualities and is also an area in which innovation can bring large sales gains. One need only think of pop-top beer cans, aerosol dispensers, clear plastic-skin packs, and L'Eggs™ hosiery to appreciate this.

PACKAGING DECISIONS

The logistics system of packaging for field service usually is based on individual unit packs, which fit into master cartons, which in turn fit into containers. The master carton is the basic unit for material handling and provides major protection from damage. The weight, volume, and fragility of the master cartons determine the configuration of transportation and warehousing.

The objective is to arrive at a configuration that is as standardized as possible in order to facilitate materials handling, high-density packing, and efficient space utilization. The ideal carton is a perfect cube of equal width, length, and depth. As the ideal is not normally feasible, care should be taken to assure an assortment of cartons that are mutually compatible, as shown in Figure 11-4.

The master carton's major function is to protect the items inside from damage. Hazards are basically of two types: physical and environmental. The most common causes of physical damage are vibration, impact, puncture, and compression, with combinations of all four forms of damage experienced whenever packages are being handled or in transit. Shock damage can best be controlled by proper loading and securing. Typical methods of securing are strapping, tie down, and the use of various dunnage materials such as wood frames and air bags, which prevent loads from shifting and absorb shocks. The best way to prevent damage is to load the vehicle in a tight pattern to prevent shifting.

Packaging requirements also influence the logistics system. The shipping practices of electronic goods provide an example. As the items are very fragile and of high value, very expensive packaging would be required to protect the products. Instead, electronic equipment is usually moved by specialized shippers who use trucks with special shock-absorbing suspensions, special handling equipment, and training to avoid damage. Although the cost of transportation is higher, the costs of packaging and damage are reduced.

Temperature, humidity, and foreign materials such as solvents, gases, insects, and rodents can create environmental damage, Many items such as photographic film and radioactive components require special refrigerated cars or secure containers that must be especially designed to accommodate them.

Packaging has a considerable psychological component.

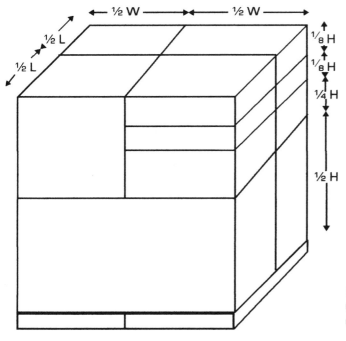

FIGURE 11-4
Compatible
Cartons.

Packaging engineers sometimes feel that the more adequately protected packages become the more careless freight handlers become.

On the other hand, carriers feel that if they handle goods more safely and carefully, packaging will be reduced and cheapened, with more potential for damage. There has been a good deal of experience with shipment of delicate large instruments that were being damaged even though they were in strong packaging.

An innovative packaging engineer suggested substituting transparent polyethylene shrouds for all the wood and cardboard packaging, with the idea that handlers would be more careful if they could see what was in the package. The method has been very successful and is now used for air freight shipments. It has the added advantage of reducing theft by making it easy to see if any component has been removed. The increased use of transparent materials also has advantages for quality control not previously possible without destroying the package.

Another problem, now attracting considerable attention, is the disposal or reuse of spent packaging. The person who invents a self-destructing beer bottle will become rich. Expanded foams and plastics are a major problem because they are not biodegradable or combustible in normal waste-disposal facilities, although cellulose "peanuts" and many similar packing materials are biodegradable.

Containerization is popular because of the cost savings. Long-distance shipments will often cost a third less when shipped by sealed container rather than by conventional methods. Wide body airliners are designed to load quickly and easily with containers that fit the shape of the aircraft's freight compartment and can be preloaded before the plane arrives and then rapidly loaded into the aircraft with mechanized special-handling equipment.

In summary, good packaging design considers many elements and provides the best balance for optimal value.

Starting with the end user and working backwards, the elements are as follows:

1. *End user factors.*
- Size
- Convenience
- Storability to fit consumer needs
- Provides instructions for product use
- Easily disposed of or reused
- Package gives utility in itself
- Environmentally acceptable
- Self-advertising

2. *Retailer/wholesaler factors.*
- ✓ Fits customer needs for resale
- ✓ Reflects customer buying habits
- ✓ Matches possible discount or special sales quantities
- ✓ Easily stored and handled
- ✓ Disposed of easily

3. *Traffic and transportation factors.*
- Maximizes loaded density
- Protects from damage
- Gains best rate
- Fits standard carrier methods and handling equipment
- Allows ease of return
- Easily marked
- Secure against pilferage
- Experience shows low damage rates

4. *Material handling and order picking factors.*
- Fits unit and multiple dimensions
- Adequate protection
- Allows package to be broken for order picking
- Easily packed or repacked
- Good markings for rapid identification
- Modularly sized
- Fits picking quantities
- Discourages theft
- Easily handled by one person

5. *Storage factors.*
- Good stacking qualities in dimensions and strength
- Cube efficiency
- Uses regular hardware

6. *Production factors.*
- Adaptable to product size, shape, and structure
- Uses existing handling equipment
- Easily filled
- Compact storage prior to use
- Allows quality control inspection without destruction
- Easily marked for internal item identification

7. *Purchasing factors.*
- Conforms to existing types
- Standard
- Low cost
- Uses free vendor consulting
- Minimal transport costs to production
- Broad tolerances and specifications

8. *Engineering.*
- Strength and rigidity in transport
- Fits product design
- Uses proven designs
- Economic

PALLETS AND CONTAINERS

Pallets are handling platforms made of wood, cardboard, metal, or plastic on which to load goods for handling. Pallet dimensions are standardized according to their use, with the most common being 40" X 48", 32" X 40", and 321" X 36". Dimensions are given in inches, the first number indicates the side where handling equipment such as a fork truck will enter the pallet. Four-way pallets that may be lifted by a fork truck from any direction are preferred but not always practical. As a general rule, the larger pallets permit more economical material handling because a greater volume can be placed on each. However, as many over-the-road trucks and trailers have interior widths of 90 to 92 inches, it makes sense to use pallets that can fit two side by side. A disposable pallet of cardboard can be made for about $1; a good hardwood pallet that costs $8 to $12 is normally returned to the sender.

Master cartons can be stacked in many configurations on a pallet, with the arrangements classed into block, brick, row, or pinwheel configuration. The stability of the load can be increased by interlocking the cartons, which is possible in all but the block arrangement. Usually the cartons are not secure enough themselves and must have additional securing. If the load is many small boxes, an overpack of heavy cardboard or plastic wrapping may be applied. Larger cartons may be strapped with steel or nylon bands, ropes, or corner posts.

Rigid containers are large wood or steel boxes into which many smaller items can be placed. The potential for increased productivity is obvious, since over half the cost of transportation is in dock handling, packaging, and claims for theft and damage.

Warehouse Functions

Service organizations are attempting to reduce the amount of required warehousing by flexible production of service parts and direct shipment from the supplier to the ordering technician. The typical service warehouse breaks down bulk shipments into "as-used" packages, stores the items until needed, and packages orders for shipment. There may be additional functions of a more technical nature to reconfigure equipment, prepare cables, load software, and even assemble all components for quality assurance before shipment. The five basic functions are receiving, transfer, storage, processing, and shipping.

Receiving usually consists of manually unloading the trucks that deliver the shipments and inventorying the contents to assure control and accountability for any damage or missing items. The goods are then transferred to a designated bin location for storage until they are required. When needed to fill an order, they are "picked" in the proper amount and moved to the assembly area for packing and shipping. Control systems determine the movements and check to ensure that the exact items are moving and that proper papers (or electronic media) are prepared for receipts, invoices, bills of lading, and customer billing. The control system should also reserve ordered parts, debit inventory when the order is picked, and trigger reordering for inventory when the quantity on hand plus on order plus in repair drops to the reorder point.

TYPES OF WAREHOUSES

Many companies agonize over whether they should own and manage their own warehouse or outsource the function to a company whose main business is operating warehouses. Initially most service managers feel that they need to run the warehouse in order to keep control of a vital function and be in touch with the customer. Eventually most service managers realize that the function can better be outsourced to a company that concentrates on running good support logistics. Economies of scale, specialized equipment, and focused effort then concentrates each of the partners on what they do best. A basic rule of outsourcing is to keep a function internal if it provides distinctive advantage. If the function will not differentiate your company from others, then outsource it to experts.

Many service companies today outsource at least some of their warehouse facilities and physical functions to third-party specialists. Use of strategic courier warehouses is an especially common strategy for high value, low use parts that must be stocked close to customers for rapid delivery. As several service companies have found, operating your own warehouse efficiently requires utilization rates of at least 75%.

Warehouses may also provide a combination facility to house marketing, purchasing, and service staff in addition to distribution people. It is common, too, for firms that handle small durable goods, such as computers and instruments, to locate a refurbishing center in the warehouse. Equipment that needs minor cleaning and repairs can be fixed on location and shipped out rapidly to the next paying customer.

Public warehouses are operated by individuals or companies that provide the facilities and services of complete warehousing to anyone willing to pay for them. Public warehouses have been very progressive in developing facilities and services that can be made available to users quickly without the high capital costs or long-range planning cycles needed for a private facility. Naturally, the variable cost of using public warehouses is higher than for private facilities, because the prices are set to recoup capital investment costs and fluctuating utilization. Charges are usually figured on the size, weight, and number of cartons handled.

The decision to use private or public warehousing is similar to the make-or-buy decision in production. As distribution is a vital link in the marketing channels, companies are naturally reluctant to turn over all responsibility to outside organizations. The potential for customer relations problems, slow or erratic service, slow reaction times, and lack of firm control are often cited as reasons for not using public warehouses. On the other hand, Choice Logistics®, Federal Express®, UPS/SonicAir®, and other stock and courier companies have proven to be a valuable supplement to a private system and handle peak loadings or low volumes in many markets. The tax situation may have an influence, as some localities do not tax goods in public warehouses but do tax goods in private facilities. The tax considerations for both kinds of warehouses can have greater impact than the potential transportation or storage savings. That is one reason for "free port" popularity, where goods can be stored free of customs or local taxes. Many states and local governments to attract industry and distribution centers that will employ local people are providing the same type of inducement.

Public warehouses have advantages in the complete line assortments they can handle and their ability to break-bulk and provide in-transit mixing at efficient rates. Public warehouses often provide local delivery service that can be shared by any firm using their facilities.

PLANNING A WAREHOUSE

Service parts should be as centralized as possible to gain economies of scale. If delivery time to customers is at least eight hours, then one location can support all of North America via next flight out (NFO) or courier service. Next-day delivery from a central stock becomes reasonably priced using Federal Express®, United Parcel Service®, or the US Postal Service. As Table 11-1 illustrated, if response delivery times must be the same day, then parts must be stocked closer to those customers. Often only a few critical parts need to be stocked close; the rest can be centralized.

The first step is to decide the location, considering required delivery time to customers, proximity to air and truck transportation in the community, and finally specific sites. This, of course, requires the establishment of objectives and detailed goals for the facility and determination of size and location requirements. The relationship of inventory locations and delivery time is shown in Figure 11-5.

Consideration must be given to nearness to customers; access to road or air transportation; utilities for light, heat, cooling, and production movement; expansion room; taxes; insurance rates; acquisition costs; and materials-handling systems. Too often a building is under construction before the internal components are planned, and an effective integration is not then possible without major alterations. The building and the functions to be conducted in and around it must be considered together in good, integrated logistics planning. Note that experience shows that service parts warehouses do not benefit

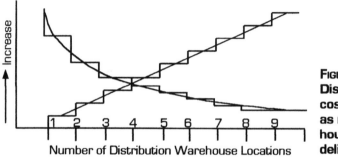

FIGURE 11-5
Distribution costs increase as more warehouses reduce delivery time.

from automated carousels and moving bins as much as routine production operations do. Service central warehouses benefit from automation in the form of wireless bar code units with planned pick sequences for minimum physical movement and quality checks of the final assembled order. This allows computers to do best what they do and humans can then do best the variable functions that unique service part picking and packing requires. The authors have seen several picking operations actually slowed by the use of automated bins that move parts to a single picker. Any service organization considering new or revised warehousing should consult with design firms that have experience with the industrial engineering of warehouses for similar service operations.

Space requirements start with forecasts of sales volumes and utilization to be expected over the next five or more years. Given the tonnage, number of units, pallets, truckloads, product lines, and other applicable quantitative facts, the planners can make detailed projections of the space required. Variations such as seasonal influences should be considered to assure high utilization; and additional space, on the order of 10%, should be allowed for increased volumes and contingency uses, which management has a way of adding to a warehouse because "they have so much space, they can find room."

The basic inventory can be numerically converted into pallet loads to determine floor and rack space requirements. Then, selection method and space can be found. Large, slow-turnover items will usually be kept in the remote storage area until they are required for shipping, but fast-turnover items may be put in a special pick area that is close to the pack line. Areas for vehicle maintenance and battery charging, offices, eating areas, break areas, toilets, and data processing equipment are also required. Special consideration must be given to safety items such as fire doors, sprinkler systems in the ceiling, air and heat flow, and firewalls. Placement of equipment in relation to these items can have a great effect on capacity and efficiency. A modern warehouse does not, in fact, have much space to spare if it is being efficiently managed (see Figure 11-6).

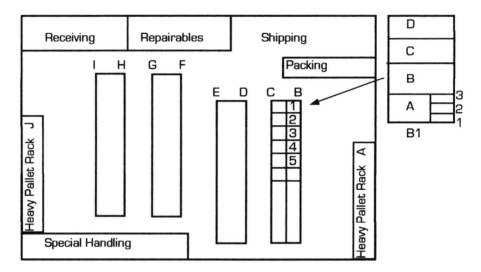

FIGURE 11-6
Layout of an efficient service warehouse.

WAREHOUSE OPERATIONS

Operations require personnel, work procedures, merchandise, control and information systems, and delivery means. So far we have concentrated on the technical systems and machines that are part of the modern warehouse. However, we sometimes overlook the most important element of the system—people. Warehousing, even automated, is a "people" business. People make the decisions and guide the machines that do the heavy work. It is not possible to have enough supervision to make up for incompetent or dishonest personnel. With dedicated people and pride in the job, a warehouse system can work at its best.

Safety must be of paramount concern to all supervisors and employees. Insurance inspectors can assist in establishing safety stations, proper markings, and safe procedures, but day-to-day operations and enforcement of hard-hat wearing, no smoking, and look-before-moving practices keeps an operation safe.

The same attitudes keep products in as good condition as that in which they arrived, assure that every outgoing item is billed, and match packed materials 100% with packing lists.

Measurement standards can be established for those items as well as productivity in terms of weights or cartons per man-hour. No such standards as absolute work factors or cost per man-hour exist to apply to every warehouse, as each is different in physical layout and items handled; but standards can be set within a warehouse based on past experience and targets, and can be compared against similar warehouses. People in the physical distribution business are usually pleased to compare figures and offer suggestions. Ideas are plentiful, but successful implementation is the most critical element to determine loss or profit.

Management Functions

Facility requirements must be part of corporate long-range and short-range plans and goals. Facility plans should be included in both functional organizations and program projects in order to assure the needed facilities are covered. The more lead-time available to those charged with acquiring new facilities, the better job they will be able to do.

It is preferable for an organization to assign or acquire specialists to form a task group to detail requirements for the facility, recommend several locations to top management, and advise on timing and purchase method. Increasing the number of inventory locations will usually improve the level of customer service through a reduction in delivery time. There is, of course, corresponding increase in the cost of carrying inventory and operating facilities, as shown in Figure 11-5.

The decision as to whether inventory should be consolidated or decentralized will include many factors besides the time and cost of transportation. Reasons for consolidating inventories include the following:

- Reduced cost of transportation from factory to distribution center
- Better warehouse management

- Consistent availability of stock items for filling orders
- Economies of scale
- Reduced total volume of safety stocks and dead and scrap items
- Reduced transfer of goods between inventory locations
- Improved inventory turnover
- High through-put for improved automation
- Volume increase for better negotiation of transportation and other services

Reasons for decentralizing inventory locations include:

➤ Customer orders more rapidly filled
➤ Reduced warehouse-to-customer transport costs
➤ Improved sales through greater availability
➤ Opportunity to use public warehousing and have costs variable with volume

There may even be reasons for putting certain items such as high-value, slow-turnover SKUs in central warehousing and those with high strategic value closer to the customer. Distribution management must be continually alert to changes and willing to aggressively operate a dynamic system if the facilities are to provide the best value at reasonable cost.

Traffic and Transportation

Traffic and transportation provide the location utility that conveys goods from the producer to the user. Transportation costs are often the greatest logistics support cost for any organization. Transportation expenditures exceed $115 billion per year, and they are increasing.

Naturally, traffic matters warrant a great deal of the total time and attention devoted to logistics management. They can be managed effectively only when they are considered as part of the total service system.

MODES

The five basic transportation modes are rail, highway, water, pipeline, and air. The relative importance of each mode is measurable in terms of distance, capacity, volume, revenue, and type of materials transported.

Railroads historically have carried the greatest number of ton-miles, although their share has declined in recent years. Railroads transport about 30% of the total intercity ton-mileage. There are presently 200,000 miles of rails in the US, and the number is declining. The capacity of railroads to transport very large tonnage efficiently over long distances is the major reason they still command a significant share of tonnage and revenues. A railroad tank car, for example, can haul six to eight times as much liquid as can a large over-the-road tank truck and do it much less expensively if it can reach both the producer and the user. Railway operations have high fixed costs and relatively small variable costs. Once goods are loaded on a train they can be transported long distances at very low cost per ton-mile. The average speed between terminals is less than 20 miles per hour.

A vessel moving on water is the oldest form of transportation. It accounts for about 28% of total intercity tonnage, a figure that is holding fairly stable. There are about 26,000 miles of improved inland waterways in the USA, including rivers and the Great Lakes, in addition to the coasts. Water transport is oriented to hauling raw materials and basic bulk commodities, as extremely large shipments can be moved at low freight rates where speed is not important. Automobile importers ship most cars from Japan and Europe to the USA via water.

Highway transportation has expanded rapidly in recent years. It now accounts for more revenues than all the other modes combined. The trucking industry presently receives about 75% of all transportation revenues and carries about 16% of the ton-miles over more than 3 million miles of roads. Relative to other means of transportation, trucks have low fixed cost coupled with high variable costs. They are more economically adapted to handling small shipments moving shorter distances. Increasing labor costs for drivers, maintenance, and platform wages are causing a great deal of pressure on the trucking industry. To counteract this trend, a great deal of' attention is being paid to improving scheduling, administrative systems, terminal mechanization, and coordinated transport systems, such as trailer on flatcar (TOFC) or "piggyback" systems. Automation and communications of major truck lines now enable knowledge of the precise location of every vehicle, what packages are on it, and approximately when it will arrive at your site; and the driver has both satellite data communications and a cell phone to arrange last-minute details.

In general aircraft is still the least utilized mode of freight transportation, accounting for less than 1% of intercity ton-miles revenue. For the service business, aircraft are vital since they enable overnight, next-flight-out (NFO), and counter-to-counter delivery of service parts. The speed of service possible between two distant points has the potential for reducing overall logistical costs through reduction of inventory, holding costs, and warehousing space. Airlines' small-package counter-to-counter service will transport small parts and documents between airline facilities on scheduled passenger flights. The costs are both monetary and human, since this requires personal delivery to the airline counter and a pickup. Even with the large air fleets of Federal Express and UPS, much air freight is transported in the belly of scheduled passenger flights. Air transport does not have as high fixed costs as rail, water, or pipeline; however, the variable costs are extremely high for fuel, maintenance, and labor. Air is expected to become even more important as the means of long-distance rapid transportation as speed of transport can trade off against reduced inventories. Getting more use from fewer assets is a priority of service logistics.

Stocking couriers

Package services such as United Parcel Service (UPS), Federal Express (FedEx), and Airborne are strong in the overnight shipping business, but also offer other services. These companies operate on a "hub" concept that brings most packages to Memphis, TN, Louisville, KY, or Wilmington, OH, in the early hours of weekday mornings, sorts and reroutes the packages, and then delivers them early the next day. These companies operate both pickup and delivery services and, because of limits on package sizes, can do an effective scheduling job. Lower cost ground shipment is also offered, which is good for return of defective parts.

FedEx, UPS, SonicAir, Choice Logistics, and others offer a stocking and delivery service of importance to service managers. For example, a consolidated inventory can be placed in the "Parts Bank" so that an order any time up to about midnight can get overnight delivery to most locations in the country by as early as 6:30 the next morning, with reduced costs for later deliveries. These companies and other couriers have developed networks of stock locations across North America and extending into Europe and Asia-Pacific counties to handle critical parts that must arrive at a customer's location within a few hours. Their services can be tuned to the needs of specific products and customers and even individual situations. Greyhound and other bus companies offer package delivery service if goods are delivered to the bus station and picked up at the other end.

RATES

Federal economic regulation covers many transportation means; however, deregulation is being implemented in airlines and trucking, which allows considerable negotiation. All products normally transported are grouped together in uniform classifications. The purpose of the classification is to consider characteristics of a commodity or product that will influence the cost of handling and transportation. The particular class assigned to the commodity or product is called its rating. A product's rating is not the price that must be paid; it is rather the classification placement. The actual price is called the freight rate, which is found in a price list called tariffs. A product rating has a very real influence on the actual freight rate.

Individual product classification is based on a relative percentage index. Class 100 is the normal class, with other classes running as high as 500 and as low as 35. A carload (CL) or truckload (TL) shipment is rated lower and, therefore, less expensive than a less-than-carload (LCL) or less-than-truckload (LTL) shipment of identical products.

Since many service shipments go by FedEx, UPS, and related services, suffice it to say that prices with those carriers can best be negotiated by consolidating volumes to achieve economy of scale. For example, subsidiaries of General Motors get very good rates because the contract is negotiated by grouping together all the many entities of the giant corporation. Smaller organizations may join consortiums to get lower rates. It never hurts to ask for lower rates. With competition driving the industry, you just might get what you ask for.

DOCUMENTATION

The major transportation documents are the bill of lading, the freight bill (airbill), and freight claims. The bill of lading provides:

- The contract for the shipment,
- A receipt for the goods shipped,
- Terms and conditions for carrier liability, and
- A title and credit instrument.

There are several variations in bills of lading. In addition to the uniform straight bill of lading, there is a uniform bill of lading whose purpose is to allow a supplier to obtain payment for goods when they are delivered and simultaneously to transfer title. As the order bill of lading is a negotiable document, it is used largely for financial purposes. There are other bills of lading for export, government goods, and livestock.

The freight bill represents the carrier's way of charging for the transportation services. The freight bill is derived from information contained on the bill of lading. As these large amounts of paperwork are expensive, some shippers are trying combination forms, and most progressive companies will be all electronic in the near future. Freight bills may either be prepaid or collect. Bills for regulated motor carrier service must be presented within seven days after the effective date of a shipment and paid within another seven days. Some firms elect to pay at the time of creating the bill of lading, thereby combining the bill of lading and freight bill into one less-expensive document.

Freight claims are documents that detail information about loss or damage to products in transit, unreasonable delay, or other problems. The shipper prepares the claim and negotiates settlement with the carrier. Shipments often go astray or get delayed en route, in which case tracing and expediting is required. If a shipper initiates a tracing action, the carrier must provide the desired information. FedEx, UPS, and now even the US Postal Service provide tracking of packages so that you can quickly find out where a package is or even who signed for it at what time. Tracking can be a help to assure rapid return of service parts and accountability to individual technicians.

Traffic Management

Because transportation is the highest single cost in most logistical systems, the traffic department should at least be consulted during product design and development and must be intimately involved in logistics planning. Traffic and transportation management is usually organized into a functional department with responsibilities that include:

- Freight classification
- Gaining the lowest possible rates consistent with adequate service equipment scheduling
- Documentation
- Tracing and expediting auditing, claims
- Research
- Performance measurement
- Negotiations
- Influencing related items such as packaging and quantities

Most of these items have been previously discussed; however, scheduling deserves specific attention. With the advent of' computers to assist scheduling, significant reductions are possible in distance traveled, optimum load composition, and timing. In the area of school-bus scheduling, which requires over $4 billion in taxes each year to support, computerized scheduling has been shown to save 15% in every case it was tried against manual scheduling and has achieved savings of 50%. These reductions in numbers of expensive school buses, mileage, variable costs, and time are very significant.

Finally, the traffic department has a research and engineering responsibility to assure that transportation is effectively interacting with the overall service logistic system. There are many ways in which transportation can be effectively used to reduce total physical distribution costs. A slight packaging change might allow a lower classification rating for a product. Even though the packaging might cost slightly more, the expense could easily be offset by a substantial transportation cost reduction. A good example of this is controlled transportation (contran), which makes it possible to obtain an almost optimal weight and volume balance of laboratory equipment being shipped by truck. The first layer of products is placed on the floor of the truck, for example, four wide and 30 deep. An over-floor is installed, and a second layer of 40 units loaded, and then a third. This loading of 120 units is a great savings over the 60 that could be loaded when machines were packaged in wood and cardboard boxes.

Physical Distribution Program Planning Guide for Durable Goods

Items that must be planned for durable goods physical distribution are listed below.

I. *Develop program support requirements.*
   A. Headquarters support (PD organization): manpower/expense/capital/facilities

B. PD operations support (field company personnel, contractors, independents, etc.): manpower/expense/capital/facilities

C. Other (computer support, legal, insurance, procurement, contract officers, etc.): man power/expense/capital/facilities

II. *Planning Support.*

A. Develops inputs to higher-level plans

B. Develop detailed functional task plans for subordinate organizations

C. Report progress against plans (task plans converted to PERT-type planning network)

D. Reconstruct plans based on revised program, product, and organization strategies or constraints

III. *Generate financial and resource factors.*

A. Generate transportation factors (machine, spares, consumables, accessories, etc.): freight $/machine (plant to DC, DC to customer, etc.):

1. Carrier costs

2. Insurance

3. Imports/exports/customs

4. Paperwork (bills of lading, invoices, reporting, etc.)

B. Generate installation/removal factors (machine and accessories):

1. Installation factors:

a. Freight to and from rigger to customer

b. Misc. $/installation (aborted installations, special handling, packaging, etc.)

c. Rigger labor, hour/installation

2. Removal factors:

a. Rigger labor hour/removal

b. Misc. $/removal (aborted removal, special handling, packaging, etc.)

C. Generate rehabilitation factors:

1. Labor hours and $/item

2. Parts $/item

3. Current overhead rate

4. Training $/location
5. Tools and equipment $/location
6. Supplies $/item

D. Inventory:
   1. Locations
   2. Inventory parts %/$ usage/turnover rates
   3. Inventory $/investment
   4. Storage space $/floor space
   5. Stock level policies

E. Parts credit:
   1. Repairable field returns (parts credit %/$ part)
   2. High-value scrap

F. Facilities factor:
   1. National distribution
   2. Regional distribution
   3. Centralized refurbishing

IV. *Central refurbishing operations.*
   A. Develop centralized refurbishing operations methods and techniques:
      1. Develop process
      2. Transportation
      3. Delivery to refurbishing location
      4. Removal/transportation/return
      5. Establish preliminary evaluation criteria for refurbishing versus more extensive rebuilding

V. *Field test and initial product observation (IPO) support.*
   A. Machine/spares/consumables/equipment control and reporting:
      1. Packaging
      2. Transportation
      3. Delivery to rigger and/or customer
      4. Removal/transportation/return
   B. Evaluate distribution support systems
   C. Develop fast response system for field test and IPO support requirement:
      1. Ordering emergency/rush parts
      2. Special parts warehousing

    D. Evaluate distribution procedures:
      1. In-transit damage evaluation
      2. Common carrier performance
      3. Rigger performance

VI. *Launch control and evaluation.*
    A. Develop flexible system to respond to launch control problems: alternate transportation, special rigger handling techniques (rapid response time), etc.
    B. Evaluate distribution systems, procedures and supply correction actions
    C. Assure distribution center, public warehouse, rigger, branch, and dealer readiness
    D. Assure proper distribution to regions/branches/dealers, etc., of allocations, start-up kits, training equipment, etc., in preparation for launch
    E. Evaluate actual inventory requirements and react according to need
    F. Review consumable distribution practices
    G. Evaluate field procurement practices
    H. Evaluate training of personnel as proved by performance

VII. *Operations support.*
    A. Implement standard distribution procedures
    B. Initiate prepack operations for spares, etc.
    C. Initiate refurbishing of defective parts and machines
    D. Activate inventory control system for automatic re-generation and physical inventory control:
      1. Supplies/parts
      2. Stock locations
      3. Equipment controls
    E. Emergency order system
    F. Vendor interactions
    G. Configuration accounting
      1. Machine/accessory/modification identification
      2. Hardware location tracking
      3. In-transit equipment control
      4. Serial number control

      5. Compatibility assurance

      6. Track machine modifications to balance spares need

  H. Traffic and transportation practices:

      1. Rigger contracts

      2. Shipment requirements (loading equipment, bill of lading, etc.)

      3. Imports/exports/customs

      4. Transportation regulations

      5. Freight claims techniques

      6. Carrier utilization

      7. Like-for-like replacement plans (timing, etc.)

  I. Return goods/parts practices (credits, rehabilitation, scrap, etc.)

  J. Warehousing operations:

      1. Public, local, regional, national, international:

         a. Customer order handling

         b. Documentation/procedures

         c. Physical inventory control

         d. Damaged goods handling

         e. Inventory control and accountability

  K. Mandatory retrofit handling procedures

  L. Order processing systems

  M. Installation/removals (contracts, controls, etc.)

  N. Field reporting analysis systems:

      1. Problems management system

      2. Physical inventory

      3. Turnaround

      4. Performance evaluation

  O. Interface requirements for manufacturing reconditioning operations

VIII. *Phase-out and termination:*

  A. Begin scrap of least valuable (problem defects/unique configuration/obsolete features) equipment first

  B. Assure financial and asset accounting evaluation and control

  C. Force decisions based on economic justification

Questions

1. What are the four utilities a product must have?

2. Select a product for evaluation. What are the channels of distribution normally used to get this product from the producer to the end user?

3. For your product example, what are the elements of the order-processing system?

4. If the physical distribution costs are 25% of sales, how many dollars of sales are necessary to cover $100 of distribution expenses?

5. What utilities does packaging furnish for your products?

6. Square beverage containers could be much more efficiently transported then existing ones. Why don't more square containers replace round ones?

7. For your products, what factors influence your decision to use private or public warehouses?

8. Could your business use faster or better-planned modes of transportation and thereby reduce warehousing?

9. Determine what freight rates are charged for three typical products. What changes might be possible to reduce the cost of transportation for these products?

10. Are transportation experts normally consulted in product design and development decisions with which you are acquainted? Should they be?

12

Call Management

*C*ustomer needs and the related service support fall into two distinctly different categories: rapid-reaction, time-driven support to corrective maintenance needs; and scheduled, cost-driven service support for installation, changes, and preventive maintenance actions. Both types of service should be planned in advance, and good service managers try to proactively manage both categories.

The sudden occurrence of failures means that corrective repairs are stimulated by factors outside the control of the service organization. Corrective service is primarily demand-driven and time-sensitive, whereas scheduled service holds the demand until the supply is efficiently available. Scheduling of installations, modifications, and preventive maintenance (PM) should be primarily driven by the cost-effective availability of skilled personnel with the necessary parts at a time that is convenient for both the customer and the service organization.

Corrective Maintenance

In order to understand the service support requirements for corrective, emergency, repair, demand-driven maintenance, let us consider the steps of a corrective service call. (You may wish to refer back to Figure 3-1.) Corrective service usually begins when a problem is perceived by customer personnel. With modern technology, error detection hardware and software will increasingly predict pending or real failures and warn the service organization to fix the trouble before the customer is even aware of the occurrence. Once a problem is perceived, the service organization is notified and a request for service is made. The response of the service organization to a request for service is one of the most critical events in corrective maintenance. The customer's mental clock runs at full stress until the customer is satisfied that his or her problem is being adequately addressed. High technology service requires high human touch. We emphasize that the customer does not care how much you know until he or she knows how much you care.

The time required for the service organization to respond by providing a telephone fix or a service technician to the site of the problem is referred to as response time. The actual response time commitment should be situational and should be dependent on the need urgency, customer rank, equipment criticality, and any contract responsibilities. Achieving the promised response time typically reflects the capability of the service organization. If the response time goal is met, the service organization is perceived as being well managed. If the response is after the expected time, the service organization is perceived as nonresponsive, unconcerned with the needs of the customer, and, thus, poorly managed. Response time typically is measured from the time the call to the service organization is made to the time the service technician arrives at the operation site. Note that times will often be stated as averages, but customers' minds often expect that to be maximum. In other words, a four-hour average response time could be achieved with an one-hour arrival at the first call and a seven-hour arrival at the second call; but the customer may be angry that the seven hours exceeded his expectation of "within four hours." Be sure that your facts equal (or are better than) the customer's perceptions and expectations.

Once the service technician arrives at the site, a sequence of steps typically follows. First, the service technician should talk with the customer management, so the decision-makers know that help has arrived, and with the equipment operator to discern his or her insights into the problem. Then the technician attempts to diagnose the problem. When the problem has been diagnosed, the service technician gains access to the faulty part or subassembly. The problem part is removed and an attempt may be made to repair or adjust it. If this is not possible, the problem part is replaced. If the part is to be replaced and a new part is required, the service technician must also order the part. Service logistics will determine the location of the replacement part and have that part packed and transported to the site. The technician will receive the part and install it in the equipment. A good support system proactively determines what parts will probably be required and delivers those parts to meet the technician.

Once the repair or replacement of the problem part is accomplished, the equipment is reassembled. Finally, the service technician will test the equipment under operating conditions to assure that the repair has been successful, essentially completing the technical dimension of the service call.

However, the service technician has two additional duties. The first is to satisfy the customer personnel that the repair has been accomplished and that the equipment has been restored to operation. The customer personnel must concur that their perceived problem has been eliminated. Good technicians make sure that the customer decision-maker also knows that the problem was quickly solved. *Fixing the customer* is even more important than fixing the equipment, although it helps to fix equipment as a major component of fixing the customer. Finally, the service technician prepares the administrative reports necessary for service management.

Two major service support functions are required for corrective service calls: the call management/dispatch function and configuration management. These functions may be consolidated into a single person to support small organizations, or they may be split into skilled specialist groups to support large organizations. The call management organization acts as the heart of the service operations function. Its purpose is to validate the customer status, determine the real customer needs, assign priorities, and pass the call to the person best qualified to help the caller. If a technician is required on site, the dispatch function receives the notification of a need for service. The dispatch function must then analyze the service personnel available to meet that need and assign a priority to that request for service with regard to all other service activities currently in operation and scheduled. Once the prioritization has been completed and service technicians assigned, the dispatch function must contact the assigned personnel and transmit to them information about the customer and the call, along with a priority rating for this call.

Call management is best handled as a central headquarters function, rather than being done at various field offices. This is because many calls can be helped over the telephone, and the information, skilled people, and computer assistance for a help desk or technical assistance center (TAC) are expensive and best managed as a central function. Software may be well managed from a central facility, since most software fixes can be transmitted via telephone modems or sent by Internet for the customer to load. Field people will argue that they know the customers best and want them under local control. Experience shows that most field customer contacts are not managed as professionally as they can be from a consolidated organization. Field managers may still have real-time access to information about their personnel and customers.

If corrective activities are scheduled only by the individual service personnel, company policy and company priorities may very well be usurped by the individual whims and personalities of the service personnel. The call management/dispatch function is critical to the performance of the service function because service policy is translated into the priorities given to service calls. When a single authority is making these judgments, company policy can be maintained. When judgment is left to individual service personnel, adherence to company policy may not be easily controlled. As an example, corrective maintenance calls for one process line may be more important than for another process line in the same plant, or one plant may have a higher priority than another plant. If this preference is not established when service calls are received, the technician may not be aware of the difference in the priorities or may not respond to service in a particular process line or plant because of some personality problem with personnel there.

Dispatch thus plays a critical function in translating service policy to operational performance. Prioritization of service calls, particularly with regard to emergency conditions under which corrective maintenance is performed, is critical. It must be maintained under strict management control and not left to the memory or personality of the individual service technician.

The second critical service support function for corrective maintenance calls is referred to as configuration management. With configuration management, the service organization is completely aware of the exact configuration of each piece of equipment it is required to service. A service technician dispatched to a specific location to repair a specific piece of equipment can know exactly what is to be repaired and exactly what tools, test equipment, and parts to take along. Such preparation requires significant management activity to maintain maintenance documentation and all configuration changes in each piece of equipment serviced. Software presents added challenges that interact with hardware. Any modification, change, retrofit, or new equipment that is added must be completely identified to the service organization to allow for provision of spare parts and proper test equipment. Configuration management of equipment is the responsibility of the service organization. Knowing the specific makeup of each piece of equipment and its requirements for support are vital to effectively maintain that piece of equipment.

Scheduled Maintenance

Installations, engineering change orders, and a preventive maintenance call and the service support it requires are best understood when put into the perspective of the elements of a planned, cost-optimized maintenance call. For example, preventive maintenance calls begin with the alert from sales or the customer or a shipper that a new installation should be scheduled. A central coordinating function or the service technician should contact the customer to arrange for a time that is most convenient to both the service organization and to the customer's operations. Once the appointment has been made and scheduled, the service technician obtains the parts needed to complete the service activity and takes them to the job site. At the site, the service technician completes a sequence of well-defined operations. Preventive maintenance activity, being well defined, can be timed very accurately to predict the duration of the call. Do note that, on some equipment, preventive maintenance (PM) can be done at the same time as corrective maintenance (CM). Any activities that require equipment down time can best be consolidated. When a CM request is received, you should check, hopefully by an automatic computer program, to see if any PM or other activity could be scheduled at the same time.

As preventive maintenance procedures can be very specifically detailed in the form of instructions and documentation for the service technician, technicians with lower skill levels can sometimes perform preventive maintenance than are required for corrective maintenance activities. Since corrective maintenance activities require diagnostic skill for unusual or difficult-to-identify problems, training for corrective maintenance requires much more technical depth. A dichotomy does exist here. Since

PM is intended to prevent failures from ever occurring, equipment in which an experienced person can tell by the human senses of sound, feel, and smell that something is not quite right may most effectively receive PM from the best technician. Equipment with dirty, routine PM and little chance for detection of future problems is usually serviced by the lowest cost, qualified person. A final check by a senior technician can assure that the job is done right and can also detect any potential problems.

After completing the preventive maintenance procedures, the service technician updates the equipment history log. According to established procedures and observations made during the accomplishment of those procedures, the service technician then determines the schedule for the next preventive service call. Rather than having the technician schedule the next preventive service call, some service operations schedule calls through a central administrative function. The service technician recommends the preventive service interval for equipment that has a variable preventive maintenance cycle, depending on the wear of the particular machine. An individual inspection by the service technician during the preventive maintenance call will ascertain how the preventive maintenance cycle should be adjusted to allow for the wear of the equipment. Finally, the service technician prepares the administrative report required by service management to complete the preventive maintenance call.

The major support activities necessary for preventive maintenance calls are retrofit management, warranty administration, and scheduling. Retrofit management has the purpose of maintaining the safety of the equipment and its safe operation as well as upgrading the equipment configuration to improve performance. These changes are often called engineering change orders (ECOs) or field change orders (FCOs). Thus, retrofit management represents an opportunity for the service organization to manage any changes made to the equipment under their control, whether those changes be to improve the safety of the equipment or to upgrade its performance. Any retrofits to equipment must be managed by the service organization in such a way as to provide accurate records of the configuration for future corrective service calls, as well as to schedule any retrofits to the machines with the appropriate prioritization. Any equipment retrofit that will significantly improve the safety of the equipment should be given a high prioity for accomplishment during the preventive maintenance scheduling or at the next corrective call. Retrofits that will provide only minor performance improvement should be given a low priority.

Warranty administration is another important support activity for preventive maintenance. Warranties for major capital equipment may be in effect only when preventive maintenance procedures are strictly followed. It is the role of the service organization to assure that any equipment warranties are fulfilled through preventive maintenance and to provide the company with the full benefits of any warranties available to them. As warranty administration can represent a significant cost factor to the service organization and the entire company, it must be considered seriously during all preventive maintenance activities. There is also opportunity to regain parts costs from the supplier when a failed part is under warranty.

Finally, scheduling is critical to the successful performance of cost-effective maintenance activities. Scheduling represents the key to optimizing the labor or expensive technical personnel. Poor scheduling will yield low service personnel productivity, poor adherence to preventive maintenance cycles, and high costs. On the other hand, good scheduling procedures can minimize idle or lost time of expensive technical personnel, help assure that necessary support resources are available, and make the customers happy.

Questions

1. Why is response time measured from the time the customer perceives the problem and requests service, rather than from the time the problem actually occurs?

2. What advantages are provided by parts that do not require adjustment and calibration over those that do?

3. How should the service department be involved in establishing company warranties?

4. Should priorities be assigned to various types of service calls, or should all be treated first in, first out?

5. Why is configuration management important to the service technician?

6. Determine what percentage of total service time in your organization is required to obtain necessary tools, information, and replacement parts.

7. Are there any scheduling advantages to time-planned maintenance rather than waiting until a product fails? What are other advantages and disadvantages?

8. How does preventive maintenance offer opportunities for lower costs compared to corrective maintenance?

9. What are the advantages of notifying service technicians of the new call as soon as it comes in instead of waiting until they've completed the one they're on?

10. Why is it important to let a customer know when service will be accomplished even though that may be much later than it was requested?

13

Customer Satisfaction

*C*ustomer relations are the most important part of a company's external relations, but one of the least understood. Interactions with people can be subjective, inconsistent, colored by personal experiences, and not well controlled. They can often accomplish (or undo) in a few words more than months of good technical effort. There are two major parts to a service technician's job, technical maintenance and customer relations. The person who answers the telephone when you call to order parts, the service representative who schedules you for maintenance and then explains why they did what they did, and the billing clerk are all critical parts of the logistics system. They form the interface between the company and the customer.

Customer perceptions are more important than quantitative numbers. For example, the customer's perception of the service reliability can be very different from the numbers indicated by a sophisticated data reporting system. The service technician may be performing scheduled preventive maintenance on the equipment, but if the manager who passes by during the call thinks, "That *!#?! instrument is broken again," his company's attitude towards the equipment will be negative. One answer to that problem is to have service personnel stay away from customers and the equipment unless maintenance is absolutely required. Sales personnel should do most customer relations calls.

People who meet customers must be trained for the responsibility. Reading a book on "how to do it" will not suffice. There must be person-to-person development, preferably using role-play for internal training, and on-the-job guidance by concerned supervisors. Success and failure should be highlighted. If a customer writes commending one of the personnel, the letter should be displayed where everyone can see it and be motivated to do likewise. Public praise should be complemented with private punishment. Lessons can be learned from mistakes, and problems can be used anonymously for training media.

Many users are presently dissatisfied, as illustrated by lawsuits, letters to your newspaper HELP! column, and a generally increasing level of customer complaints. On the other hand, organizations providing good customer service are seeing significant increases in business and profits.

The typical American has grown accustomed to the conveniences provided by over 33 electromechanical devices in the home, with many more at work and in leisure activities, as illustrated in Figure 13-1. Customer satisfaction must be the overriding concern in all those elements. Many service organizations organize separate customer service departments to provide the functions of information exchange, order entry, installation scheduling, claims and credits, and warranty management.

Information exchange is important to provide product specifications and use information, prices, sales and delivery terms, to handle demonstrations and samples, and to respond to inquiries.

Order entry will make sure that orders from salespeople are correctly entered into the sales system and that customer credit is acceptable. It is also used to schedule shipments, trace order

Can Opener   Hi-Fi   Trash Compacter   Dehumidifier   Vacuum
Freezer   Air Conditioner   Shoe Buffer   Watch   Camera
Automobile   Typewriter   Tape Recorder
Electric Toothbrush   Radio   TV   Refrigerator   Ice Crusher   Shop Tools
Iron   Floor Polisher   Garage Door Opener
Hair Curler   Garbage Disposer   Clock
Dryer   Boat   Blender   Toaster   Sports Equipment
Projector   Shave Cream Dispenser   Dish Washer   Clothes Washer

Figure 13-1
We depend on many home appliances.

status, and handle orders for nonstandard products or services.

Complaints should be routed to the customer service department, which should handle claims and assure that credits are issued if necessary, and also handle warranty management, including establishing and administrating warranties.

Customer service should also take an active role in planning and controlling customer service performance and cost. Table 13-1 lists requirements for good product service. The main activities of this function should include:

➤ Define the necessary elements of customer service.
➤ Determine the customer's viewpoint.
➤ Design the competitive service package.
➤ Establish the value of the package in terms of performance and cost.
➤ Gather actual performance and cost data.
➤ Compare the actual performance and cost against standards.
➤ Identify the problem area.
➤ Stimulate and follow up on corrective actions to improve service to standards.

Table 13-1
Good Product Service Requirements.

Pre-Purchase Information	Ease of Use
Fast Order	Preventive Maintenance
Prompt Delivery	Rapid Repairs
Smooth Installation	Termination-Replacement

Naturally, in many small service organizations these functions may be part of the service manager's duties.

Marketing Concepts

The marketing concept is simply a planning philosophy that seeks to identify customer needs and direct the firm's resources to serve them at a profit. All systems of the company—engineering, production, finance, marketing, and service—must be aimed at this fundamental goal. Three statements form the foundation for the marketing concept:

1. Customer needs are more basic than the product.
2. Products must be viewed in an end-user concept.
3. Volume is secondary to profit.

Potential markets must be studied in depth to determine the customer's true needs and wants; the product and services can then be designed to fill them. A product must have four utilities: form, time, place, and possession. Profits result only if all four utilities are integrated and satisfy the customer.

Keep in mind that the marketing concept is a corporate orientation and not directly related to performance of the marketing department.

MARKETING MIX

Marketing mix is the term given to the parts of a firm's marketing plan. The major elements are shown in Figure 13-2. The name "mix" comes from the fact that all the items are blended together into an integrated effort. The mix gives customers a total package of goods and services in the hope of attracting their business.

KEEPING CUSTOMERS REDUCES COST

In a recent nationwide survey of 100 major US companies, it was shown that the average cost of acquiring a new customer was

$118.16, whereas maintaining existing customers costs only $19.76. This 6:1 ratio is of major importance to service, as it is service's main job to keep the customer. The working relationship already established and familiarity with each other opens the way to providing additional products and services.

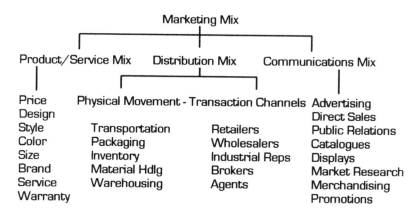

FIGURE 13-2
Elements of the marketing mix.

SERVICE STRATEGIES FOR CUSTOMER SATISFACTION

By definition, satisfaction implies complete fulfillment of one's wishes, needs, and expectations. If satisfaction is delineated for the industrial customer, it includes contributions to fulfillment of business purpose, mission, financial goals and objectives, safety, and growth needs for the firm, as well as fulfillment of the specific wishes, needs, and expectations of individuals involved including design engineers, manufacturing, purchasing, and administrative managers, professionals, and other personnel. Customer satisfaction is an evasive concept, yet it is a principal determinant in developing or modifying an industrial positioning argument. There is no better measure than satisfaction to express the ultimate in expectations, delivered benefits, and value received by customers.

Czepiel, in the *Combined Proceedings of the American Marketing Association* (1974), suggests four major groupings of elements that influence satisfaction: product related, process related (pre-sale service aspects), psychosocial, and postpurchase (after-sale service and environmental aspects). This perspective suggests that major contributors to customer satisfaction are service oriented, thus supporting the idea that the successful positioning of industrial products requires considerable attention to the array of pre-sale and post-sale customer services that are offered and provided to customers.

The industrial marketer must be sensitive to needs and demands of the industrial customer. Customer perceptions aren't necessarily the same as those of the marketing staff, advertising department, or sales and service personnel that manage and service the customer accounts. Industrial customers sometimes view a supplier's marketing mix through spectrally distorted glasses. They often only see quality defects, unfilled orders, unavailability of service and parts, back orders, and unmet promises. Correspondingly, purchasing agents and buyers appear to have computer-like brains with large-capacity memory systems that are capable of instantly accessing every price increase or unmet delivery promise for each of a hundred vendors over the past 18 months.

SATISFYING THE COMMERCIAL/INDUSTRIAL CUSTOMER

Studies of over 30 business and medical equipment markets, including copying equipment, data processing equipment, computer and communication terminals, medical electronics and health care systems, office copying equipment, facsimile equipment, etc., describe factors-of-importance in the selection of equipment by users. Table 13-2 illustrates a summary of these factors in rank order of importance by user customers. Each factor in the reported results has been classified according to the five primary elements of the marketing mix: product, distribution, price, customer service, and promotion. Isn't it interesting that the top five factors involve industrial market's secret weapon, customer service? These examples highlight the importance of service elements in the positioning argument for industrial companies.

CUSTOMER SERVICE PERSPECTIVE

Several years ago, a major, multi-line industrial company conducted an in-house seminar for its various manufacturing divisions. The company had designated a corporate-level function, Total Customer Service (TCS), which supported a corporate objective dedicated to product quality and customer service. Each of the company divisions had a TCS executive with direct reporting responsibility to the corporate senior executive vice president—to administer and report on each division's customer service performance. Sixty-one representatives from 32 divisions comprising the TCS executives, general managers, marketing managers, service managers, and sales managers attended the conference. The TCS chairmen were appointed from divisional middle-management ranks, with an accountable person from each of the functional departments including marketing, sales, service, manufacturing, traffic, and engineering. An important feature of the seminar was for all attendees to participate in a workshop in which product-market groups identified customer service elements and listed their priority. Table 13-3 displays the results, illustrating perceived customer service elements and their priority, which reflects their importance to customers. An interesting result occurred because the groups were asked to

TABLE **13-2**
Factors of importance in the selection of equipment (listed in rank order of importance by users, on a scale of 1-5, 1 being highest).

Rank	Factor	Rating	Classification of Factor in Marketing Mix
1	Reliability of Equipment	1.48	Product/Service
2	Quality of Copy/Image/Reproduction	1.72	Product/Service
3	Field Service Response Time	1.76	Service
4	Ease of Operation	2.39	Product/Service
5	Cost of Service	2.84	Price/Service
6	Machine/Printer Speed	2.92	Product
7	Cost of Paper/Supplies	2.94	Price
8	Communicating Capability (of Product)	2.95	Product
9	Timely Delivery of Equipment	3.16	Distribution/Service
10	Previous Experience with Manufacturer	3.61	All Elements of Mix

include quality and price in their listing. Two groups ranked price second, three ranked it sixth (last on the list); and one group eliminated price because none of the group members wanted to assign any of the weighted points to price as compared to other elements. This illustrates that customer service elements rank significantly with product quality in industrial marketing.

TABLE 13-3
Priority listing of customer service elements.

ELECTRICAL PRODUCTS

Utilities	Industrial
1. Quality (Reliability)	1. Product Quality
2. Competitive Price	2. Price
3. Correction of Troubles	3. Customer Communications
4. On-Time Delivery	4. On-Time Delivery
5. Contract Administration	5. Assistance in Bidding & Selling
6. Delivered As Ordered	6. Contract Administration
7. Communications Responsiveness	7. Product Availability
8. Parts Availability	8. Technical Service Support
9. Equitable Claim Settlement	9. Request for Quotations
10. Scheduling Flexibility	10. Product Service

PROCESS EQUIPMENT

Heavy	Standard
1. Product Quality	1. Product Quality
2. Product Availability	2. Delivery
3. Meeting Shipping Dates	3. Field Service
4. Frequency of Calls	4. Technical Support
5. Communications	5. Product Availability
6. Price & Price Information	6. Price & Price Information

WHEELED VEHICLES

Agricultural	Industrial/Commercial
1. Product Availability	1. Product Quality
2. Communications	2. Parts Support
3. Service (Dealer/Field Sales-Service)	3. Product Availability
4. Repair Parts Availability	4. Advance Warning
5. Product Quality	5. Training & Sales Tools
6. Pricing	6. Meeting Shipping Dates

SERVICE AS AN ELEMENT OF STRATEGY

In the early 70s, Pitney-Bowes tried two diversification efforts—one a startling failure, the other equally as much a success. The first, which was a venture into electronic cash registers, carried them outside their normal market into retail establishments. The move failed, yielding a $20 million net loss and a $70 million write-off. The venture failed when product problems and inadequate service support destroyed credibility with customers. It was the typical failure of many new products. Engineering and manufacturing shortcomings couldn't be eliminated without going back to "start." Interestingly, the problems experienced in the electronic cash register business enabled Pitney-Bowes to more adequately prepare for their entry into the office copier market two years later. This is the strategic program that won Pitney-Bowes the Sales and Marketing Management Grand Award for 1975.

Pitney-Bowes' competition was formidable. Xerox was the number one in the computer and office equipment market. Pitney-Bowes and Xerox are two of America's most successful corporations, both firmly entrenched in the office products market; both with totally self-sufficient sales and service organizations. The authors were on the Xerox side of this competition.

The man selected as vice president and general manager of Pitney-Bowes' copier division had gained experience with one of the competitive businesses. Pitney-Bowes immediately established a market-sensitive management. The strategy evolved.

The product was targeted for the medium-copy usage market segment. The machine was designed to use plain bond paper and was to be second to none in quality and performance. The general manager began his employment while prototypes were on field test. He initiated recall of all prototypes for disassembly and complete analysis. The prototypes were rebuilt for testing and demonstration. This degree of concern for quality and reliability continued in the production stages.

Distribution was scheduled for a branch-by-branch introduction—several branches at a time. Initially, sales were confined to a 25-mile radius of each branch. This assured adequate service support during the hiring and training program for 300 service recruits. They were able to handle all service calls within two to four hours, which was critical for satisfaction.

As you can see, the program emphasized attention to details, for it was a lack of detail planning that caused the electronic cash register program failure. Pitney-Bowes now had product quality, reliability, service support, and management awareness of the marketing requirements.

The four-hour limit on service calls was deemed critical in assuring renewal of rental agreements, which was the usual method of procurement. The 25-mile introductory radius was enlarged to 50 miles after service performance was assured.

Promotion activities included distribution of product brochures and a 35mm slide viewer illustrating product features. Presidents of potential clients received personal invitations to product demonstrations by Pitney-Bowes' board chairman. Salespeople also handed out personal invitations to demonstrations.

Salespeople were provided with all available information on competing models, particularly those in the same product class. Each salesperson participated in a two-day training session on a branch-by-branch basis, scheduled with the product introduction. The training emphasized product features and benefits, application details, competitive practices, use of backup films, and advertising. Role-playing sessions were conducted to practice sales presentations and handle objections

A structured sales commission plan ensured that salespeople maintained close contact with customers during the initial evaluation period. A higher commission was awarded for extended rental plans beyond the normal 12-month period. In response to competitors' rental fee cuts, Pitney-Bowes initiated a volume discount system to continue their market position advantage.

In a recessive economic period, with industry sales off 15 to 20 percent, Pitney-Bowes won orders for over 3,000 machines the first year, with a two-to-three fold increase for the second year of 5,000 to 10,000 machine placements.

Although the Pitney-Bowes copier program achieved only

two percent penetration for the medium-volume user, sales attained a $100 million annual rate and Pitney-Bowes' diversification objective was achieved, providing significant sales growth for the corporation.

A strategy that achieves a "first" in sales has advantages over competition. Analysis indicates Pitney-Bowes' primary strategy elements were a product to suit a market niche, adequate promotional support, strong emphasis on personal sales, and a strong product service program. Eliminating any of these elements, including Pitney-Bowes' distribution network of company branches, would have resulted in failure. *Sales and Marketing Management* reported comments of industry analysts: "Pitney-Bowes' sales topped the net new replacements of both major competitors in the medium-copy usage market in the introductory year."

DEVELOPING SERVICE STRATEGY

The Pitney-Bowes example illustrates that a company's management team must be attentive to conditions in the marketplace with evolving customer needs and satisfaction. Awareness to change enables a company to modify goals and objectives and reformulate strategy elements.

Customer service elements should always be components of a company's marketing strategy package for a product offering. Variations are based on the choice and combination of servicing elements. Several of the product groups shown in Table 13-3 can be used to illustrate the differences of how the most beneficial strategy mix will be tailored to the unique product characteristics and specific requirements of customers in the served market.

Electrical switchgear and pole hardware for transmission lines are purchased by utility companies for installation and maintenance of the lines. Contract construction crews make the initial installations and the utilities' line crews perform maintenance and replacement functions. Vendor-supplied technical service and sale-services are important in the pre-sale stage. The regularly employed line crews routinely provide after-sale services. Utility companies maintain stocks of replacement components to suit anticipated requirements, particularly the demands arising from storm damage. Wear-out and product service of operating equipment is not a problem. Customer service elements for utility products excludes the typical product service functions but includes parts availability as a low-priority item.

In contrast, agricultural wheeled vehicles owned and operated by farmers have a high-priority requirement for after service and repair parts. These functions are satisfied by a dealer organization, so some of the strategy provisions of the manufacturer must be "passed down the channel."

While the managers of the utility electrical products division do not view product service and parts as particularly important strategy elements, the managers of agricultural wheeled vehicles must pay particular attention to these service elements in their strategic planning, operational management, and control.

In all cases, these and others involving consumer durables, and the broader varieties of industrial products and process equipment, the planning and management of marketing strategy is a most important part of the management task. Managers must strive to establish the best balance of products, distribution structure, pricing, promotion, and service support. Figure 13-3 illustrates the approach to formulate and implement the service strategy as a component of the overall marketing strategy.

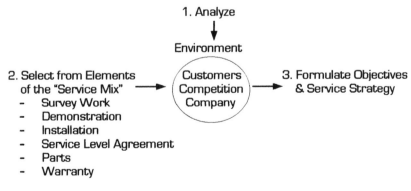

Figure 13-3
Objective setting and strategy formulation process for service.

Central to the strategy process is the essential requirement to monitor the served market, with continuous attention to the levels of customer satisfaction and market share performance relative to competition. Customer satisfaction is a central concern in this process.

Pricing and Billing

A substantial percentage of service inquiries are related to billing questions, prices, and discount structure. Customer service personnel must have a thorough understanding of the company's pricing structure, payment terms, discounts, credit, and billing practices. Prices over the long run tend to be determined by the familiar supply-demand ratio. In the short run, however, price may be unrelated to that ratio or to the cost because the company's marketing strategy may dictate artificially high or low prices. When a company is introducing a product or attempting to penetrate new markets, the following cost-related strategies that affect service may be employed:

- ☐ Psychological pricing
- ☐ Skim pricing
- ☐ Penetration pricing
- ☐ Quantity discounts
- ☐ Trade discounts
- ☐ Service discounts
- ☐ Payment term discounts
- ☐ Promotional discounts

Psychological pricing is used when a high price will tend to denote high quality, and where the emotional desire for a product is the most important factor that determines the decision to buy.

Skim pricing involves setting initial prices at a level substantially higher than that expected to later become standard. Skim pricing helps recover high research and development costs for unique products that may have little initial competition. Electronics and pharmaceutical industries often use skim pricing.

Penetration pricing involves setting a very low price, sometimes below cost, to encourage maximum distribution of the product in order to get "a foot in the door." The price may later be adjusted to a more profitable level once the market has been penetrated.

Quantity discounts involve reducing the unit price as a function of the total quantity purchased. For example, discounts would be allowed for buying a case of consumables at one time or, in the case of larger quantities, complete truckloads.

Trade discounts may be given to wholesalers and agents as partial payment for their marketing services.

Service discounts (or increases) may be tied with special short response times, a shorter delivery cycle, or for a high level of support. Special discounts may also be given if customers will take delivery for longer periods of time or if they will accept a longer response time or a higher level of back-order.

Discounts may also be provided for prompt payment For example, if payment is received within ten days of delivery, a 1% discount may be allowed.

Promotional discounts may be useful to increase sales on excess inventory, in connection with advertising displays, to stimulate new product introduction, and to draw attention away from competition.

There are also five major types of geographic pricing policies that may be utilized: uniform delivered pricing, base-point pricing, free on board (f.o.b.) pricing, freight equalization, and zone pricing. F.o.b. pricing requires that the customer pay for all freight charges from the plant to the customer's location.

Uniform delivered prices will be an advantage to some customers and a disadvantage to others, and will simplify billing. All customers pay the same delivered price regardless of their geographical location because the company simply allocates the total transportation cost among all customers.

Zone pricing is a modification of uniform delivered pricing. All customers within a given geographic zone are charged uniformly. This system is used by the US Postal Service, while several other carriers vary price by zone.

Base-point pricing allows customers to order from designated shipping points with no freight charges if they are located within the basic point area. Customers located beyond the area boundaries are charged the base price plus the cost of transportation from the nearest basing point to them.

Freight equalization is a tactic for meeting price competition from manufacturers closer to the customer. The seller absorbs some or all of the freight charges in order to eliminate those costs and hopefully stimulate sales. Freight charges are usually then calculated from the competing location nearest the customer rather than from the actual company location.

LEGAL CONSIDERATIONS

There are legal constraints to each of the above pricing considerations, as well as many other aspects of service business. It is important that service management and customer care personnel have a thorough understanding of the legal implications of pricing, delivery, warranties, and other aspects of service.

Three major acts—the Sherman, Clayton, and Robinson-Patman—must be obeyed in pricing service and logistics. The Sherman Anti-Trust Act of 1890 and the Clayton Act of 1914 had the objective of promoting free competition through the elimination of artificial restraints of trade. In particular, large-scale collusive action by business firms, to the detriment of the general public, was to be eliminated. The main effect of the Sherman Act was to forbid persons or firms engaged in interstate commerce from discriminating in price between purchasers if the effect was substantially to decrease competition. Although the idea behind the law was noble and did prevent some mergers and eliminate some unfair practices, giant business firms continued to dominate many industries. The Robinson-Patman Act of 1936, an amendment to the Clayton Act, specifically mentions three major areas of cost that might justify quantity discounts to customers purchasing commodities of like grade and quality, manufacturer, sales, and delivery.

The act says in part, "It is unlawful...to discriminate in price between different purchasers for commodities of like grade and quality...when the effect of such discrimination may be substantially to lessen competition or tend to create a monopoly in any line of commerce or to injure, destroy, or prevent competition with any person who either grants or knowingly receives the benefit from such discrimination, or with customers with either of them...provided that nothing... shall prevent differentials which make only due allowance for difference in the cost of manufacture, sales, or delivery."

As a practical matter, cost savings and manufacturing have been difficult to defend. Court interpretations of the Robinson-Patman Act have required uniform allocation or fixed costs. Many firms have found it difficult to justify their arbitrary cost allocation, and for this reason have entirely abandoned quantity discounts.

For firms wishing to maintain quantity discounts schedules and justify them before the Federal Trade Commission (FTC), logistics cost evidence appears to be the best justification, not only because of the reduction in average cost per unit of goods transported in large quantifies, but also because detailed documentation accompanies transportation activities. As the Robinson-Patman Act allows quantity discounts less than, but no more than, justifiable decreases in cost and quantity sales, many logistics organizations have the task of determining whether the transportation and handling savings are sufficient to cover the amount of the suggested quantity discounts.

Call Management/ Help Desk/Dispatch Function

One of the more important functions in service is the management of customer calls for assistance. Customer-service personnel interface with the customer and direct the service technicians. Their main functions are to:

1. Receive the customer communication and initially pacify the customer.

2. Identify the customer and level of support authorized.

3. Record information properly for transmission to a service technician and for necessary record keeping.

4. Help the customer to solve the need, if possible. Considerable coaching, software assistance, and operating advice takes place during telephone assistance.

5. If a technician or parts are needed, determine the technician, arrange the parts, and dispatch the call.

These functions may be all done by one skilled person in a small service operation, or there may be thousands of people on Help Desk with thousands more field technicians plus logistics support, in which case the functions should become specialized by product, customer type, and even by the language spoken. Calls resolved over the phone help the customer fast and usually result in high satisfaction ratings while costing much less than calls that require a technician visit to the site.

Customer communications are usually received on the telephone, but more and more are coming over the web or by e-mail. The normal source is from the operator who discovered the fault in the equipment. Other sources may include customer management, organization sales personnel, or related organizations such as installation riggers. Telephone procedure for people answering customer calls is particularly important, as the customer is usually upset and unhappy with defective equipment. The receiving call representative must be courteous at all times and also be fast and efficient. It is very helpful if each machine has its own identifying number that can be easily given by the calling customer, either the serial number or a specific code number attached strictly for service identification. An example of such a tag that could be prominently displayed on a machine is shown in Figure 13-4.

For Service Call 689-6650
Please Tell the Help Desk
This is Machine No. 364-C

FIGURE 13-4
Sample dispatch tag put on equipment.

Many people calling to request service will not have noticed the dispatch card or will not give a hoot, and figure it is the company's responsibility to know that information. The call management organization should have immediate access to a computer system that has equipment records cross-filed by product code, machine serial number, customer name, address, and telephone number. That way, if a customer who calls up does not know the machine number, looking at the customer master list will tell the dispatcher that machine 364-C is at that location. This information is easily kept online in a computer system so that typing any of the data on the keyboard will display all necessary information. The customer problem can be entered immediately in the call record. If the machine is normally assigned to a specific service technician who is expected to be available in the near future, the call can be dispatched to await action. If the service can be provided by the next service technician available, it should be put in priority order in dispatch. The workload waiting for each service technician should be displayed on a Gantt chart form. There ae several systems available to do this, with the simplest being lines displayed on an 8-hour chart indicating the length of time projected for each service call. If a motherboard call is normally expected to take 1.5 hours, then 90 minutes would be blocked off on the service technician's workload chart.

The need for service should be communicated to the service technician at the earliest possible opportunity, usually by pager, radio, cell phone, or personal appearance. The normal message will give the customer and machine by code number, indicate the problem, and give the call sequence number. The sequence number enables the service technician to keep track of all calls and not miss any. If call 5 arrives and call 4 has not preceded it, the service technician should check to resolve the discrepancy.

A code for machine location and problem is used both to speed communication over restricted airwaves and to keep competition from gaining too much intelligence if they monitor the transmission.

Many organizations use a telephone recorder to communicate routine information from the service technician back to dispatch. The recorder can take down the completion times for every service call and any special information that should be noted. At a convenient time, the dispatcher can clear the tape and enter the information on proper records. The combination of pager and telephone recorder has proved to be efficient, significantly reduce communication time, and make the dispatcher more available to service technicians and customers when they are needed instead of tying up telephone lines with low-priority conversation.

Experience shows that relying on telephone dispatch and call closing results in considerable waste time for technicians on "hold" and wrong part numbers communicated. The better solution is to provide technicians direct digital access to receive calls, check history, report status, and close calls with all details. This can be done on wireless hand-held computers, laptops, and similar devices. The advent of two-way pagers enables technicians to receive and reply to communications and to close calls including part numbers, while the cost of both the "beepers" and transmissions is low.

It is common practice in many service organizations for the service technician to call the customer within ten minutes of receiving the dispatched call message, to allow the customer to make alternate arrangements if necessary. The customer is most upset from the time he detects the defective equipment until he knows someone is working on it. The return telephone call from the service technician appears to alleviate this concern even though the machine may not be back into operation until a long time later.

If radios are not effective or too expensive, telephones offer the next alternative. In remote areas where radio transmission is not effective, the service technician should call the dispatcher at the beginning and end of every day and preferably after completing every service call. The dispatcher in these remote areas may be a local telephone answering service rather than a centralized company dispatch. Concerns over lack of status and efficiency are usually overcome by the local activities of the service technician. Finally, of course, some service technicians operate from the dispatch location or arrange to drop in occasionally. This is not desirable because time is wasted any time a field representative comes to the service office. The reason usually given for having service technicians come to the office is to pick up parts. If parts distribution efficiency can be improved there will be little need for people to assemble at the office.

Meanings of Customer Satisfaction

RESPONSE TO SATISFACTION-DISSATISFACTION

The concept of utility suggests that customers shop for and purchase benefits, not just products. As these benefits are realized, customers enjoy satisfaction, which is the ultimate reward of product acquisition and use.

By previous definition, satisfaction implies complete fulfillment of one's needs. It follows that degrees of satisfaction or dissatisfaction, which are manifestations of need fulfillment, may result throughout the process of selection, acquisition, use, and disposal of a product. A consumer example illustrates the satisfaction outcomes. Mary Smith lives in a sparsely furnished apartment, including an old television set. Mary's little sister is planning a visit, for the first time since Mary rented the apartment. Mary knows that her sister will want to watch some of her favorite television shows, but may be displeased with the poor color and occasional fading of the picture. The following sequence of events takes place:

1. Sister visits and Mary turns on TV set. Both notice fading and low-quality picture. Mary is dissatisfied.

2. Mary sees newspaper sales ad for a large-screen color set with warranty and one-year in-the-home service agreement at a price she can afford, with generous trade-in allowance for "any old set." Mary anticipates purchase and feels satisfied.

3. Mary purchases set, with promise that it will be installed

that day. Mary feels satisfied.

4. Evening comes and the new set is not delivered. Mary is dissatisfied and calls store to complain. She is greeted by an answering machine saying the store is closed and to leave a message. Mary is dissatisfied with the store's performance and complains that they broke their promise to deliver the set.

5. The store delivery person arrives early the next day. The delivery person is unkempt and surly, but installs the new set and adjusts it. Mary is now satisfied with the new TV set, but is dissatisfied with the store and delivery person.

6. That evening, Mary and her sister are watching television when the picture blacks out. Mary becomes very angry and expresses her dissatisfaction with the television set, the store, and all the people at the store.

7. The next morning Mary calls the store and complains to the store owner. He is very understanding and apologetic. He promises to have the problem taken care of by noon that day. Mary feels relieved, but is still dissatisfied.

8. The owner personally delivers another new set, listens to Mary's complaints, installs and adjusts the new set, and apologizes for the inconvenience. He gives Mary his home phone number and asks her to call him personally if she has any more trouble. Mary feels pleased and satisfied with the store's performance and the new television set.

9. Two days later the store owner calls Mary and tells her that he has put the delivery person on probation, pending improvement in appearance and attitude. He thanks Mary for her business and patience with his store. He repeats the request that she call him if she has any further problems. Mary feels satisfied.

This example illustrates the complexity of the satisfaction concept in a relatively simplified situation, as compared to what one might anticipate for an industrial product situation. If you measured Mary's level of satisfaction/indifference/dissatisfaction with the old TV set, the new set, the store, and the store's personnel throughout the process, there would have been a broad variety of responses. Mary's experiences with the television set and the retail store illustrate that two aspects of customer attitude are particularly important insofar as the meaning and measurement of satisfaction is concerned:

➢ Word-of-mouth promotion
➢ Repurchase expectation

Word-of-mouth promotion occurs when people share their feelings about products and the performance of sellers and providers to other people who may be prospective purchasers or users. This type of promotion contributes substantially to building or destroying seller or provider credibility and is important to the process of selling/acquiring products and services.

Repurchase expectation is the inclination of the owner of a product or the user of a service to repurchase the same brand of product or service from the same seller or provider.

SURROGATE MEASURES OF CUSTOMER SATISFACTION

Although many companies may not have direct measures of customer satisfaction, all have one or more surrogate measures that indirectly communicate customer attitudes and purchase intentions.

Sales levels and share-of-market are probably the most frequently used surrogate measures; fluctuations in customer satisfaction will be reflected by increases or decreases in sales levels and market share. It is assumed that this performance ultimately reflects customer attitudes, specifically the level of satisfaction.

More directly, opinions of sales and service representatives reflect customer attitudes, particularly dissatisfaction. This feedback is haphazard and may do little more than amplify what is already suspected or known from sales performance statistics.

For those industrial companies with a few major accounts, the feedback from sales and service representatives may be an adequate source of information about satisfaction-indifference-dissatisfaction. Service reports are particularly valuable, because a service representative has opportunity to communicate with the variety of people within an organization who are exposed to the product and servicing activities. Unfortunately, as the example of Mary's experience with the unkempt, surly delivery man suggests, direct feedback from sales and service personnel may skirt a problem or lack objectivity. A large number of firms define satisfaction in terms of complaints. If customers do not complain it is assumed they are satisfied. Reality shows differently!

The surrogate measures reflect many other factors including level of advertising, representation in the marketplace, pricing, competitive effort, and shifting technology; and should not be trusted to be representative of customer attitudes.

SATISFACTION DEFINED

The definition of satisfaction used here is offered by Howard and Farley in *Consumer Behavior: Theory and Application* (Boston: Allyn-Bacon, 1974):

Satisfaction is defined as the buyer's cognitive state of being adequately or inadequately rewarded in a buying situation for the sacrifice he or she has undergone. The adequacy is a consequence of matching actual past purchase and consumption experience with the reward that was expected from the brand in terms of its anticipated potential to satisfy the motives (needs, drives, desires) served by the particular product class.

The primary elements identified are thus *reward* and *sacrifice* and the comparison of these factors throughout the buying situation. Howard and Farley view satisfaction as serving the purposes of a *feedback mechanism* which exerts influence on attitudes and confidence after purchase and full comprehension of the "value set" that has been acquired.

Diagrammatically, the purchase-satisfaction process and its effect on motives and our cognitive state can be illustrated as in Figure 13-5. This view suggests that satisfaction is the alteration of motives and is the technical explanation for "fulfillment of one's wishes, needs, and expectations," an earlier definition.

An important point is illustrated in Figure 13-5: The *consumption/utilization* experience is an ongoing process (i.e., comparing rewards and satisfactions with expectations), thus altering motives/satisfaction. This ongoing experience involves all aspects of the product and service-provider relationship. It is easily seen that the satisfaction response (satisfaction-indifference-dissatisfaction) may be more dependent on aspects of after-service rather than the product itself.

Since the user experience is ongoing, the satisfaction response is an important aspect of the overall marketing process, and the measurement of satisfaction is essential to business planning and strategy formulation.

Measuring Customer Satisfaction

A review of the marketing literature leads to the conclusions that there is little consistency in the definition of customer satisfaction or its measurement. Also, most marketing literature tends to neglect the service functions and the importance of specific servicing activities to marketing success. Predominately in this literature, the marketing variables are limited to the "four

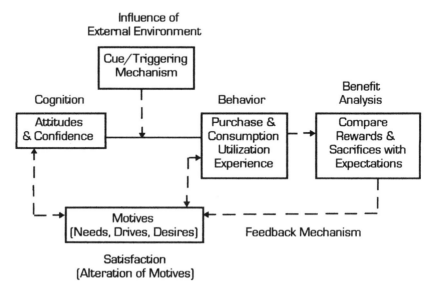

FIGURE 13-5
The purchase-satisfaction process.

P's": product, place (distribution), promotion, and price. Most literature refers to service as "part of the product," thus tending to overlook the existence and importance of the whole array of service elements illustrated in Figure 13-3—survey work, demonstration, installation, service level agreements, parts, and warranty. The view held in this discussion is that the meaning of customer satisfaction is highly dependent on service elements and their influence on the product utilization process.

CHARACTERISTICS OF SATISFACTION

Satisfaction has been defined in a previous section, but in order to measure customer satisfaction, the characteristics of satisfaction must be understood. There are four elements that characterize satisfaction. These four elements are identified and described in the following paragraphs.

Intensity of satisfaction. The intensity of satisfaction is a measure of the value of the specific activity relative to your personal needs or the needs of a company. When a doctor has just saved your life, you are intensely satisfied. When your paperclip order arrives a day ahead of schedule, you are satisfied, but not with the same intensity as with the life-saving activity of the doctor. Put into a more industrial setting, when the lubricating oil for the production line arrives one day ahead of time, you have little intensity in your satisfaction. When, however, your production line has shutdown and the critical spare part needed to restore production is hand-carried into your plant, allowing the plant to quickly restore operation, your level of intensity is much greater than that from the lubricating oil arriving a day early. Thus, the satisfaction level is directly related to the value of the service provided. The more valuable it is, the more intense will be the level of satisfaction. Often the service provided is of such a hgh quality that its full value is not recognized. Good maintenance service can deter a product from catastrophic failure, but only a severe failure can intensify service satisfaction levels under "normal," nonfailure conditions.

Figure 13-6 diagrams an interpretation of the effects when a technician requests a part from the stockkeeper. If no part is available (below the horizontal zero line) the level of pain is great. If the part is available the level of satisfaction is only moderate. After all, having the part is expected normal performance. If there were two parts available but the technician only wanted one, then no one really cares about the second part. However, about the time the vice president of finance finds out that there are several expensive parts languishing under the dust of no use, then there is a different type of pain.

Congruence of satisfaction. The congruence of satisfaction is a way of stating that the difference between actual and expected satisfaction will directly affect the level of satisfaction. Prior to the performance of a service or the delivery of goods, a customer has a level of expectation. How closely the actual goods or service meets that expectation will determine the amount of congruence between the expected and actual level. As these two come closer together, the level of satisfaction will increase. If a customer expects a service technician to arrive on site within two hours, his satisfaction expectation is based on a two-hour response time. If, in fact, the service technician does not arrive for four hours, the difference of two hours will dramatically change the level of satisfaction. The drop in satisfaction level will probably not be linear as the delay increases. Doubling the tardiness from two hours late to four hours late will probably not double the drop in level of satisfaction. This difference between expected and actul performance works similarly when the actual results exceed the expectation level. Using the same service technician example where a two-hour response time is expected, if the technician arrives within an hour and a half, the actual

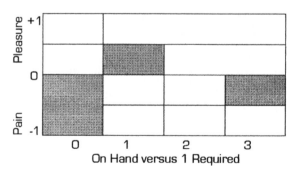

FIGURE 13-6
There is more pain from too few parts than from too many, and both overwhelm the pleasure of having the correct quantity.

versus expected performance is one half-hour better, and the level of satisfaction will be somewhat greater than had the technician arrived within two hours. On the other hand, if the technician were to arrive within one hour, improving the response time twice as much as the one-and-one-half hour arrival time, it is not likely the customer's improvement in satisfaction would be double that of the hour-and-a-half arrival time. The key point is to recognize what the expected level of performance is for the customer, and it is important for actual performance to match that expectation as closely as possible.

Some believe that the congruence aspect of service is, in fact, a two-factor component, consisting of a dissatisfaction component and an acceptable/neutral component. If response time is within an expected value, then the customer is accepting or neutral in his or her judgment. If response time is poorer than the anticipated level, then the zone of dissatisfaction is entered. They are not points on a continuum; they are separate scalar continuums.

Ambiguity of satisfaction. The level of satisfaction by the customer can be directly related to how clearly the customer understands what goods or service he has been provided. In many service support areas the customer is not specifically aware of what has been done. Going back to the original example of the doctor saving your life, there was no doubt as to what the provided service was and its value to you. Obviously, the ambiguity of the satisfaction was zero. On the other hand, many service activities can be very ambiguous unless specifically directed otherwise. For example, preventive maintenance on equipment can be a very ambiguous service if the customer is not educated with regard to all of the activities involved in the maintenance service provided. The frequency with which contract maintenance occurs, and the improved reliability of the equipment that results from the service, too often falls into ambiguity due to lack of customer education. When the preventive maintenance contract is offered, the customer questions both its costs and its value. A simple solution to this problem is to direct the service technician to make sure the customer is aware each time a preventive maintenance call is made, the number of activities that were involved in the call, and by pointing out both the value of the call and the lack of machine problems in the interim periods. Thus, ambiguity of satisfaction can be eliminated through customer education.

Periodicity of satisfaction. The frequency with which service is provided to a customer will also have dramatic impact on level of satisfaction. If the customer never sees anybody performing service on his equipment he would certainly wonder whether his service contract has value. Implicitly, he should also think that his equipment is extremely reliable and service free. The other extreme would be when he is conscious of the frequent presence of a service technician and wonders, perhaps, whether he has an unreliable piece of equipment and whether its value to him is really what was expected when the purchase decision was made.

For each class of equipment there is a nominally perceived frequency that customers would expect to have service performed on their equipment. For high-technology electronic equipment, customers perceive the need for corrective maintenance two or three times per year. As the owner of an automobile, you would certainly not expect to have the need for service more than one or two times per year. Certainly, you would be very concerned if you had a pacemaker attached to your heart and it required service on a weekly basis. On the other hand, you would be very concerned if you had paid for a preventive maintenance contract on a piece of industrial equipment that indicated you should receive a minimum of four calls per year, yet at the end of the year only two service calls had been performed.

Satisfaction will be maximized when the periodicity of the service comes in congruence with the customer's expectation of the frequency with which service should be provided. Too frequent service can be just as harmful as too little service and can have the same negative effect on the level of satisfaction. When a company understands how these characteristics of intensity, congruence, ambiguity, and periodicity contribute to the satisfaction with its products and services, it should enjoy a substantial advantage over its competitors, not the least of which is the opportunity to enhance customer brand or company loyalty for all future purchases.

MEASURES OF SATISFACTION

Historical measures of customer satisfaction tend to compare product performance with pre-purchase expectations. If your product is a conveyor lubricator, and an automobile assembly line is shut down because service and parts for the lubricator aren't available, then customer satisfaction doesn't have much to do with a design engineer's pre-purchase expectations for the lubricator. Suddenly, the plant superintendent and maintenance foreman are on the scene and customer satisfaction has taken a new twist.

Realistically, a product cannot be treated as an island unto itself when customer satisfaction is at stake, particularly as it relates to pre-purchase analysis and purchase decisions for products, maintenance, repair and parts, supplies, and product rebuild or retrofit. We must take the view that concern for customer satisfaction has a future rather than past perspective. How much, and in what way, does customer satisfaction affect future business opportunities?

MEASUREMENT CRITERIA

Measurement of customer satisfaction relates to attitude or cognitive state. It is a measurement of perceptions. This type of measurement is one that psychologists have been working on for many years, and it requires an approach unlike that within the realms of engineering and technology. Measurements are qualitative, but they are quantified on a numeric rating scale that indicates differences in expectancy between markets, including relative importance of various components of satisfaction for individuals. Attitudinal measurement cannot be tied down to an absolute scale as is done in the physical sciences, such as measures of temperature, speed, time, and distance. Rather, in attitudinal measurements the points are normalized against individual standards. These scales are similar to converting a raw score in statistics to a "Z" score allowing comparisons between non-identical elements.

In terms of a measurement of satisfaction, it doesn't matter if dissatisfaction results from one or three failures causing one hour or three days of down time. What is important is that both the person affected for one hour and the one for three days is very unhappy. The resulting rating is the same for both.

Companies that measure customer attitudes and customer satisfaction use survey methods of mail, telephone, e-mail, and personal interview. The results are tabulated, validated, and statistically analyzed for significance. Many companies categorize the measurement of customer satisfaction in the broader range of market research, and they rely on staff personnel or consultants who specialize in this work to develop the measurement instruments and to perform analysis for them.

The criteria for implementation of a customer satisfaction measurement program should include at least the following four points:

1. *Sampling.* Identify and develop a survey sample that will be representative of the customer base. It is important that any measurement of customer satisfaction be representative of the customers that the company is serving. All components of the customer mix should be included. The sample should be geographically representative as well as market-segment representative. This requires a "good database" often found missing in even the more sophisticated organization. There should be equal likelihood that any customer be included in the sample.

2. *Instrumentation.* Develop a series of instruments that can be used for data gathering. Survey instruments typically include components such as a measure of the total level of satisfaction with the company, a rating of the equipment, a rating of the product service, a rating of the other support services, and a rating of other aspects of the company, including sales support. The factors chosen for measurement should be representative of the more important elements required for maintaining a high

level of customer satisfaction.

3. *Analysis methodology.* Conceptualize the statistical, analytic approach that will assure the maximum ease of quantifying the responses from customers. Without a statistical approach to reduce the data gathered from the instruments, meaningful conclusions would be impossible. Hence, prior to the initiation of the program, the appropriate statistics must be identified.

4. *Resource allocation.* Assure that the organization will both analyze and communicate the results of the satisfaction measurement program to appropriate line management. In this way, company resources can be properly allocated to achieve the level of customer satisfaction set by executive management. Quite often it may be desirable to use an external research firm due to availability of requisite knowledge and skills, as well as the ability of such a resource to approach the project in an objective manner. A member of an internal group might not want to indicate that their group is partially responsible for low customer satisfaction. The tendency in such a situation would be to structure the measurement instrument and analysis so that some other group is also held accountable.

Measurement Techniques

Several techniques in the measurement of attitudes are reviewed now to illustrate methodology. Results of several studies were reported in the early part of this chapter. These are used to illustrate the measurement process, as related to customer satisfaction with service. Results of studies illustrated in Table 13-2 assist in identifying typical factors that concern commercial customers. As noted, these factors were found to have a degree of importance designated on a 5-point scale. Only one of these reported measures—field service response time—was singularly indicative of service performance. The point to be recognized is that delivering customer satisfaction is a team effort, illustrating the importance of including non-service factors in the instrumentation. Note that customer perceptions were reduced to numeric values by using an attitudinal measurement scale and asking customers to select a word combination or number to indicate their attitudes. Figure 13-7 combines both approaches:

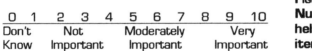

FIGURE 13-7
Numerical scales help people rate items.

Another technique is to use a ranking method, with the customer being asked to assign points, or to rank one or more factors in accordance with their value or importance. This approach, requiring forced choice, is sometimes used to determine the importance for one factor as compared to another. For example, the following listing could be provided with the instruction to rank order the factors (1-6) in order of importance:

_____ Product quality
_____ Parts support
_____ Technical service support
_____ Repair service support
_____ Product price
_____ Training

In effect, this was the process used to determine the ordering of data illustrated in Table 13-3. Once the factors to be measured are designated, an instrument is constructed for the survey. The designs are specialized for personal (face-to-face) and telephone interviewing, or mail surveys. In any case, services of a research specialist should be used to assure validity of results.

SERVICE SATISFACTION AND ITS MEASUREMENT

Several case examples illustrate methodology, findings, and corrective action for customer satisfaction studies, one involving retail and the other commercial customers. Retailco periodically uses a telephone survey to measure satisfaction with its appliance service. Through the years they have determined that three categories of response are of value to them in measuring customer satisfaction with the service itself: promptness, courtesy, and repair effectiveness. They also measure other factors: overall service satisfaction, convenience, courtesy of service order writer, cost of service, etc.

Surveys are conducted with a representative sample of customers on a semi-annual basis, allowing comparison of the "service satisfaction index" from period to period. Corrective action is taken between surveys to improve deficient areas. Retailco services a variety of appliance products, and the service effectiveness is tabulated over time by service/satisfaction factor (as promptness, etc.), by date (at six month intervals), and by product category (as ranges, TV sets, etc.). Thus, the database is filed in a three-dimensional matrix: product type, satisfaction index factor, and date. A Service Satisfaction Index (SSI) is the satisfaction score for any designated factor at any point in time. This index can be expressed as a percentage of customers satisfied or as a score value—such as 52% satisfied, 1.4 on a 1-5 scale (1 being highest), or 6.7 on a 1-10 scale (10 being highest). In discussing satisfaction levels, the "numbers" can be used conversationally by responsible employees to represent the actual and targeted measures of satisfaction.

Retailco employs trained telephone interviewers who use a prescribed questionnaire form. Customer response is entered numerically into "punched card format"—card columns are designed for response to each question. The following question and response alternatives illustrate the format:

Based on what you have experienced or heard, how would you rate the speed with which Retailco answers calls for service, compared with most other companies—better, the same, or worse?

Better	*1*	*Worse*	*3*
The Same	*2*	*Don't Know*	*4*

The interviewer enters response (as 1, for "Better") in the proper card column. Interviewers can record data on forms to be entered into the computer at a later date, use mark-sense cards, or enter data directly into the computer.

In a typical interview series, telephone interviews were conducted with 1,027 repair-service customers. All respondents had used the repair services in the previous month. The person interviewed was "the person who can best tell me about how satisfied you are with the service you received on (product)." The reporting of findings by Retailco is extensive, typified in Table 13-4 for one factor (prompt service), and product (ranges), over time. Similarly, Table 13-5 shows results for all products, over time.

In reviewing this data, you quickly realize that any deteriorating SSI has been flagged. Effects of seasonality for ranges, freezers, air conditioners, and TV sets is suggested by the differences in the SSI values in the spring of the year as compared to fall. If a range is causing trouble during the holidays, or if the TV isn't working during the football season, one can expect different customer response as compared to the spring of the year.

To determine the overall satisfaction with service levels, specific SSI values can be designated for key satisfaction factors.

TABLE 3-4
Over time, percent mentioning prompt service as reason for satisfaction with their ranges.

	11/97	11/98	11/99	Base Units
Ranges	60%	54%	71%	156

TABLE 3-5
Over time, percent mentioning prompt service as reason for satisfaction with all products.

Prompt Service	Ranges	Washers	Dryers	Refrig	Freezers	A/C	TV
11/97	60	73	74	63	67	85	49
11/98	>54	>71	75	65	>65	>80	51
06/99	71	>70	>73	67	77	>65	65

For example, Retailco has determined that promptness is the most important factor for their products with retail customers. This being the case, what might the minimum standards be for prompt service? How would you respond to the above data if you were director of service for Retailco and the date was June 30, 1999?

COMMERCIAL SERVICE EXAMPLE

A major, multidivisional business equipment firm, designated Busequipco, has a national field service organization that is responsible for all after-sale service for the company's products. Busequipco's vice president of technical service was concerned with the level of customer satisfaction from the service operation and decided to conduct a customer survey. An evaluation of internal staff responsibilities and capabilities led to contracting for the study. A consulting firm, designated CAL, which had considerable prior experience with field service organizations was selected. CAL was given the responsibility to conceptualize the program, design the measurement instrument, and devise the methodology for sampling and data analysis. The following program resulted:

Busequipco's service planning staff and CAL decided that the survey should emphasize those variables defined as being important to the customer. Questions were arranged in three distinct sections:

1. *Demographic information.* The data necessary to characterize the company's market segments. Questions related to the following:
- Type of service contract with customers
- Primary business activity of customers
- Customer company size as measured by number of employees and gross receipts

2. *General and specific customer service factors.* The measurement of satisfaction levels for general areas and specifics about service:
- Broad marketing factors such as product quality, sales sup-

port, operator training, technical service support

- Specific factors that allow evaluation of the service operation, down to each service technician and his ability to maintain products

3. *Overall corporate capability.* The overall measurement of satisfaction with Busequipco's ability to satisfy the customer:

♦ Total levels of satisfaction with products and support services
♦ Identification of product types and satisfaction with each
♦ Solicitation of suggestions to improve Busequipco's service image and capability.

The final section was necessary because of the breadth of Busequipco's product line and the importance of pinpointing the product group and all company measures. The final question allowed the respondent to recommend how Busequipco could improve, although many respondents used this opportunity to specify what was wrong with the company, its products, and service at the present time.

CAL designed the questionnaire based on the assumption that multiple aspects must be considered in evaluating customer satisfaction with the service organization, since they affect the overall and specific service satisfaction measures. The most comprehensive approach would be to measure satisfaction in total, for each major functional area, and with specific detail for each area, including service factors.

The factors considered in the measurement were the overall level of satisfaction, service representative performance, equipment quality and performance, service support, aspects of sales support, invoicing speed and accuracy, operator training, and equipment operability.

The sequence of questioning was deemed important. After consideration of the detailed questions regarding service, refresher questions were used to draw out attitudes about the satisfaction state.

The instrument was mailed, with additional follow-ups to customers who failed to respond. Additionally, a sub-sample of nonrespondents was interviewed personally. The purpose of this additional effort was to validate that the respondents were, in fact, representative of the total customer base.

Each satisfaction question in the second section (general and specific customer service factors) was evaluated on a scale of 0-9 (10 points). The central score of 4 and 5 was for "average," 2 and 3 for "below average," and 6 and 7 for "above average." The extreme points of the scale were 0 and 1 for "poor," and 8 and 9 for "excellent." This quantification of qualitative descriptions in equal-appearing intervals allowed for the statistical analysis of returns.

The questionnaire was designed by CAL so that it could be sent to the customer with a cover letter and, with a simple folding procedure, act as a return, self-addressed, postage-paid piece. This overall approach was aimed to minimize mailing costs to Busequipco, while anticipating a high rate of response.

Busequipco decided to sample one-fourth of the customer base each quarter of the first year. At the end of the year, the entire customer-base had been sampled and measured relative to the customers' satisfaction. At the completion of this program, the questionnaire was redesigned and shortened, allowing for the implementation of a sampling strategy to reduce costs while maintaining input information on customer satisfaction. The questionnaire and letter were sent out over the signature of the vice president of technical service. Anonymity was provided customers through use of a central mail location and return site. Thus, the possibility of a customer's fear of local repercussions over a bad response could be minimized.

The data was subjected to numerous analyses. For each of the demographic items, frequency of response was calculated. This allowed profiling of customer groups by size and geography to determine customer satisfaction levels and need for improvement.

For each of the factors, satisfaction levels were computed, yielding a mean (average) value and the frequency of selection of each response score, for example, "poor" (0-1 score). The comments responding to the open-ended suggestions of how Busequipco could improve the delivery of service were categorized by type and tallied, indicating areas needing attention. Each specific comment was analyzed and referred to the responsible local manager, or headquarters, for handling.

Using product information in the last section, the responses were categorized to determine satisfaction levels by product category. By performing the study and analysis, it was possible to do the following:

- ❑ Compute demographic profiles for customers with measures of satisfaction
- ❑ Compute geographic (regional, district) profiles, with measures of customer satisfaction for each factor
- ❑ Determine servicing effectiveness down to each administrative unit and individual service representative
- ❑ Compute customer satisfaction profiles by product categories
- ❑ Analyze comments to determine "trouble spots"
- ❑ Establish base lines for measures of customer satisfaction

Statistical analysis included determination of levels-of-significance for various data. (The .05 level was used as the criteria of significance.) While some measures were statistically significant, more often the findings were of a trend nature to be observed over time to see if management action was indicated at a later date.

In general, members of Busequipco's management team found the results and techniques employed to be powerful and useful. They were warned of areas needing improvement, specific problems were identified, and they were alerted to conditions that needed watching.

SERVICE STRATEGY

These two examples, Retailco and Busequipco, illustrate methodology to measure customer satisfaction. In initiating programs of this type, it is imperative to establish objectives and measurement criteria. The central idea is to determine the customer impact of service variables and to use that information to continuously reallocate resources to improve results.

Perhaps a program aimed at measuring customer satisfaction might have an objective as follows: "By (date), install on-going program to measure levels of customer satisfaction, to recommend desired satisfaction levels for designated service elements, and to periodically reallocate resources to maintain customer satisfaction at the desired levels." This objective aims to provide an unemotional means to judge effectiveness of service strategy, then to "fine tune" the strategy mix to maximize results.

To assist in the determination of desired service levels, it is important to have criteria to judge the importance of measured customer satisfaction levels. To this end, it is useful to find out from customers not only their level of satisfaction but also the level of importance of the item. For example, assume the level of customer satisfaction is 8.5 (on a scale of 1-10) and the customers indicate that a 5.0 level is acceptable. If it costs $100,000 annually to maintain the 8.5 level as compared to 7.0, $150,000 as compared to 6.0, and $175,000 as compared to 5.0, then a good decision is to reduce the level of customer service to 6.0 and reduce costs by $150,000 annually.

To provide guidance for these decisions, Donald Blumberg identified a model to compare "supplier performance" to "importance to customer." This model has been adopted and Table 13-6 illustrates the comparison for several factors measured in the Busequipco study. The values for "importance to customer" factors come from a national study of office equipment customers. The following comparisons are drawn:

TABLE 13-6
Importance to customers determines the emphasis on the performance rating. (Values are on a scale of 1 to 10, with 10 being highest.)

Set	Busequipco (Actual Performance)	National Study (Importance to Customer)
A	Professional Behavior—7.95	Professional Attitude—4.50
B	Response Time—7.08	Ability to Respond Rapidly—6.75
C	Parts Availability—4.50	Ability to Repair—6.35

If one accepts the thesis that the upper and lower limits of desirable performance vary somewhat as shown in Table 13-6, based on importance to customer, it follows that the high priority concern of Busequipco is to improve Set C, parts availability, thus to improve its ability to repair defective customer products.

It is quickly noted that the professional behavior of Busequipco's service reps and response time is adequate. Although professional behavior of service reps is above the suggested upper limit, it's unlikely that Busequipco's service management would want to reduce the level of performance.

The Service Strategy Map, Figure 13-8, is a format to compare values of actual versus desirable levels of the factors that influence customer satisfaction. The band of desirable performance is based on the premise that supplier performance should be referenced to the customer's perception of importance. The Map is divided into four quadrants: NE—performance is optimum, maintain service level. NW—performance exceeds customer expectations, reallocate resources, reduce service level. SW—service level is below customer expectations but the service factor is of minimal importance to customer, improve performance, low priority. SE—factors are of critical importance to customer and performance by supplier is at a low level, improve performance, high priority. The Map abscissa (importance to customer) and ordinate (performance by supplier) are designated as scales of 0-10, with 10 being highest. Those desiring to reference the Map using data based on other scales (as 5-1, with 1 being highest; 1-4, with 4 being highest, etc.) can use ratios and inversions to convert data to the 10-scale.

Caution: in analyzing data it is easy to be lulled into complacency if average values (means) for a customer satisfaction score are at a tolerable level. Note the following example. Instrumentco conducted a study of their customers to determine "total satisfaction with factory service." The results were as follows:

30% Excellent   47% Good   14% Fair   10% Poor

(Mean: 7.41 on a 1 to 10 scale, where Excellent = 10, Good = 7.5, Fair = 5.0, and Poor = 2.5)

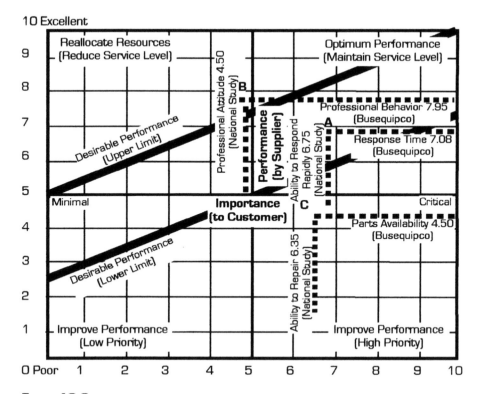

Figure 13-8
**Dick Berry's Service Strategy Map is a good tool
to compare Busequipco with national information.**

In analyzing this data, Instrumentco's management noted
that the average performance was "good," and that the majority
of respondents found the performance to be "excellent" or
"good." The 7.41 mean value would probably look impressive
on the strategy map, Table 13-6. However, it should be noted
that 10% of the customers reported that their level of satisfaction
was "poor." Can we interpret this to mean that 10% of the
customers were dissatisfied and would not use Instrumentco's
products and services in the future? Probably.

Instrumentco's management must decide whether or not
they want to improve their service level to reduce future "poor"
ratings. Analysis of detailed response to the study indicated that,
as compared to competitors, their performance was "poor" on

the following selected factors (greater than 10 percent "Poor"):

- Time required to return instruments (13% Poor)
- Proper response to special instructions (13% Poor)
- Provision of educational services (14% Poor)
- Provision of technical field services (14% Poor)
- Time required to satisfy orders for parts (16% Poor)
- Back ordering of critical items (18% Poor)

These are the priority concerns of Instrumentco's director of service. Management must determine the tolerable lower level of "poor" ratings.

This section has explored the meaning and measurement of customer satisfaction from the perspective of the product service function. Emphasis has been given to servicing relationships with commercial and industrial customers, detailing the importance of various customer-serving functions in building a firm's overall marketing and service strategy.

Special Efforts

Sales and service organizations share responsibilities for customer satisfaction. Many actions performed by service directly affect the ability of the sales organization to meet its objectives, while in turn the actions of sales affect the service organization. It is a good idea to single out special areas throughout the year for extra attention. Examples of activities that will return high value if given special attention are:

- Installation
- Sales coordination
- Equipment requirements
- Balancing activities to avoid "month-end crunches"
- Operator training
- Supply sales
- Competitive supplies
- Cancellation prevention

Interest and attention tend to fade over time, and service management should be continually restimulating specific areas for improved customer satisfaction. Management should keep in mind that customer perceptions may be more important than facts, and sooner or later the customer is always right.

Questions

1. Why should sales personnel instead of service technicians do most customer relations calls?

2. What kinds of information does your service department provide to customers before they order equipment?

3. What are the functions of dispatch in your organization?

4. Does your organization follow the marketing concept that the customer is buying a capability, not just a product?

5. Determine the approximate cost for acquiring a new customer for your business and the cost for maintaining an existing customer.

6. What is the general pricing policy of your service organization?

7. What government organizations and regulations affect pricing in your business?

8. What values are there to conducting audits of how satisfied your customers are?

9. Should a service technician tell the customer decision-maker when equipment is repaired or just quietly leave and avoid confrontation?

10. Why are installation, commissioning, and the initial period of use particularly sensitive times?

14

Information Systems

S ervice information systems are changing at an exponential rate. Personal computers on most desks and laptops, hand-held communications terminals, and two-way pagers provide very effective tools for exchanging information about the business of service. It is important, however, to note that the computer is only a tool. It provides the means for a manager to retain large amounts of data about his business for rapid, thorough, accurate analysis.

The computer can not do any of these tasks without the program guidance from humans who describe exactly what the computer is to do. A computer system must be carefully directed by service professionals to perform their exact demands. Once the programs are coded and implemented, the computer system becomes a strict disciplinarian. We assume that a person wanting to know how computers work can easily find that information in many bookstores or training programs.

We concentrate here on how information systems should help service management. Note the change in terms over recent years. What were called Management Information Systems (MIS) have dropped the word *management* and become information systems (IS). One reason for this change is realization by management that the most valuable use of information is to provide it to everyone who might benefit and to enable the lowest level people to become empowered by information that will help them do their job better. This requires a change in management thinking as well as the technology to enable the information and its communication.

Challenges of the Information Process

Information systems considerations include:

1. Reliability
2. Validity
3. Redundancy
4. Quality
5. Relevance
6. Insufficiency
7. Timeliness
8. Cost

Looking at these problems one by one, we can get a better understanding of the desirable and undesirable characteristics that should be considered in service information systems. Reliability of information reflects the degree of consistency just as does the reliability of any item of hardware. The reliability of information can be readily measured, whereas validity, the degree to which information contributes to the goals of the individual or organization, is not so readily measured.

We often refer to validity as comparing apples with apples and not with the fruit basket. In other words, does the information mean what you think it means? Information becomes distorted because of filters and differences in perception between the transmitter and receiver. In humans this is sometimes referred to as "impedance between the ears." In service, one person may be thinking *orders* while another person interprets the information as *issues,* while a third person may believe it means *usage.* Those differences in the ways different people see specific data can cause major disconnects and business problems. It is important that service managers delve deep enough into information to make sure that the technicians are putting in the correct data and that it is correctly used as information. Artificial intelligence is no substitute for the real thing!

Noise is a disturbance or outside interference that can not be identified with any part of the message, but presents another problem in evaluating the transmission. This is static of the human kind. If, for example, technicians are pushed to account for every minute of the work day, then they may start with the required eight hours and calculate backwards to fill in the times. This is a problem that can be avoided by on-the-spot data entry.

Redundancy is that part of the message that is unnecessary, in the sense that if it were missing the message would still be complete. It unnecessarily increases the volume of data that has to be handled and may distort the significance of the information. Do you ever get so much e-mail that the important messages get hidden in the mass of trivial subjects? Most managers, rather than suffering from a lack of relevant information, suffer more from an overabundance of irrelevant information. Most of what we need to know is available; the challenge is being able to find it quickly. Optimal decision making requires up-to-date relevant information. The World Wide Web (www) has transformed information gathering in recent years. The author's paper files that used to consume several racks of filing cabinets are now held in three drawers of one cabinet. Most operating information is in the computer. If up-to-date information is needed, a search on the Internet will probably reveal up-to-date facts.

Time is most problematic when the information required

involves conditions external to the company, such as technological development, government policies, and competitive practices. We all appreciate the significance of computerized data
processing in being able to process large amounts of data in a
short period of time. More information can be processed on a
laptop computer today than could be handled on a large computer ten years ago. Another time-saver is the ability to transfer
files electronically over the Internet as e-mail attachments.

Finally, the cost of information is a fundamental problem.
Gathering data is an expensive undertaking, even though personnel within the organization may gather the data. Even though
service technicians, repair foremen, auditors, and others are
permanent employees, if they are required to seek and report
information, that effort is an expense. Fortunately, most service
organizations appreciate the value of good information and are
willing to determine and spend the costs necessary to get good
information.

Information Users

Service information is needed for the three main user functions of 1) operations, 2) technical, and 3) financial management. Operations needs include labor time, travel, utilization,
productivity, training, overtime, and other human items. Technical needs include failure problem/cause/action analysis, uptime,
availability, parts use, and similar items for feedback to technical
training, engineering design, manufacturing, and quality assurance. Financial needs include contracts, costs, invoicing, and
related business concerns.

Data needs

Master records that are necessary for a service management
information system include:

1 Customers/Users
2. Equipment
3. Personnel
4. Parts

Contents of these master records should be flexible and include subsections. The Customer/Users data includes name, mail address, contact person, e-mail address, and phone number; equipment installed; contracts; and billing specifics. Equipment records should include major sections for equipment identifiers, configuration, and preventive maintenance. Personnel records will include all contact information, qualifications and certifications, regular customer and equipment assignments, and training. Parts records include everything necessary to uniquely identify parts and link them to stock locations, equipment, vendors, and optimum inventory management factors.

Detailed analysis, financial profit and loss, productivity, and similar evaluations are possible once data has been collected in the system. The needs of service organizations are typically 80-90% common, and a relatively small portion is unique. The use of soft code tables makes it possible for data to be validated online, using terms that are unique to a specific organization and thereby assure accurate information in real time. Flexible report writer software now allows any data in the database to be gathered for any period of time and evaluated against almost any desired parameters.

Typical Functional Sections

Service management programs typically require the following as minimum capabilities. Naturally, the capabilities of most must include the ability to enter new data and change what exists, within security restrictions. "Read only" capability can be placed by person on some information. For example, the selling price of a part may be displayed so a customer quote can be prepared, but only a few financial people should be authorized to write new price data.

The person who gets the immediate information should modify addresses, contact people, telephone numbers, and similar frequently changing data. In past years, that information was gathered and maybe checked before a database administrator allowed it to be entered. Not only was that wasted effort, but the information was often not available for use until the problem was past. Instant updates have more useful value. The software can maintain a tracking log of who made what change.

SERVICE CALL

♦ Service call receipt
♦ Telephone help desk assistance
♦ Remote diagnostics
♦ Frequently asked questions (FAQs) advice
♦ Service call status and close postings
♦ Estimate labor and materials
♦ Active service call status
♦ Inspection/PM due (with flags for overdue)
♦ Historical service calls (sortable by customer, equipment, organizations, and/or employee)
♦ Active service call
♦ Re-open historical service call
♦ Dispatcher report
♦ Alert parameters
♦ Management alerts
♦ Return materials authorization
♦ Work demand schedule load
♦ Work supply schedule capacity and planning
♦ Schedule control

EQUIPMENT

• List equipment
• Equipment status and history
• Equipment configuration
• Change management
• Preventive maintenance

- Unique equipment PM
- PM status
- Parts for equipment
- Installations, moves, and changes
- Assign employees to equipment

CUSTOMER

- Customer name, address, contact, phone, and unique items
- Customer's equipment
- Contract terms and conditions
- Customer list
- Financial information probably as a confidential interface

SUPPORT AND WARRANTY AGREEMENTS

- ☐ Equipment installation and warranty dates
- ☐ Equipment installations pending
- ☐ Service level agreements
- ☐ Support agreement plans and pricing
- ☐ Pricing history
- ☐ Agreements and warranties due to expire, with action notifications
- ☐ Quote preparation
- ☐ Support agreements canceled, for follow-up
- ☐ Service history, costs, and profit for a support agreement
- ☐ Revenue and Cost Reports

STANDARD CODES

- Craft/certification/qualification
- Part commodities
- Equipment documents
- Activities
- Delays
- Equipment precautions
- Organizations
- Problem, cause, and action
- Status codes

- Products
- Procedure checklists
- Stockrooms
- Service tax
- Billing codes
- Discounts
- Warranty/support agreement action codes
- Part nouns
- List of all codes

It should be mentioned that codes can be a shortcut and they can also be confusing. Technicians have a lazy way of finding a code that fits many situations and using that whenever possible without exerting additional effort to find an exact match. With modern Windows® capability drop-down menus can often be used so the authorized selections display and the best item can be easily highlighted and selected from the list. Write out the words whenever possible so there is no confusion about what the numbers or initial codes mean.

Acquiring an Information System

The current term for an all-inclusive service management system (SMS) is customer relationship management (CRM), which also includes sales support. A CRM system is a subset of the larger enterprise resource planning (ERP) system. The concept is that all information systems within an organization should tie to each other. These 'seamless interfaces' are a goal of SAP, Baan, Oracle, PeopleSoft and similar software companies that are trying to handle all corporate functions on the same applications software.

Unfortunately, at this time none of those companies has a good service management capability in their software, though Oracle is coming close. The difference can be generalized by saying that ERP covers the 'back office' activities of finance, human resources, production, and supply chain management.

CRM covers the "front office" processes where interactions occur with customers. The customer processes tend to be done in real time as individual contacts. Back office activities can be done in batch mode, for example processing invoices once a week. The challenge is where the front and back activities meet. ERP vendors seem to believe that all users should change to conform to their way of doing business, and that all programs they provide should operate the same way. Relationships with customers must be much more flexible!

Acquiring good service information capability presently requires that a service organization tie a good CRM package like Clarify, Metrix, Siebel, or Vantive to the large ERP system. Most of these CRM software packages are more than just technical service, they also cover help desk, phone fixes and other activities involved in the total customer satisfaction. Service parts are different from manufacturing parts for 16 reasons. LPA software, Management Metrics Services, Inc., and Servigistics are among the best providers of service parts forecasting and planning information. It will be interesting to look back at these words in a few years to see which companies have merged, been acquired, or succeeded on their own.

There are several ways to acquire a computerized service management system. The basic approaches are either to purchase a standard package or to design and program your own. Before you can do anything, you must have a good written requirements document.

This determination of needs should involve all possible users and the solicitation of their needs and wants for consideration. The need for involvement of knowledgeable service persons in this phase can not be over emphasized. Considerations for selection will include the following:

1. Ability to meet needs with minimum modification
2. Compatibility with existing computers and staff
3. Support by experienced, knowledgeable service professionals
4. Ease of use (human friendly)

5. Initial data load requirements
6. Timeliness of introduction
7. Training of operators, users, and managers
8. Documentation (online help)
9. Life cycle costs (acquisition plus on-going expenses)

Costs are the last item listed because they are a function of most of the prior factors. Computer systems are expensive in both money and effort. The initial software acquisition cost is only a third to a half of the total costs. Preparing and loading initial data can be quite laborious. Any data on other computers should be transferred electronically via tape, diskettes, or direct connection. Some data will have to be key entered and cleaned up by humans, which can be both time consuming and expensive. Once initial data is entered, bar codes, optical character readers, and hand-held portable teletransaction computers can aid fast, accurate data entry. It will take several days of training in procedures to gain full benefit from any computer system. This should include training for management in what reports are available and how to use the information. Documentation, preferably online, is necessary for preparing modifications, detailed understanding of intricate areas, and retraining in case of personnel turnover. A telephone support facility should be provided to quickly answer small questions. Enhancements should be provided to users when better ways become available to perform functions.

Packaged programs have many advantages over self-development. Computer programs often take longer to accomplish and cost more than planned, and even then they may have "bugs" that linger a long time. Proven programs not only have most of the bugs out, but also can spread the high cost of development over several purchasers so that each system typically pays only about 1/4 of what the same effort would cost as a custom project. Don't try to do the programming yourself. The talents of most service managers are put to much better use managing service than playing with computer programming. If programs are to be developed in-house or a package extensively modified, the programming may be done either by internal staff, by a contract software organization, or by the package developer. The original developer will be able to do the job fastest and probably at lowest cost, and can also then be held responsible for the complete system.

Service Manager Questions

These are questions that a modern service manager will need answered by a computerized service information system (SIS). Add your special questions to this list, and delete any you do not need.

CALL RECEIPT AND DISPATCH

- Who requested a particular service call?
- Whose customer is this?
- How urgent is this call?
- How is this call to be prioritized?
- Is this call already in the system?
- How long should this call take?
- Which employee is assigned to the call?
- What is the status of a parts order?
- Is this call linked to another call (incomplete, or closed call)?
- Need to estimate expected response time.

ACTIVE CALL MANAGEMENT

- Need to find a call number.
- What is the status of a specific call ?
- What is the status of all open calls?
- What percentage of calls are related to hardware versus software?
- How long will it take to finish the open calls?
- What is the call ageing status.
- What is the PM/ECO/Installation status?
- Which open and/or recently closed work orders are beyond time or cost estimates?

- How many times has someone called about a particular problem?
- Which calls are in an escalated status?

CALL MANAGEMENT PERFORMANCE

❑ What is the first call fix rate?
❑ What problem is causing the most delays?
❑ When and how was a specific completed call handled?
❑ How much did the service call cost the organization?
❑ Are the expenses associated to a service call reasonable?
❑ Were the parts used on the service call reasonable?
❑ What is the cost associated with a PM?
❑ What is the percentage of phone fixes?
❑ What is the call volume received by the call management center?
❑ What percentage of calls are related to a customer calling for service?
❑ What is the Mean Time To Repair?
❑ What is the Mean Time To Respond?
❑ What is the Mean Down Time?
❑ What percentage of calls are planned?
❑ What is the travel versus on-site ratio? Billable versus meetings and other overhead?
❑ How is the call management center performing?
❑ How long does it take to complete a call?
❑ What are the percentages of different call types received?

ASSET/EQUIPMENT MANAGEMENT

➤ Where is this equipment located?
➤ Is a piece of equipment under warranty? When will it expire?
➤ Can you recommend this product based upon its reliability and maintainability?
➤ How much equipment is under warranty?
➤ Does the warranty reimbursement cover warranty expense? What about installation?

➤ What are the products, both hardware and software, that we support?
➤ How is the customer's equipment performing?
➤ Given a particular equipment problem, what is the likely cause and recommended action?
➤ Which particular pieces of equipment are giving us and our customers trouble?
➤ Which parts are unreliable?
➤ What is the Mean Time Between Failure?
➤ If we terminate support for a product, what parts go with it?

CUSTOMER MANAGEMENT

- Is this a top priority customer?
- What equipment has been installed there in the past?
- What is the credit rating of this customer? Is it approved?
- Need quick access to customer's address or phone number.
- How many customers do we have? How much does each pay us and at what margin?
- How is a customer's system performing?

EMPLOYEE MANAGEMENT

• How do I contact a specific employee or group of employees?
• What is the work backlog?
• What is the current work force capacity?
• Who works for whom, by territory?
• Who is assigned to a particular site?
• Who is trained in a particular geography?
• Who is trained in a particular skill?
• Do we need to train anyone in this product?
• How much overtime is being generated? Is it excessive?
• What is the productivity and utilization of field personnel?
• What is the effect of training or experience on productivity?
• How many people do I need now and in the future?
• How do you account and plan for vacations, holidays, and sick time?

SERVICE SALES

➤ What is the forecast versus actual T&M and contract workload?

➤ How much would it cost to support a product not on the list?

➤ What prices and conditions were quoted to a particular customer?

➤ What is the status of proposals sent out to customers?

➤ What is the price for a particular service?

➤ When did the invoice go out and how much was it for?

➤ What is the status of this invoice?

➤ Which invoices need to be collected?

➤ What is our customer retention rate?

➤ How many new customers did we gain this month?

➤ What is the volume of external part sales?

➤ Which parts are customers buying?

➤ Am I making money on service?

CONTRACTS

♦ What are the terms and conditions of a particular customer's contract?

♦ When does a contract expire?

♦ When should a new contract be pursued?

♦ Which sites and equipments are covered by a contract?

SYSTEMS

- What is the configuration of hardware and software at this customer?

DISTRIBUTION AND INVENTORY MANAGEMENT

❑ Is a particular part available, and where is it?

❑ Is there a substitute for this part?

❑ Need shipping information for a stockroom.

❑ When is a physical inventory needed?

❑ What were the last inventory variances between physical and systems counts?

❑ When will an order from a vendor or repair be received?
❑ What is the volume of orders, shipments, and all parts transactions this month?
❑ What is the quarterly shipping expense?
❑ What is the volume of parts due in from the field.
❑ What is the average defective or excess part return time?
❑ What is the dollar cost of parts on order?
❑ What is the number of months of supply on-hand, or turns?
❑ What is the part number of this unknown part?

PARTS PLANNING

- What is the value and service level met by the current inventory?
- Is a parts order required? How many should be bought?
- How many units and dollars in excess parts?
- How is the overall stock performance versus plan?
- What are the parts that are on back order or are in danger of going on back order?
- List all the parts in a product
- What is the individual parts forecast, and the total volume forecast, for the next year?
- What parts should be stocked and where?
- What is the average carrying and ordering cost?

REPAIR MANAGEMENT

- What is the repair workload?
- What is the status of a particular workorder?
- How much does it cost to repair versus replace?
- Is this part repairable?

VENDOR MANAGEMENT

➢ Which suppliers should we use? Are some better than others?
➢ What is the vendor's lead time promise versus actual?
➢ When will an order from a vendor or repair be received?

Human Interfaces

It is natural for every person getting involved with a computer system to ask, "What's in it for me?" Some people eagerly look forward to the new tool. Others expect that this technology will enable management to time-study their performances and demand more work for the same pay. Most managers are apprehensive about the knowledge power contained in a computer system. They probably cannot type fast (which is presently necessary to give instructions to most information systems) and are envious and even fearful of young people who know how to use the computer and are perceived as having a powerful advantage.

When considering a computer information system, the critical principle is participation. Get everyone who may have anything to do with the system involved in the planning. Solicit their needs and communicate plans. A project team should be used to plan the selection, development, and implementation of the new system. A typical team will be composed of a team leader from service, an IS (information systems) computer expert, an experienced consultant, and team members from major functional organizations. A plan should be established with goals to be met at specific dates. Project progress (with corrective actions for any delays) should be communicated to everyone affected. Formal training should be given to each person, with hands-on time at terminals to actually use a training database. The best learning and enthusiasm comes from actually pushing the keys yourself so you experience what happens. A technique to gain involvement is to have each person enter his own name, address, and other information into his personnel record. This occasionally takes considerable time to "hunt and peck" the right keys, but the positive emotions involved make the effort worthwhile.

Even with the best computerized information system, service can not be managed from behind a desk! Managing with detailed information requires balance. Often the detailed data appears to show that a technician is doing a poor job. Take that information as general direction and go visit that person on the job. Service information is usually good across a group of people or equipment or customers, but specifics have to be personally evaluated. Remember that the technician who is criticized for not working eight-hour days will either start at eight hours and work his report backwards to justify what he thinks management wants, or will cut back his typical effort and work to the clock instead of to complete the job and satisfy the customer.

A good service information system can be a very effective tool for service management. To be successful, the manager must get involved.

Internet and WWW

The Internet provides many opportunities for your technicians and customers to help themselves by accessing frequently asked questions (FAQs), technical bulletins, software downloads, chat rooms, and even e-mail contacts. Many customers gain satisfaction from participating in the solutions to their own problems and even by helping others in similar situations. Your organization can develop an effective web site and allow both your own people and customers access to information to help themselves. Technicians can relieve themselves of huge stacks of manuals and documentation that are rarely up to date. With the web, or even a compact disk (CD), they can have timely information that can be quickly sorted to find the specific material they need. When the service business and our products change so frequently, instantaneous electronic updates are really the only way to keep current.

The web has major cost advantages too because local phone access from many Internet service providers (ISPs) such as America OnLine (AOL) do not incur the long distance charges that would otherwise occur. One update from headquarters can be sent to or requested by anyone and everyone who might find the information useful.

Top Ten Techniques
for a Successful Service Information System

Yes, there are Top Ten Techniques for Service Information Systems as well as for service parts, and several other areas of service. The authors find that compacting this complex service business into ten or fewer priority items helps to concentrate on the critical few.

1. *Gain management support.* This will be number one on all Top Ten lists. The best ideas will fail unless the people in charge promote them. "What's in it for me?" is a common, if unspoken question. Management must commit to the project and sell the SIS to everyone involved. Dollarize activities into financial terms wherever possible. Stimulate active participation of everyone affected by the SIS.

2. *Buy packaged software and tune it.* Given that there is not a standard approach to managing service you should document your requirements, survey the SIS solutions already available, and select the one that best matches your service business. Develop a list of questions that you normally need answers to, and assure that the SIS will provide direct answers. See the functions in software demonstrated with your data, rather than in sales documents. Prototype any changes and add details later.

3. *Up front work is most important.* The most critical part of an SIS is the planning and implementation to assure that good service business principles and practices are supported by all elements of the system. The tendency is for service people to go off fighting fires and allow IS to take over. Insist on service team involvement through the entire process.

4. *Plan and procure the complete capability.* An SIS is expensive in money, time and effort. Be prepared to pay several times the software cost for process improvement, data conversion, communications, new hardware, training, tuning, and implementation assistance. There will be an initial bulge in required resources.

5. *KISS—Keep it satisfyingly simple.* Assure that user interfaces are intuitive, minimal, standard, and receive real time validation of correctness. Standard does not mean inflexible. There will be frequent evaluation needs that require the ability to search information for gems of wisdom. Enable special analysis by users.

6. *Don't abdicate your responsibility for total success.* You, the service organization customer, are the majority owner in this SIS partnership. You must set the strategy and tactics that the SIS will support. Reward the SIS supplier for results. Agreements should clearly state what items the supplier does and what items you do.

7. *Set measurements and goals.* Recognize that the computer is only a tool that supports and disciplines management's strategy and tactics. Goals, measures, and controls must be set by humans to tell the computer what to do. Prioritize by importance, criticality and essentiality. Concentrate on the critical few.

8. *Emphasize customer satisfaction.* Restoration goes beyond response. Provide everything a customer might need. Think of all the problems that might occur, and eliminate them. Then be ready to solve more. The person who claims a foolproof system has probably underestimated the quality of the fools who will try to use it. Change software rather than trying to change people. Help customers help themselves.

9. *Minimize personnel delays.* Eliminate, simplify, and standardize processes prior to computerization. Personnel delays are often the tip of an infrastructure problem iceberg. Enable personnel to directly enter update information and keep an audit trail, rather than funneling all changes to a control point. Information and knowledge are perishable commodities, so provide answers in real time.

10. *Close loops.* Two monologues do not make a dialogue. Assure that 'To Do' lists with due-dates are held open to a responsible person until closed by completion of the action. Frequent reviews should be held to assure satisfactory results. A service call is not complete until the customer is happy, required information is validated, and payment is in the bank.

Questions

1. Why do we more readily accept information that is computer-printed, typed, or printed in a publication than we do handwritten or vocal information?

2. What changes could be made in computerized information processing that would make input and output easier?

3. What is meant by validity of information?

4. What is meant by reliability of information?

5. Discuss whether a manager can ever receive too much information.

6. List the field reporting systems necessary for your organization.

7. Why is field information desired more by durable goods service functions than by those dealers who simply sell the products?

8. What is the relationship between field reporting systems and forecasting?

9. What are the advantages of an exception reporting system over one that reports all activities?

10. Why are many service organizations "data rich and analysis poor?"

15

Economics, Accounting, and Finance

Financial matters seem to overwhelm many service managers. Dollars (or other currency) are the language of necessity for communicating with top management. Money is the common denominator by which nearly all efforts can be measured and compared.

The objective of this section is to familiarize readers with the terms commonly used in relating money to service activities. By necessity, this chapter is a shallow overview of monetary subjects. Practicing service managers must have a working knowledge of economics, accounting, and finance if they are to successfully evaluate alternatives, determine the value of their efforts, and have significant influence on reducing life-cycle costs and improving profits of service systems. Several topics, including budgets, FIFO, LIFO, and forecasting, are covered in greater detail in other sections. The principles of US tax law are generally observed, as they have a major influence on monetary activities.

Time Value of Resources

It is well known that money in hand today is worth more than money in the future, because of the risk inherent in the future and inflation. Therefore, if you lend money to someone or put it into a savings account, you expect to be paid interest that will increase your deposit in absolute amount. Conversely, if you borrow money, you expect to pay interest on it. The amount of interest is governed by the prime rate, which is the interest percentage charged by banks to their best customers. You will expect also to pay a higher interest rate for long-term loans than for short-term borrowing. The common symbols used in interest calculations are:

P = principal
i = interest rate per period
n = number of periods
S = sum

Simple interest is Pin, which is the initial principal invested times the interest rate per period times the number of periods. For example, if we invest $250 for one year at 6% interest, we expect to receive $15 as simple interest.

$$\$250 \times .06 = \$15.$$

This simple interest method is used to determine the sales tax on an item: 7% sales tax on a $7 purchase equals 49 cents tax, for a total cost of $7.49. Conversely, if someone were to get a 15% discount on a $15 item, he would pay $12.75, as $15 - (.15 x $15) = $12.75. An alternative method is to subtract the 15% discount from 100%, leaving 85%, which is multiplied by the original cost, giving $15 x .85 = $12.75.

A compound interest formula is used to determine the future value (FV) of money. The formula is $S = P(1 + i)^n$. Thus, if we invest $50 at 6% interest per year for 3 years, we will have at the end $59.55, as $50 $(1 + .06)^3$ = $50 (1.191) = $59.55. Future value compound interest is often known as SPCA, which stands for single payment compound amount. Most financial books have tables showing the factors for the future worth of $1 at various rates for different periods, as shown in Table 15-1 at the end of this chapter. The alternative question is, "How much do I need to invest now in order to have a sum S in n interest-compounding periods?" The formula for the single payment present worth (SPPW), also called present value (PV), calculation is:

$$PV = S \frac{1}{(1 + i)^n}$$

This present value calculation is very useful in service management to determine the amount of the unit cost that must be invested in a product to equal the operating and support expenditures required in the future (see Table 15-2 for factors). Another question often asked is, "If each December I invest $2,000 from my yearly bonus in a stock account that earns on the average 8% annual interest, how much will I have at the end of 30 years?" This uniform series compound interest amount (USCA) is formed by the formula:

$$USCA = P \frac{(1 + i)^n - 1}{i}$$

Using Table 15-3, for 30 periods at 8% we find a factor of 113.2832.

$$\$2,000 \times 113.2832 = \$226,566.40$$

The same factors are often titled "Future Value of Annuity of $1 in Arrears." To convert those tables to values of an annuity in advance, add one more period and subtract 1.000 from the factor. A uniform series present worth (USPW) formula is used to answer the question, "How much do I need to invest today if I can get 8% interest rate and wish to be paid $2,000 at the end of each year for 30 years?" The formula is:

$$\text{USPW} = S \left[\frac{(1 + i)^n - 1}{i(1 + i)^n} \right]$$

We can also use Table 15-4 to find the factor 11.258, which is multiplied by $2,000 to find the answer $22,516, the same as given by using the formula.

The capital recovery (CR) formula is used to answer the question asked for repayment of an auto loan, "If I borrow $3,000 to be repaid over two years at 24% interest on all unpaid balances, how much do I pay each month?" The formula is:

$$\text{CR} = P \times \frac{i(1 + i)^n}{(1 + i)^n - 1}$$

For monthly payments, there will be 24 payments in two years, and the interest rate is equivalent to 2% per month. If we look at the attached Table 15-5 for 24 periods we find a factor 0.05287. Multiplying that factor by the $3,000 initial payment gives $158.61 per month. If you wish to know the total amount that will be paid, multiply that by 24 payments which gives $3,806.64, including interest over the two years. Note that this is quite different from borrowing $3,000 for two years and paying back the entire amount plus interest at the end of that time. The cost of borrowing would be $1,612.80 in interest, in addition to the $3,000 principal, which would have to be paid as a lump sum. People usually find it mentally easier to repay or save on a budgeted routine basis rather than having to pay back the entire lump sum at one time.

Banks, in order to attract more funds from savers, have discovered that compounding for short interest periods can give a higher effective interest rate than if the interest is compounded monthly, quarterly, or yearly. Effective interest rate (EIR) for discrete compounding uses the formula:

$$EIR = (1 + i)^n - 1$$

when there are n compounding periods during the year. Thus, an account that is set at a 5.5% yearly interest rate can yield 5.65% if compounded daily.

Capital Items

A capital expenditure represents an investment of capital either to acquire property with a useful life of more than one year or to make permanent improvements that increase the life of the property. Buildings, trucks, machines, tools, and office furniture are capital items. The cost or other basis of these assets is generally recoverable through annual depreciation deductions. You may deduct each year, as depreciation, a reasonable allowance for the exhaustion, wear and tear, and obsolescence of depreciable property used in your trade or business or held for the production of income.

Salvage value is the amount that you expect to realize upon the sale or other disposition of an asset when it is to be retired from service. For example, if you plan to buy a truck for $10,000 and run it until it is worth $50 to the junk man, then the salvage value is $50. On the other hand, if you plan to use the truck for three years and then sell it for about $4,000, the salvage value is $4,000.

The major methods of computing depreciation are straight line, declining balance, and sum of digits. Straight line depreciation means that an equal percentage is taken during every period. If, for example, you are depreciating a machine over five years, then 20% (one fifth) would be taken as depreciation each year. The declining balance method uses the same depreciation rate each year, but the preceding year's depreciation is subtracted from the cost or other basis of the property before computing next year's depreciation. Thus, the same rate applies to a smaller or declining balance each year, which gives a larger deduction initially and a smaller depreciation deduction in succeeding years. Different items have different maximum rates relative to the straight line method. For example, a new machine with a useful life of three years or more may be depreciated at a maximum of twice the straight line rate. Used equipment has a maximum rate of one-and-a-half times the straight line rate.

The sum of digits method adds the total number of digits and uses the respective fraction for each period. For a five-year term, the sum of digits $5 + 4 + 3 + 2 + 1$ is 15, so the first year $5/15$ of the value may be depreciated, $4/15$ the second year, and so forth. A comparison of the methods is shown in Table 15-6.

Assume a new machine costs $10,000 and is expected to last for five years. Its salvage value is estimated to be $1,500. Table 15-6 shows that the double declining balance method of depreciation gets the greatest deduction in early years, with sum of digits the next greatest, and straight line being the slowest method of early investment recovery. You may use different methods for different accounts and items but are restricted to one method for each case, once it is established. Depreciation may not exceed the value of the item. Also, if the item is sold for more than the estimated salvage value, the positive variance is taxable. The market value of an item may be the same as its book value, higher, or lower, depending upon inflation, technological obsolescence, the condition of the item, and other factors that may change its value from the forecast.

Acquisition Economics

Unit cost is the factor of merit of most importance during the acquisition phase. The objective is to keep the cost of acquiring a new item as low as possible. It is only recently that the operating and support costs have been equally considered, with life-cycle costs used to evaluate the total system. A major reason for emphasis on unit costs is that they are incurred today and can best be controlled, whereas risk and uncertainty are associated with future costs. As a product concept proceeds through the phases of development, all costs already incurred are considered to be sunk and not recoverable. If the product concept were canceled right now, the organization would cut its losses by

TABLE 15-6
Comparison of depreciation methods.

STRAIGHT LINE METHOD

End of Year	Cost or Remaining Basis $	Rate %	Depreciation Allowance $	Reserve $
Start	8,500	NA	0	1,500
First	6,800	20	1,700	3,200
Second	5,100	20	1,700	4,900
Third	3,400	20	1,700	6,600
Fourth	1,700	20	1,700	8,300
Fifth	0	20	1,700	10,000

DOUBLE DECLINING BALANCE METHOD

End of Year	Cost or Remaining Basis $	Rate %	Depreciation Allowance $	Reserve $
Start	10,000	NA	0	0
First	6,000	40	4,000	4,000
Second	3,600	40	2,400	6,400
Third	2,160	40	1,440	7,840
Fourth	1,500	40	660	8,000
Fifth	1,500	40	0	8,500

SUM OF YEARS-DIGITS METHOD

End of Year	Cost or Remaining Basis $	Rate %	Depreciation Allowance $	Reserve $
Start	8,500	NA	0	1,500
First	5,667	5/15	2,833	4,333
Second	3,400	4/15	2,267	6,600
Third	1,700	3/15	1,700	8,300
Fourth	567	2/15	1,133	9,433
Fifth	0	1/15	567	10,000

simply terminating the project and not throwing any more "good money after bad."

Costs are usually classified as either fixed or variable. The fixed costs include the facility, utilities, machines, and other expenses incurred whether one or one thousand items are supported. Variable costs will fluctuate in proportion to the items produced, mainly for labor and materials. If the expenses can be related to specific items, they are termed direct; if they cannot be so related, they are called indirect or overhead. General and administrative (G&A) expenses are those necessary for top management, payroll, and other administrative support.

Transfer pricing is a subject of interest to service management as many items are exchanged within a company. For example, an integrated company may have an iron mine that supplies ore to a steel mill, which in turn supplies steel to an assembly plant, which in turn supplies spare parts to the service organization. The two basic alternatives for pricing intracompany transfers are some version of market price or cost. The market price approach is essentially an opportunity cost notion, where the price is equivalent to prices prevailing in an outside market at time of transfer. It treats individual divisions as if they were separate companies. Transfer prices based on cost or cost plus some markup have a different orientation. Cost often includes not only conventional product costs but also a portion of administrative and research costs. Cost-based transfer prices that insure recovery of costs often fail to provide any incentive to control costs. The whole area of transfer pricing is filled with problems of huan relations and the need for careful accumulation and analysis of relevant data for pricing decisions. Transfer price policies must be workable in the sense that they should neither require excessive management time nor interfere with overall company goals.

OPERATIONS AND SUPPORT

As a personal example of operations and support expense, once you have acquired a family automobile, you must still pay operating costs for insurance, gas, oil, and license. You will also have occasional support costs for maintenance, such as lubrication and repairs. As operating expenses are incurred over a period of time, present value calculations are vital for determining what those costs are worth today.

Operating and support (O&S) costs may usually be categorized as:

- Dependent on time
- Dependent on use
- Dependent on specific events

Your car, for example, requires expenses based on time for licensing, insurance, and obsolescence, even if it just sits in the garage. It incurs expenses based on use for gas and oil; it also has expenses related to specific events, such as the need for snow tires and antifreeze when winter comes to you northern readers. Operating and support costs are always expensed, that is, they are immediately deductible from gross income as a cost of doing business.

Lease or Buy

Just about any capital item that can be purchased may also be leased. Although leasing costs more money in the long run, it does not require the initial investment for a purchase, and the lease costs may be expensed. An outright purchase, on the other hand, requires a large amount of initial money recoverable through depreciation. Companies with a great need for funds prefer leasing, as the total lease package will cost only slightly more than borrowing money from the bank to purchase the equipment and gives them funds that might not otherwise be available.

Evaluations

Some methods of financial evaluation most common to the service profession include:

> ➤ Break-even analysis
> ➤ Cash flow
> ➤ Efficiency
> ➤ Expense revenue
> ➤ Payback period
> ➤ Price earnings ratio
> ➤ Return on investment ratio
> ➤ Turnover

Break-even analysis is used to determine how many units must be sold before costs are recovered. You may want to refer back to the break-even diagrams shown in Figure 4-1.

The formula is:

$$C_F + n\,C_V = n\,R_U$$

where C_F = fixed cost, C_V = variable cost, n = number of units, and R_U = revenue per unit. If, for example, we are setting up a repair process for printed circuit boards that will require $5,400 in fixed costs and variable costs for parts and labor of $20 per board, we want to know how many boards we must repair in order to break even if we charge $60 each:

$$\$5,400 + n\$20 = n\$60$$
$$40n = 5,400$$
$$n = 135 \text{ units}$$

We could change any of the variables in order to analyze how much we should charge in order to break even at 100 units, or what limits should be placed on fixed costs if we know what the variable costs and our transfer price or selling price must be. This general analysis form will be used also for making repair or discard decisions.

Cash flow is of particular importance when people are not paying your invoices as fast as your suppliers expect you to pay them. This can be a particular problem when transportation is involved, as credit terms for transportation are usually C.O.D. (cash on delivery) or net within four days. If you order a large shipment, you may have to make payment immediately, even though you will not be able to sell the goods or receive payment for them for many months. All good managers will project their cash requirements and calculate them against the cash income, to know in advance when they will require bank credit and not be taken by surprise. Cash flow is one key to Dell Corporation's success. Since they build computers to order, if I order a computer and pay for it with a check or credit card effective when shipped, Dell gets my money when they ship me the computer and then owes their suppliers on 30 or 45 days terms. Thus the growing business finances itself to a large extent. Growth of a service business otherwise requires considerable funds for people, parts, facilities, vehicles, tools, etc.

It is worth mentioning that paying your suppliers promptly is a good way to enhance cooperation and motivation on your behalf. The opposite can bring problems. If somehow invoices are lost, or your account did not get in this week's checks and will be a week late, or even if checks are processed on the due date so they are approved the next day and snail mail delivers them a week after they should have arrived; then the level of cooperation will drop. Make sure that whomever pays your bills understands that the motivational value of paying on time earns far more return than does keeping the funds for a few extra days.

Efficiency factors are used in service to evaluate cost, time, and quality. Some of the more common evaluations are:

$$\text{Process Efficiency} = \frac{\text{Output}}{\text{Input}}$$

$$\text{Financial Operating Efficiency} = \frac{\text{Total Revenues}}{\text{Total Expenses plus Profit}}$$

$$\text{Relative Cost Efficiency} = \frac{\text{Incurred Costs (labor, materials, etc.)}}{\text{Standard Costs}}$$

$$\text{System effectiveness} = \text{Capability \%} \times \text{Availability \%} \times \text{Dependability \%}$$

Cost-benefit analysis is a special application of systems effectiveness evaluation. This type of analysis seeks to relate the expected results of a projected program to its cost. Thus programs that measure benefits in the same terms may be compared to determine their effectiveness relative to each other. The benefits are often computed in monetary values in order to assess more accurately the total impact of programs in which several types of benefits may be realized. Where the cost flow and the monetary benefit flow differ significantly over a period of time, discounting may be introduced to get the present values of program costs and benefits. It should be understood that the two concepts of efficiency and effectiveness are separate and distinct. The efficiency system provides no clue about the potential revenues that may be available from the system's operation. In like manner, a system's effectiveness bears no necessary relationship to the cost of operating it. But together, these two measures provide a means for evaluating total system performance.

Expense/revenue ratios provide a measurement of how well an organization such as service is keeping costs in line with revenues. The ratios will vary by industry and even in products, but form standards such as a "10% service expense to sales revenue" against which performance may be judged.

The length of the payback period is frequently used to decide whether an investment should be made. Many companies have criteria, such as a one-year payback period for current product field equipment or a three-year payback period for new test equipment. As a simple example, if we presently spend $20,000 per year for all costs associated with repairing relays and can develop and manufacture a new relay for $50,000 which will eliminate these costs, the payback (disregarding financial costs of money) is 2½ years. You can see that the true payback period is slightly longer, as we are investing $50,000 today and getting a return flow over a future period of time, but nevertheless it is well within a three-year limit. Service business tends to require initial investment and will then pay back over several years, with accelerating returns. This causes a problem with investors like venture capital funds, who expect a quick return and who are not willing to wait for the high long-term rewards.

Return on investment (ROI) is the most common form of financial evaluation. It tells the rate of payback we have received from our money invested. It may be either absolute dollars, in present value terms, or shown as an incremental difference. ROI is found by using the interest and present value formulas covered earlier. As a large portion of the invested funds may be borrowed, the variation called Return on Assets (ROA) is often used, particularly as a base for company profit-sharing plans.

Opportunity costs, the costs of foregoing an opportunity because the limited available resources are used for another alternative, should be followed rather than any direct cost of capital. If, for example, you can borrow money from the bank at 11% and would get only a 5% ROI through your internal efforts, then it is better not to borrow the money and, in fact, better to put available funds into an investment, which would undoubtedly earn more than your internal efforts could. But if you could earn 15% through your internal efforts, then 15% is the opportunity cost, rather than the 11% cost of borrowing from the bank.

Turnover ratios are used to evaluate how rapidly assets are being converted into cash. Inventory turnover can be measured in either dollars or units, with a high ratio indicating a slow-moving inventory. Turnover is a a good measure in production, but is a fourth order factor in service parts. Of greater importance are support level, demand satisfaction, and even safety stocks. A sign of potential danger is a turnover ratio that is rising or higher than a competitor's. On the other hand, the company may deliberately carry large inventories to reduce the loss of sales caused by inadequate stocks and to avail itself of economies of large purchase or production of lots. Nevertheless, a rising ratio is evidence of a decline in liquidity, high carrying costs, and potential future losses from obsolescence. Because inventories are listed at gross cost rather than sale price, turnover is best measured by cost of goods sold or used/inventory average value. The same purpose can be served by calculating sales $/inventory $. Make sure both parts of the ratio are in the same parameter of units, costs, or sales. The turnover of accounts receivable is of major concern. If, for example, we have sales of $100,000 per year and average receivables of $10,000, then the receivables turn over approximately ten times per year, which means an average collection period of 36.5 days. That low figure would be very good. Most companies find receivables tending towards 60 days, even when terms are net 30. Just what collection period is satisfactory depends on the company's term of sales, which in turn often are governed by industry practice.

The low ratio relative to the terms of trade indicates either a vigorous collection activity or a tight credit policy, or both. Highly selective granting of credit leads to a rapid receivables turnover but may unduly restrict sales. A loosening of credit standards will often increase receivables by a larger percentage than the increase in sales, but the increase in profit may be considerably higher than the company's desired rate of return on the added investment. If a company's credit policy has not changed, however, a change in receivables turnover or in the collection period from one year to the next may help explain changes in the overall return on investment.

Life-Cycle Cost and Profit Analysis

Life-cycle costing (LCC) is a fundamental concept in service planning and management. The concept operates on the premise that everything has an associated cost, and every cost from the earliest idea through the last termination must be considered. Various terms such as "cradle to the grave" are used to describe the duration of the life cycle, though "womb to tomb" is more correct. LCC is the total cost of ownership.

Life-cycle costing is a tool, a technique, and a philosophy that insures that each individual item is measured against its impact on the "bottom line" profit. Very few people have the talent, ability, experience, or knowledge to realize all the implications of their decisions. Even if they could, many would be biased by the person who writes their performance appraisal, or the hard-nosed supervisor, or by the small segment of the system they are accountable for. Most people will try hard to meet any realistic goal set forth. LCC provides a means of insuring balance to all parts of a system. Historically, the major emphasis has been on production costs. The support costs, which are usually two to seven times greater than the original build costs, have often been forgotten until the products are built, and then it's too late!

Most government contracts require life-cycle costing as a specific requirement, to know that the item can be supported at a planned cost. Otherwise, a contractor could reduce design and production costs and make exorbitant profit on a poor product that costs a fortune to support in the field.

Life-cycle costs have a close relationship to "design to cost/price." Once the "affordable" costs for each segment of the life cycle are determined, targets are set and the user-producer relationship established. Activities and costs associated with LCC include all research and development, investment, acquisition, production, operation, support, maintenance, and termination items.

Reliability, maintainability, and other support factors can often be improved by "better"—and usually initially more expensive—components. Does it pay off? LCC helps say yes or no. Once items are dollar-valued, the differences in time and cost or payback (cash flow) relationships must be computed to a common base. Present value (PV) and return on investment (ROI) are common financial measures for achieving this. If most costs are incurred at the time of manufacture and payback is spread out uniformly, then simple sensitivity ratios or graphs can be used. A simple ratio such as "$100 production cost = $1 service cost per thousand hours" is helpful. This type of information can be carried in everyone's mind and used quickly without referring to complex, and sometimes distrusted, graphs or formulas.

A life-cycle cost/profit model can be very useful to service management, because it provides a tool for accurate, valid financial calculations that add credibility to service efforts.

In summary, we have covered the major economic, accounting, and financial terms used in the service profession. A major question asked by many frustrated service managers is, "How can I get management's attention?" The best approach is to put your arguments in monetary terms so that your efforts have a direct impact on the organization's bottom-line profit.

TABLE 15-1
Future value of $1.00 (single payment compound amount).

			$FV = P[1+i]^n$			
Periods	2 %	4 %	5 %	6 %	8 %	10 %
1	1.0200	1.0400	1.0500	1.0600	1.0800	1.1000
2	1.0404	1.0816	1.1025	1.1236	1.1664	1.2100
3	1.0612	1.1249	1.1576	1.1910	1.2597	1.3310
4	1.0824	1.1699	1.2155	1.2625	1.3605	1.4641
5	1.1041	1.2167	1.2763	1.3382	1.4693	1.6105
6	1.1262	1.2653	1.3401	1.4185	1.5869	1.7716
7	1.1487	1.3159	1.4071	1.5036	1.7138	1.9488
8	1.1717	1.3686	1.4775	1.5938	1.8599	2.1436
9	1.1951	1.4233	1.5513	1.6895	1.9990	2.3589
10	1.2190	1.4802	1.6289	1.7908	2.1589	2.5938
11	1.2434	1.5395	1.7103	1.8983	2.3316	2.8532
12	1.2682	1.6010	1.7959	2.0122	2.5182	3.1385
13	1.2936	1.6651	1.8856	2.1329	2.7196	3.4524
14	1.3195	1.7317	1.9799	2.2609	2.9372	3.7976
15	1.3459	1.8009	2.0709	2.3966	3.1722	4.1774
16	1.3726	1.8730	2.1829	2.5404	3.4259	4.5951
17	1.4002	1.9479	2.2920	2.6928	3.7000	5.0545
18	1.4262	2.0258	2.4066	2.8543	3.9960	5.5600
19	1.4568	2.1068	2.5270	3.0259	4.3157	6.1160
20	1.4859	2.1911	2.6533	3.2071	4.6610	6.7276
30	1.6114	3.2434	4.3219	5.7435	10.0627	17.4495
40	2.2080	4.8010	7.0400	10.1857	21.7245	45.2597

TABLE 15-2
Present value of $1.00 (single payment present worth).

$$PV = S\frac{1}{[1+i]^n}$$

Periods	4 %	6 %	8 %	10 %	20 %	30 %
1	0.962	0.943	0.926	0.909	0.833	0.769
2	0.825	0.890	0.857	0.826	0.694	0.592
3	0.889	0.840	0.794	0.751	0.579	0.455
4	0.855	0.792	0.735	0.683	0.482	0.350
5	0.822	0.747	0.681	0.621	0.402	0.269
6	0.790	0.705	0.630	0.564	0.335	0.207
7	0.760	0.685	0.583	0.513	0.279	0.159
8	0.731	0.627	0.540	0.467	0.233	0.123
9	0.703	0.592	0.500	0.424	0.194	0.094
10	0.676	0.558	0.463	0.368	0.162	0.073
11	0.650	0.527	0.429	0.350	0.135	0.058
12	0.625	0.497	0.397	0.319	0.112	0.043
13	0.601	0.489	0.368	0.290	0.093	0.033
14	0.577	0.442	0.340	0.263	0.078	0.025
15	0.555	0.417	0.315	0.239	0.065	0.020
16	0.534	0.394	0.292	0.218	0.054	0.015
17	0.513	0.371	0.270	0.198	0.045	0.012
18	0.494	0.350	0.250	0.180	0.038	0.009
19	0.475	0.331	0.232	0.164	0.031	0.007
20	0.458	0.312	0.215	0.149	0.026	0.005
21	0.439	0.294	0.199	0.135	0.022	0.004
22	0.422	0.278	0.184	0.123	0.016	0.003
23	0.406	0.262	0.170	0.112	0.015	0.002
24	0.390	0.247	0.158	0.102	0.013	0.032
25	0.375	0.233	0.148	0.092	0.010	0.031
26	0.361	0.220	0.135	0.084	0.009	0.031
27	0.347	0.207	0.125	0.076	0.007	0.001
28	0.333	0.198	0.116	0.069	0.006	0.001
29	0.321	0.185	0.107	0.063	0.005	0.001
30	0.308	0.174	0.099	0.057	0.004	-
40	0.208	0.097	0.046	0.022	0.001	-

TABLE 15-3
Annuity of $1.00 in arrears (value of a uniform series of $1 pay-

$$USCA = P\frac{(1-1+i)^n - 1}{i}$$

Periods	2 %	4 %	5 %	6 %	8 %	10 %
1	1.0000	1.0000	1.0000	1.0000	1.0000	1.0000
2	2.0200	2.0400	2.0500	2.0600	2.0800	2.1000
3	3.0604	3.1216	3.1525	3.1836	3.2464	3.3100
4	4.1216	4.2465	4.3101	4.3746	4.5061	4.6410
5	5.2040	5.4163	5.5256	5.6371	5.8666	6.1051
6	6.3081	6.6330	6.8019	6.9753	7.3359	7.7156
7	7.4343	7.8983	8.1420	8.3938	8.9228	9.4872
8	8.5630	9.2142	9.5491	9.8975	10.6366	11.4360
9	9.7546	10.5628	11.0266	11.4913	12.4676	13.5796
10	10.9497	12.0061	12.5779	13.1808	14.4666	15.9376
11	12.1687	13.4864	14.2068	14.9716	16.6455	18.5314
12	13.4121	15.0256	15.9171	16.8699	18.9771	21.3846
13	14.6803	16.6268	17.7130	18.8821	21.4953	24.5231
14	15.9739	18.2919	19.5986	21.0151	24.2149	27.9755
15	17.2934	20.0236	21.5786	23.2760	27.1521	31.7731
16	18.6393	21.8245	23.6575	25.6725	30.3243	32.9503
17	20.0121	23.6975	25.8404	28.2129	33.7502	40.5456
18	21.4123	25.6454	28.1324	30.9057	37.4502	45.6001
19	22.8406	27.6712	30.5390	33.7600	41.4463	51.1601
20	24.2974	29.7781	33.0660	36.7856	45.7620	57.2761
30	40.5681	56.0849	66.4388	79.0582	113.2632	164.4962
40	60.4020	98.0255	120.7998	154.7620	259.0565	442.5974

TABLE 15-4
Present value of annuity of $1.00 in arrears
(uniform series present worth).

$$PVA_n = S \frac{(1+i)^n - 1}{i(1+i)^n}$$

Periods	4 %	6 %	8 %	10 %	20 %	30 %
1	0.962	0.943	0.926	0.909	0.833	0.769
2	1.886	1.833	1.783	1.736	1.528	1.361
3	2.775	2.673	2.577	2.487	2.106	1.816
4	3.630	3.485	3.312	3.170	2.589	2.166
5	4.452	4.212	3.993	3.791	2.991	2.436
6	5.242	4.917	4.623	4.355	3.326	2.643
7	6.002	5.582	5.206	4.868	3.685	2.802
8	6.733	6.210	5.747	5.335	3.837	2.925
9	7.435	6.802	6.247	5.759	4.031	3.019
10	8.111	7.360	6.710	6.145	4.192	3.092
11	8.760	7.687	7.139	6.495	4.327	3.147
12	9.385	8.384	7.538	6.814	4.439	3.190
13	9.968	8.853	7.904	7.103	4.533	3.223
14	10.563	9.295	8.244	7.367	4.611	3.249
15	11.118	9.712	8.559	7.606	4.675	3.268
16	11.652	10.106	8.851	7.824	4.730	3.283
17	12.166	10.477	9.122	8.022	4.775	3.295
18	12.659	10.828	9.372	8.201	4.812	3.304
19	13.134	11.158	9.604	8.365	4.844	3.311
20	13.590	11.470	9.818	8.514	4.870	3.316
21	14.029	11.764	10.017	6.649	4.891	3.320
22	14.451	12.042	10.201	8.772	4.909	3.323
23	14.857	12.303	10.371	8.883	4.925	3.325
24	15.247	12.550	10.529	8.985	4.937	3.327
25	15.622	12.783	10.675	9.077	4.948	3.329
26	15.983	13.003	10.810	9.161	4.956	3.330
27	16.330	13.211	10.935	9.237	4.964	3.331
28	16.663	13.406	11.051	9.307	4.970	3.331
29	16.964	13.591	11.156	9.390	4.975	3.332
30	17.292	13.765	11.256	9.427	4.979	3.332
40	19.793	15.046	11.925	9.779	4.997	3.333

TABLE 15-5
Capital recovery (uniform series with present value of $1).

$$SCR = \frac{i(1+i)^n}{(1+i)^n - 1}$$

Periods	2 %	4 %	5 %	6 %	8 %	10 %
1	1.02000	1.04000	1.05000	1.06000	1.08000	1.10000
2	0.51505	0.53020	0.53780	0.54544	0.56077	0.57619
3	0.34675	0.36035	0.36721	0.37411	0.38803	0.40211
4	0.26262	0.27549	0.28201	0.28859	0.30192	0.31547
5	0.21216	0.22463	0.23097	0.23740	0.25046	0.26380
6	0.17853	0.19076	0.19702	0.20336	0.21632	0.22961
7	0.15451	0.16661	0.17262	0.17914	0.19207	0.20541
8	0.13651	0.14853	0.15472	0.16104	0.17401	0.18744
9	0.12252	0.13449	0.14069	0.14702	0.16008	0.17364
10	0.11133	0.12329	0.12950	0.13587	0.14903	0.16275
11	0.10218	0.11415	0.12039	0.12679	0.14008	0.15396
12	0.09456	0.10655	0.11283	0.11928	0.13270	0.14876
13	0.08812	0.10014	0.10646	0.11296	0.12652	0.14078
14	0.08260	0.09467	0.10102	0.10758	0.12130	0.13575
15	0.07783	0.08994	0.09634	0.10296	0.11683	0.13147
16	0.07365	0.08562	0.09227	0.09895	0.11298	0.12782
17	0.06997	0.08220	0.08870	0.09544	0.10963	0.12466
18	0.06670	0.07899	0.08555	0.09236	0.10670	0.12193
19	0.06378	0.07614	0.08275	0.08962	0.10413	0.11955
20	0.06116	0.07358	0.08024	0.08718	0.10185	0.11746
21	0.05678	0.07128	0.07800	0.08500	0.09983	0.11562
22	0.05663	0.06920	0.07597	0.08305	0.09803	0.11401
23	0.05467	0.08731	0.07414	0.08126	0.09642	0.11257
24	0.05287	0.06559	0.07247	0.07968	0.09498	0.11130
25	0.05122	0.06401	0.07095	0.07823	0.09368	0.11017
26	0.04970	0.06257	0.08956	0.07698	0.09251	0.10916
27	0.04829	0.08124	0.06829	0.07570	0.09145	0.10826
28	0.04698	0.06001	0.08712	0.07459	0.09049	0.10745
29	0.04578	0.05888	0.06605	0.07358	0.08965	0.10873
30	0.04465	0.05783	0.08505	0.07265	0.08883	0.10608
40	0.03655	0.05052	0.05828	0.06646	0.08386	0.10226

Questions

1. Why does money in a savings account that compounds interest daily at a 5.25% annual interest rate pay more than an account that pays the same 5.25% annual interest rate compounded quarterly?

2. Why do service analysts need to utilize present value (PV) calculations?

3. Select a typical product. How many years of life would you assign to it? What would you expect the salvage value to be at the end of that time?

4. If you want to get the largest possible depreciation next year for the above product, what method of computing depreciation should be used?

5. If you have a large amount of money already invested in a new product that probably won't be profitable, should you proceed to try to get back some of the spent money or cancel the product now?

6. What costs are variable in your service organization?

7. Should intracompany transfer prices from manufacturing to the service organization include a profit for the seller? Why?

8. For your selected product, what operating and support costs are usually categorized as dependent on specific events?

9. If your service organization needs to acquire one million dollars worth of electronic test equipment, what considerations would you weigh to decide whether you should lease it or purchase it outright?

10. If your service department's inventory turnover is three and the industry standard is five, what should you do?

16

Service Marketing

*T*here are two different meanings to the term "marketing." Some people think of marketing as selling, influencing, and persuading the potential customers. Others think of marketing as being sensitive to corporate and human needs and how to serve those needs. This chapter on service marketing emphasizes the second meaning: being sensitive to serving and satisfying both corporate and human needs. Sales is considered to be a subset of marketing.

The marketing concept basically holds that the problem of all business firms is to develop client or customer loyalties, and to provide satisfaction within these loyalties. Marketing is the key to doing this. Marketing provides the organizational focus to establish and identify the needs of the customer. Obviously, the short-run problem is more specific, and that is to persuade existing customers and clients to purchase existing products and services. The long-run objective is to create services and products that customers and clients need and further to insure that both the customers and clients are aware of the availability of these services and products.

In general, companies are formed to service the interests of particular groups. That is, entrepreneurs of new-product business entities in larger corporations look at market segments, understand the interests and needs of those market segments, and then develop products and services to satisfy those needs. Unfortunately, the end results of service activity are most frequently only identifiable in terms of intangible criteria, such as improved efficiency or improved skills. Sometimes, it is a matter of improving productivity or even as intangible as the well being of an organization. Customers or clients are often reluctant to buy this intangible product or service. To complicate the matter further, the customer or client must have a method of evaluating successful performance and outcome at the end of the service provision. Thus, the marketing of service must include not only a keen awareness of the customer's interests and needs, but also an awareness of the necessity to provide a means of evaluating the service. Many times this evaluation refers not only to the immediate impact of the performance, but also relates to the longevity of the effect that it has produced. With the marketing of a service, guarantees of performance become extremely difficult to substantiate. This is much more so than for goods where the actual product performance can be measured. A useful summary of the similarities and differences between the goods and services is provided in Table 16-1.

The marketing process for service consists of a number of discreet steps, each of which is identified below. These steps are given on a very general basis, since it is the intention of this text to provide a structure that would be applicable to many areas of product service rather than to any one particular segment. In any event, it must be clearly understood at the outset that the marketing of service will always consist of four components: the service product identification; the pricing of that product within

TABLE 16-1
Products and services have both similarities and differences.

	PRODUCT VERSUS SERVICE	
Classifications	Similarities	Differences
1. Product Characteristics	Described as Features with Associated Benefits	Services not Patent Protected
Source of Ideas		
Warranty	Marketplace	None
Branding	Similar	Service Warranty May Have Less Liability
Development	Similar	None
Inventory	Some Stages	Services Done Quickly
Manufacture	Few	Services Can't Be Inventoried
	Few	
2. Promotion Advertising		Services are Simultaneously Manufactured & Consumed
Promotion Selling	Objectives	Can't Show Product
3. Pricing Basis	Same Media	Can't Display Product or Provide Samples
Variation	Same Techniques	No Demonstration Possible in Service
4. Distribution Location Channel	Value or Cost	
	Adjust to Meet Local Competition	Not Easily Compared with Competition
	Depots Similar to Manufacturing	Often Bundled
	Can Use Brokers/ Agents	Dispersion Preferable for On-Site
		Little Change or Conflict

the context of the customer needs and the competitive environment; the promotion of the product through advertising, sales promotion, and direct customer contact; and the distribution of that product to each of the individual customers or clients. The general steps in the marketing process for service are:

1. Develop an accurate but generic definition of all of the services to be offered by the organization.

2. Segment the market into homogeneous subsections that have common or similar key characteristics or requirements, so that the marketing function can concentrate marketing resources on the sections of the market that will offer the greatest profit potential and/or will meet other corporate criteria.

3. Each of the individual market segments should be approached with presentation, timing, and exposure that are geared specifically to the needs of the individual target market. Too often, marketing programs become generic and try to be all things to all clients in all market segments.

4. Collect and analyze data on individual clients or customers, the competition, and the business environment. Too often, service executives will make service product decisions and pricing decisions based on their gut feelings or on the conditions of the market when they were actively involved in the day-to-day customer service or support. Since the market appears to be continually changing with increasing rapidity, it becomes evident that the collection and analysis of data should be an ongoing activity performed as frequently as quarterly, and certainly at least once a year.

5. Evaluate the elements and their resources, capabilities, experience, or reputation that will create special values in the minds of the customers. The purpose of this evaluation is to identify service products that can be differentiated from those of the competition and that have particular value to the customer population.

6. Select the proper mix of communication channels to reach, educate, and convince potential clients of the value of the service products being offered. In the following sections, we will discuss the various pros and cons of the types of communications channels that are appropriate for service products.

7. Integrate all of the service marketing activity to ensure that the multiple marketing tools in use are not self-canceling and,

further, to optimize the use of limited marketing resources. Too often, marketing is done on a piecemeal basis, product by product, or area by area, communications channel by communications channel, so that mixed messages are provided to customers of multiple products, many times causing confusion as to the image the company is presenting to the customer or confusion about the role that the service offerer intends to play. The obvious solution is the integration of all the various marketing activities, that each one reinforces the other, and that the communications information is complementary and not in conflict.

8. Monitor changes in the business environment and company performance. As mentioned earlier, the business environment continues to change, as will company performance. The constant monitoring not only of the performance of the service organization but also of the service organization in light of the competitive business environment must be evaluated on an ongoing basis, even though performance may continue to be provided on a consistent basis. The business environment may, in fact, be causing customer needs to change or the perception of the value of service products to change. For example, as the cost of a field service call increases, the value of the call may not increase in the same proportion as the cost, and, hence, the customer needs may put a greater value on depot service and a lower value on field service. Service marketing must continue to address not only the service offering but also the value to the customers of the services themselves.

9. Obtain periodic, reliable audits of achievements, objectives, use of resources, market opportunities, and competitive threats. All too often organizations look to the outside as reasons that they are not performing to their own levels of expectation. Obviously, the need for a critical self-examination on a periodic basis, like a physical examination of your own personal health, should be done to assure the organization that the organization performance and vitality are healthy, that there are no signs of oncoming illness, nor are there any indications of internal malignancies or dissension that could cause performance deterioration in the future.

Product

Of the four elements of marketing—price, product, promotion and distribution—product is the most important, for without it price, promotion, and distribution have no meaning. In order to understand the difference between the service product and the hardware product, consider first some of the basic product concepts. Quality is derived from performance of service products, not from physical characteristics as it is with hardware products. The appropriateness of the idea and the level of skill with which the product is delivered determine success. Hence, value added has only one level since the service product cannot be resold. The input must be recast to represent only supplies consumed, depreciation of capital goods used, and labor in the production of the service, which is significantly different from value added for hardware products. Services have time, place, possession, and satisfaction utility, instead of the time, place, and form utility for hardware products. They also have life cycles, just as hardware products do. Services can be classified by durability, tangibility, and commitment. The criteria for durability, tangibility, and commitment are shown in Figure 16-1. It is particularly interesting to understand the two caveats of this classification system. One is that the classification is determined by the buyer, not by the seller, and the other is that services are viewed by most buyers to be durable, specialty, and of a shopping nature.

PRODUCT DEVELOPMENT

When developing a service product it is important to distinguish between providing a new service product and a new method of delivering an existing service. A comparison of new service products and new methods of delivering a service are identified in Table 16-2. The conventional steps of exploration, screening, business analysis, development, testing, and commercialization apply to service products as well as to hardware products. However, because the new service products will be intangible, the development phase is bypassed. The behavioral

Examples for Service Products Classification	*Durability*	*Tangibility*	*Commitment*
On-Site Repair	Perishable	Makes Tangible Product Available	Short Term
On-Site Preventive Maintenance	Perishable	Adds Value to Tangible Product	Short Term; Can Be Postponed
Contract Service	Perishable	Adds Value to Tangible Product	Short Term; Can Be Postponed
Depot Service	Perishable	Makes Tangible Product Available	Short Term
Phone Support	Perishable	Adds Value to Tangible Product	Short Term

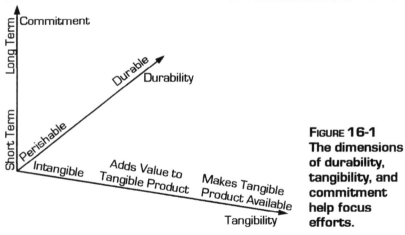

FIGURE 16-1
The dimensions of durability, tangibility, and commitment help focus efforts.

sciences aspects are relatively more important in the development of a new service product than the physical sciences. The physical sciences are, however, relatively more important in the development of a new means of delivering the service.

CHARACTERISTICS

Since there is no transfer of ownership in the sale of a service, relationships between buyer and seller in control of the use of the service product are indeterminate. The fact is, the services are sold and then produced and consumed simultane-

TABLE 16-2
Examples of service product innovations.

Type of Service	New Service Product	Service Product Improvement
On-Site Emergency	Remote Diagnostics	Programmable Tester
On-Site Preventive	Life-Time Lubricants, Throwaway Modules	Quick-Access Modules
Depot Repair of Products/Assemblies	Built-In Diagnostics, Specialized Transportation	Courier Unit Replacement, Overnight Replacement
Telephone Support	Built-In Support Software	Dedicated Help Desk

ously, so that the capacity and capability to produce a service must exist before any transaction can take place.

Unused service facilities or capabilities are perishable products, and, hence, for each moment that they are unused, the service product perishes for that moment. In addition, it is very difficult to attain uniform performance standards since each deliverable service product is different. In order to accommodate these product characteristics, traditional functions of marketing must be recast. Let's identify those functions and how they will be recast for service.

1. Transportation is now viewed as the concept of location of the service facility, rather than transporting a hardware product from the manufacturing operation to the customer.

2. Storage, which has typically been inventory of hardware products, can be conceptualized as available capacity to perform a service.

3. Risk-taking in hardware manufacture is not available for service, since the service itself cannot be used as collateral.

Service products cannot be purchased and resold, but brokers can represent them. Since services cannot be owned, there can be no product possession, but there can be product performance; therefore, pride, rather than being on the part of the owner, becomes pride of the service deliverer. Because the services are not owned and cannot be accumulated or displayed, and because the buyers' greater dependence is on the service seller, the purchase of services is likely to proceed from rational buying motives rather than emotional motives and would be planned rather than purchased on an impulse.

PRODUCTIVITY

Since the service product is simultaneously manufactured and delivered, productivity is a key element in understanding the service product. For this reason the following discussion is provided to identify the key components of productivity for the service product. The qualitative output element is an overriding factor in any attempt to measure productivity, and since services are performed and not produced, there should be a greater concern with performability than with productivity. In trying to assess productivity, it is important to understand that there is typically buyer participation in the consumption of the service. Thus, productivity measurements can be confounded by buyer involvement.

In order for the services to be performed, service facilities must be in place and operational before they can be used, and the services themselves cannot be stockpiled or inventoried. The fact is that the services are produced and consumed simultaneously, typically at the customer site. Since no title passes and no "thing" is bought or sold, ethical values on the seller's part are relevant to the product delivery.

Improvement in productivity of the service product is equivalent to improvement in the service product itself. Consideration must be given to the fact that the buyer often has the option to do it himself, as he contends with high cost and low productivity. Improvement of productivity through standardization of performance in mass production can be one of the keys to maintaining the cost of service delivery. Productivity can be most easily improved through technological means of performing the services, and that can occur through the use of automated diagnostics, remote diagnostics, or other technological assistance provided to the service technician. Finally, productivity can be improved by shifting attention from measurable units of input and output to custom measures that would relate more to the value of the service to the customer or, more specifically, the performance of the service to a specific operation of the equipment being serviced.

Price

There are four market environments for the service business, namely, a purely competitive environment, monopolistic competition, oligopoly, and a pure monopoly. Examine each of these four market environments to understand in which it is most likely for the service market to operate.

Pure competition is probably not present in the service business community because the knowledge of conditions on the other side of the market are imperfect and are definitely unequally distributed among the various service providers, with the buyer being especially disadvantaged. In addition, the service product, being non-standard in nature, provides a very difficult target to identify clearly in a purely competitive environment. Hence, we can reasonably conclude that the service market will not operate in a purely competitive environment.

Monopolistic competition may be most appropriate because each of the service sellers has unique products and, hence, can often establish a monopolistic position, primarily due to his labor force, the aptitude of those laborers, and the skills that are available for them. In addition, the service seller may have a reputation that typically enables him to charge higher prices. The monopolistic element can be particularly well achieved through service location, the amenities of the service offering, the development of the service image of the provider, and the personal selling and advertising of the service organization. Based on these criteria, it is reasonable to conclude that much of the service market is in a monopolistic competition.

An oligopoly market may be present in some situations because there may be few sellers and the performance of the services may be substantially substitutable. This is particularly true for third party operation. In these areas, we will typically see that nothing much would be gained through price reduction, and the price increases have little risk. In this situation, there are very few service providers, but those that are present are substitutable, one for the other.

In certain circumstances a pure monopoly may be present. This will occur when technical skills that may result from technology advances are limited to one company, which will maintain itself as a monopoly until other service providers can develop the skills. In addition, trade secrets may restrict the service providers as a result of drawings and parts not being available to competition. However, as products age, the monopolistic position may deteriorate and open the door for movement from the pure monopolistic market to either the oligopoly or monopolistic competition. One further reason that a pure monopoly market may exist is that the product liability associated with the service provider may dramatically limit the competition and, in fact, may restrict it to the provider of the product.

PRICING POLICIES

Pricing policies in service marketing are affected by five differentiating characteristics: 1) the limited standardization of services, 2) the difference between routine and sporadic services, 3) the buyer's knowledge of sources of supply of the services, 4) the market condition associated with it, and 5) the nature of the service product. Some of the pricing policies that could be considered that would accommodate these characteristics are further described in the following paragraphs.

The *single-price* policy does not usually operate in the service marketplace because in many cases the geography of the service prohibits the one price to all people. The cost of delivering a service to midtown Manhattan would be substantially different from providing a service to a rural community of western Texas. The geographical nature will add significantly different costs depending upon the location of the customer site. Another reason for not using single-price policy is that the time of day for service delivery can vary dramatically. Whereas many customers require service only during the eight to five Monday-through-Friday time frame, there are other customers who are looking for after-hours service through the week or possibly Saturday service; and there are customers who will require service 24 hours a day, seven days a week, 365 days a year. Providing one-price service for each of these different kinds of customers would be disadvantageous in many areas. In fact, many customers may be very concerned if they must pay the same price for first-shift service as they would for after hours and weekend services. Another reason not to use the single-price policy is that scheduled and unscheduled calls typically have very different cost elements, a scheduled call being much more cost effective due to the fact that the customer requirements are known in advance so that parts, tools, test equipment, and documentation are available when the call is made. The unscheduled call, on the other hand, can cause a disruption of the ongoing scheduled calls and may require special trips to pick up emergency parts and/or have special test equipment or tools brought to the site. Finally, the cost of living in various areas of the country may impact the single-price policy. Cost of service delivery in New York City is much greater than the cost of living in a rural environment of the Midwest or the South. Metropolitan areas typically have higher costs of living than do the suburban, rural, and non-metropolitan areas of the country.

Another service policy is to provide one price to all under given conditions. This service policy is perhaps most used in the service industry because it accommodates the restrictions noted in the single-price policy. Hence, the cost of living prices, the type of call considerations, the time of day for a service delivery, and the geographical location of the customer can all be accommodated under the given conditions; hence, pricing can be rationalized to the customer while simultaneously maintaining approximately the same margins for each of the given conditions.

The third pricing policy is to use variable prices, that is, provide different prices to different buyers of the same product under the same conditions, depending only upon the competitive situation and bargaining power of the buyer. This price policy is not usually used in service except under the following types of conditions: 1) the buyer may be willing to pay only a certain price that is less than (or, perhaps under certain conditions, more than) other buyers; 2) there is a lack of any explicit pricing policy of any kind, which is most often prevalent in small service organizations; 3) it is used to acquire a new account, with sales or profit potential in other areas; 4) it is used to establish a technology capability in a given area or in a given product area; 5) it is used in order to establish a local presence. Standardized services that permit the measurement of units of service purchased are commonly discounted for quantity.

Pricing Methods

There are two broad classes of pricing methods: cost-oriented and market-oriented. Cost-oriented pricing requires understanding the fixed costs involved with delivery of a service and an accurate measure of the variable costs involved with the service delivery. The market-oriented method, on the other hand, requires knowledge of competitive prices, understanding of psychological pricing, and promotional pricing. If prices are based on the cost of service, the cost will be determined through a formula of which the major element is labor. Pricing according to the difficulty of assignment to give pricing flexibility for multiple levels could modify the formula of service. An alternative is rate of return pricing, which is used primarily when service is capital intensive. Here, the price is set to achieve a desired rate of return on the dollar invested in the capital equipment. It's used primarily when services also can be standardized.

In competitive pricing, labor costs are common to the various competitors, which allows only limited flexibility for price competition. One of the controversies in competitive pricing contends that large service organizations with high overhead cannot compete with the smaller service organization with low overhead. The counter argument to the high overhead, higher price organization versus the low overhead, lower price service organization can be equated to insurance policies. The low overhead, low competitive price, small service organization represents a very simple insurance policy with limited coverage. A larger service organization with a high overhead provides economies of scale for more efficient administration but, more importantly, more comprehensive support and higher probability of problem resolution. Hence, the counter argument is that the larger the organization, the more likely it is to be able to resolve all the service problems. Another comparison would be to look at a one-string football team versus a football team with a number of backup players. In the case of the one-string football team, should one of the players be hurt or not be able to perform adequately, there is no backup for him. In the larger, multisquad football team, when one player is hurt or is not performing adequately, there is a backup player who can come in and fulfill the requirements. One final point to make with regard to competitive pricing is that price-cutting often implies to buyers a reduction in the quality of service, and, hence, competitive pricing in the service business does not have the same features as hardware price-cutting. Thus, price-cutting does not have the same value and should be seriously reviewed before any price cutting approaches are applied to the customer base.

Demand-oriented pricing is another pricing method, and in this methodology buyers have a difficult time providing meaningful price comparisons because the services are invisible and typically non-standard. The buyers also may be reluctant to display price sensitivity because of their perception of the relationship between the buyer and the seller. They may not wish to jeopardize that relationship by being seriously concerned about pricing. For many of the services that are purchased, there may be no substitutes available, so demand-oriented pricing is appropriate. Certainly, demand of a crisis nature that is not subject to postponement is usually price insensitive; this is particularly true of emergency service calls when operations have stopped as a result of a machine malfunction. A note of concern, however, is that industrial buyers are becoming much more conscious of the price of service alternatives and are, in fact, looking for options. Under these circumstances, using demand-oriented pricing may be one way of being rejected by the industrial shopper.

PRICING ISSUES AND TACTICS

The five dimensions of service output that could provide criteria for effective pricing strategy are 1) the time required to perform a particular service, 2) the extent to which capital goods are utilized in the service, 3) the quality of the performance of the service, 4) the degree of specialization in the content of the performance, and 5) the value of the performance of the service to the buyer. Once these five conditions have been reviewed, there are a number of pricing tactics that can be considered in that light. These pricing tactics are noted in Table 16-3. Each of these tactics has a particular value for the marketplace and should be selected in accordance with the overall marketing strategy. Given a review of the tactics and a selection of the proper tactic, the price that will be finally offered to the customer should consider the following four points:

1. The marginal profit of the service contract or the marginal profit of the service product that is being announced.
2. The marginal loss that may occur if the contract is lost or if the product is not offered to the customer base.
3. The probability of success for any given price within the specified customer environment.
4. The calculation of expected profit from the service offering. Expected profit will be computed according to the equation: Expected Profit = (Marginal Profit x Probability of Success) - (Marginal Loss x Probability of Failure). In this case, the probability of success plus the probability of failure equals one.

In closing the subject of pricing, the objectives of pricing should be clearly identified and reiterated. The two objectives of pricing are to obtain new business and to insure the profitable continuance of the firm.

TABLE **16-3**
There are several tactics for pricing service.

Tactic	Description	Effect
Loss Leader	Deliberate Low Price to Obtain Business	May Establish Ceiling on Pricing; May Establish Revenue for New Territory/Market
Offset	Low Basic Price with Extras Charged at Higher Prices	May Generate New Business but Astute Customer can Control Extent of Extras
Diversionary	Low Price on Selected Services	May be Effective but Should Not be Used as "Bait & Switch"
Discount	Priced Subject to Discounts on Predetermined Criteria, e.g., Volume, Timing	Encourages Customer to Based Structure Service on Mutually Favorable Basis
Guarantee	Price Includes Commitment to Achieve Specific Results	Moves Competition to Value Area; Favors High-Quality Service
Price Lining	Price is Kept Constant but Quality or Extent of Service Adjusted to Costs	Removes Price as Major Negotiating Point

Promotion

The goals of any promotion program within the marketing operation are to inform, to persuade, and to remind. Service promotion, it should be pointed out, differs as a result of the concepts of the role of promotion in service marketing and the execution of promotion. There is a tendency in the promotion of service to stress quality of performance and reputation as the most valuable form of promotion. This tendency strikes a responsive cord, because as the service product is identified it is noted that, along with the intangibility, performance and reputation represent significant areas. It should be clear that service promotion differs more in terms of objectives and form than in the significance in quantity of the promotion. The promotion of service must include the following points:

1. Promotion methods are clearly defined and agreed upon.
2. Targets of the promotion are identified and are practical.
3. Message to be conveyed through the promotion is effective and clear.
4. Coordination of the promotion throughout the marketing organization and the organization as a whole is achieved.
5. Feedback occurs as a result of the promotional effort.
6. Evaluation of the promotion itself, even if only approximate, should be accomplished.

To put the promotional goals into perspective, the chart in Table 16-4 indicates the relationship of promotional objectives, promotional methods, and promotional media. Reviewing each of these together indicates the many possible ways in which promotion can be achieved for service products.

For service and service products, the superior form of promotion is in the sale of an idea. Quality of performance and reputation can identify an image, but it is the sale of the idea that

TABLE 16-4
Service promotion relationships.

Objectives	Methods	Media
Concept Promotion	Press Releases Advertising	Trade Journals Visionary Speeches
Image Development of Specific Service	PR Activity	Radio/TV Interviews Magazine Articles
Build Atmosphere for Service	Academic Support	Directories CEO/CFO Periodicals
Improve Level of Customer Knowledge	Direct Mail Company Tours	Films/Cassettes/CDs Presentation Rooms Web Site
Sell Cluster of Support Factors	Exhibitions Partnerships	Academic Press
Sell Size/Reputation of Company	Sponsored Activities Packaged Offerings	Seminars Executive Breakfasts

provides the differentiation between one service provider and another. In the sale of the idea, it is important to stress the amenities of the service and the convenience of the facilities, to describe how the work is to be performed, to stress any status symbols that might be related to the performance of the service, and, in particular, to stress achieving any objectives such as cost cutting or improved productivity that might result from the performance of the service. Services have typically been traditionally viewed as undifferentiated products, and service providers have been willing to allow buyers to make their own differentiation on the basis of experience, with no effort to differentiate their products from their competition's products. Recently, service firms are making increased use of trademarks and trade names as a form of differentiation. The concern in most service operations is how to promote undesired services, such as the ability to repair equipment that fails. The sales organizations typically take the position of not wanting to tell the customers that the equipment is going to break down. However, it is reasonable to promote undesired services, and this can be accomplished through 1) describing the "in being" nature of repair services, and 2) describing the availability of services that might be available to prevent crises from occurring or minimizing the impact of the crisis itself. As one sees the number of alternatives for promotional paths, there are some factors that will affect the promotional mix. These factors include:

1. The details of professional constraints
2. The extent of promotion in any one market area
3. The size of the geographical market served
4. Customs and traditions within that particular segment
5. The degree of sophistication of the customers themselves

Media selection is usually based on the suitability to inform buyers of the availability of the services, the ability to describe their benefits, and the staying power of the media, which is why most service organizations select magazines as opposed to television or radio. The advertising message content used in the promotion must relate to the prevailing characteristics of the buying process. If that buying process has changed, it is important that the advertising message change with that buying process. The advertising should stress dependability in order to engender confidence, since the service is intangible. The message should also be designed to hold the present customers as well as to attract new ones. For promotional campaigns designed for services that will be purchased only when needed, such as emergency service, the message that should be used is one that will keep the potential customer aware of the availability of the service, that is, the "in being" aspect of the service operation. Persuasive messages serve no purpose unless the advertiser is encouraging preventive services. Where the buyer attitudes and practices must be changed if a transaction is to occur, then the message must attract the attention of latent users and develop a sufficiently strong interest to generate some initiative on the part of the buyer. Benefits are typically stressed through the use of testimonials of satisfied users, comparisons of before and after experiences, and the identification of personal satisfaction that is derived from the service delivery.

When using press advertising, the emphasis should be on the utilities and the customer benefits of the services delivered rather than on the technical details of the service process, the diagnostic capabilities, or the skills of the service technician, which may not be related to the satisfaction of the customer needs and desires. Thus, the advertising must rest strongly on the promise of performance and the benefits that will ensue.

The promotional process in service has its value in image utility. Image utility is the ability of a service provider to provide satisfaction through the user's perception of the commercial and corporate meanings of the service. In addition to image utility, there is possession utility, which is the satisfaction resulting from the rendering and receipt of a service.

Of critical importance and value for service providers is place utility, which is the accessibility of a service at the place that is required, and time utility, which is the accessibility of a service at the time that it is required. These utilities are the real values that can be attributed to the service product.

The use of direct mail may be a major advantage in the promotion of service, and it is possible to target the message accurately to the firms and individuals to which it is directed. Direct mail can be controlled in its timing and rate of dispatch to exploit environmental factors and to cope with replies so that the service organization is not overburdened with a deluge of responses for which it does not have handling capacity. Finally, direct mail provides more opportunity to explain the service product than does advertisements in various media. The objectives of direct mail are to get attention and, more importantly, to develop product business immediately. A review of the merchandising techniques for service is provided in the chart shown in Table 16-5.

WEB SITE

Every service organization should have a web site. The Internet has made possible a relatively inexpensive means of communicating with prospects and customers around the globe. The advantages of obtaining up-to-date information are considerable. The authors, who do have fancy print brochures for their companies, have used only a few since their web sites were established. If someone calls and asks for information, you can simply refer them to the web site. On the other hand, they may search the web for information and find you.

Web-site design, like good print material design, is an area where you are well advised to hire experts who know graphic design and also understand how to show your material best. They will display small graphics since large photographs take a long time to load, and will use colors and type styles that will please prospects using different internet service providers and computer capabilities. With modern software available to do your own web site, you may be tempted to do it yourself, but remember that the display must appear professional and its image is your image to the outside world. Keeping information up-to-date is a web challenge. You can't do a site once and leave it. It must be refreshed frequently to keep people interested.

Once you have the site designed and operating you could update much of the material yourself.

Make sure that you have good key words in your web information so that search engines will find you quickly. For example, *www.supportparts.com* can be found searching for *service parts, logistics, service parts planning,* and the most common query is a phrase we don't like, s*pare parts.*

Dell, Gateway 2000, Hewlett-Packard, and most high-technology companies have developed excellent web sites to enhance shopping for new computer systems, finding answers to frequently asked questions, and providing information so that customers can help themselves. The image of service is built into

TABLE 16-5
Merchandizing techniques for service.

Technique	Description
Trial Offer	Test of Service with "No Commitment" Break Clause
Gifts (Advertising Specialties)	Practical Material Such as Size Calculators, Wrist-Watch Calendars, Desk Accessories
Literature	Brochures, Displays, Signs, thanksgiving Cards
Special Events	New Premises, Link with Environmental Factors, "Birthdays," Unveiling of New Services
Packaging	Attractive Bindings for Quotations End Reports, Novel Forms of Literature Presentations & Sales Aids
Sponsored Events	Financial &/or Promotional Backing for an Event Related or Not to the Firm's Activities
Users Group	Creating Users Group for Liaison & Communication Between Customers & Firm
Sponsored Conference	Conference Mounted to Present Information on a Subject Related to the Service Firm's Expertise, Usually with Independent Speakers as Well as Firm's Speakers
Web Site	Company Highlights on WWW, White Papers, Training, Seminars, Publications, & Easy Request for More

those web sites, and is a major marketing tool for companies that effectively use the web. The web is certainly better for selling hard goods of known configuration than it is for selling services. In a typical week, books on service management, like the one you are reading, are sold via www.supportparts.com to people in Sweden, Italy, Africa, and Texas. That world market could not be reached by any other means. Services can also be stimulated over the web and instant information exchanged to greatly reduce the time required for negotiations. Information on training courses and the annual Service Executives Logistics Roundtable are put on the web site, and registrations with credit card payment are returned the same way. The Internet is speeding communications and reducing service costs.

Distribution

Distribution, the fourth major element of marketing, is characterized as location and channel. For service operations and service marketing, location refers to the distribution of people and facilities prepared to perform services. Channel refers to a network designed to deliver services to the end user. The marketing channel contributes time and place utility to the intangible service product. The relative importance of time and place utility is greater for the delivery of services than it is for the case of goods.

The inability to store or ship intangibles and the need to have service facilities in place and operational to meet intermittent and random demand at various times suggests that the price paid for services reflects a substantial portion of time and place utility in the total value of the service product.

Services are classified by distribution location in three ways: they are either concentrated, dispersed, or the location may be irrelevant. This is based on where the service is performed. In general, field service has dispersed location. Depot service, on the other hand, indicates that the locations may either be concentrated or the location may be irrelevant. Dispersed services have acknowledged the preeminence of demand factors, thus the need for the services to be dispersed throughout a large geographic area. The demand factors force the local availability of service in order to acquire the service. Concentrated services, on the other hand, find supply considerations to be the overriding factor; thus, specialized service depots may concentrate in order to accommodate each other's unique needs.

The nature of service and the characteristics of demand reward the service seller who positions his facilities in terms of the needs of the buyer. Specialization within services encourages the concentration, so that the specialist can turn quickly to complementary assistance, and thus, the concentration of depot services. Which category a particular service falls into is determined by the buyer, and the same service may be classified in all three categories by various buyers. Over a period of time, the classification of particular services can change, as other factors such as technology and needs change, so that which may require a dispersed service today may require a concentrated service in the future. A major factor in the propensity to buy services rather than self-performance is the location or accessibility of the service, which reinforces the fact that most field service operations are dispersed.

At the beginning of the service marketing channel is the creator or performer of the service. At the other end of the service marketing channel is the end user. The service channel that is confined to the performer and the end user is equivalent to the direct marketing of goods from the manufacturer to the user. The two intermediaries possible in service marketing channels are agents and brokers. However, there is no uniformity in the functions that are performed by either of these intermediaries. The service broker acts on behalf of the service provider, and the agent can act on behalf of the buyer, so the maximum number of components in the distribution channel is four: the seller, the broker, the agent, and the buyer. Dispersion of the distribution channel can result through either branching (that is, having many branch offices) or franchising. The fact is that any standardized service is an appropriate candidate for franchising, but the more nonstandard a service is, the more difficult it is to establisha franchising function.

The small service firm can compete with the multibranch service firm or franchises, but it must do so by forming either cooperative networks or affiliations with other small service firms; otherwise, the advantages of place and time utility will be in favor of the multi-branch service firm or franchise.

Selling

Selling service requires a different approach, since you do not have a finite hard product to demonstrate. The steps illustrated in Figure 16-2 start with learning the needs of the top management decision-maker and making sure that she or he has the money to obtain the services needed. Listening is the most valuable selling skill a service person can have. Building a service relationship requires that you understand the prospect's real needs. Those needs are not usually learned in the first few minutes of conversation. Resist the temptation to tell the prospect how good you and your company are. Instead listen to what her problems are and then suggest how you might help solve those problems.

Many service commitments are obtained without the customer's ever seeing a demo or visiting a facility. That is difficult for a hardware salesperson to understand. Consultative selling often starts long-term relationships that can be very profitable for both parties. Signing the service agreement can become almost incidental to continuing the selling process. The relationship and process are most important because the results can be very flexible.

Technicians can be the most effective salespersons an organization has. Many technicians build a long-term relationship with their customers and become trusted advisors on matters within their expertise. If the customer is considering new equipment, the technician is often casually asked for his opinion. By personality, technicians will usually give honest opinions that will help the customer even though the result may not sell more of the company's products. Basic sales training should be part of the curriculum for all service people. Whether they are accidental or incidental salespeople makes little difference, they have great influence on customers.

The multitudes of technicians who are with customers should keep their ears open for leads—perhaps notice that the customer is low on consumable supplies, for example. Prepare the technicians to ask if the customer would like to place a supplies order. If a large opportunity such as an equipment upgrade or an extension to the service agreement are mentioned by the customer it will usually be best for the technician to pass those leads on to the professional salespeople who support service.

Selling service is different from selling product. Service should have its own staff of salespeople who are rewarded for selling service agreements. Experience sshows that having hardware salespersons sell service is not a good solution. Certainly the hardware salesperson should offer the customer enhancements to the product warranty at the time of original sale, but that is the limit of what can be accomplished well by those persons. Salespeople should specialize on selling service in order to be effective.

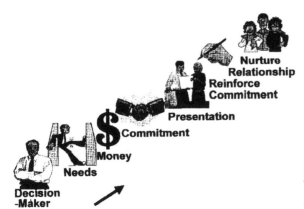

Nurture
Relationship
Reinforce
Commitment

Presentation

Commitment

Money

Needs

Decision
-Maker

Figure **16-2**
The steps of
service selling.

In conclusion, sales and service have often been at crossed purposes with each other. It has been said, "Sales places the product and Service sell it." Effective service organizations realizes that service needs sales, but that selling service is very different from selling hard goods. Selling a service contract at a profitable margin should be emphasized as compared to pushing for high market share without regard for the profit.

Historically, if business got tight, the service organization was usually called upon to sacrifice budget and resources. Now, smart service organizations realize that emphasis should be put on raising revenue, rather than on always cutting costs. Marketing and sales must be strong functions if a service organization is going to make good profits.

Questions

1. What are the conceptual differences between product marketing and services marketing?

2. What would you do to differentiate your service products from the competition?

3. Compare pricing on similar services and explain the differences in terms of the services offered. Which pricing model was used for each?

4. Develop a trade journal ad for emergency repair service for personal computers.

5. How would you advertise a service over the radio?

6. What new service products will result from the additional microprocessor electronics being used in automobiles?

7. How would you market contract repair services to a regional hospital chain?

8. Why would a service organization want to use a broker?

9. How would you market equipment services to have little or no price competition?

10. How would you verify that the services offered were not appropriate for your customers? How would you conclude that your offerings were "better" than the competition?

17

Service Quality

*Q**uality* is one of the most over-used and complex words in our business vocabulary. Among the definitions from dictionaries and common professional terminology are:

➤ Fitness for Use
➤ Conformance to Specifications
➤ Grade, Class, Category, Brand
➤ Distinguishing Features
➤ The Quality Function
➤ An Organization

The central issue is *fitness*. For service, the degree of fitness is established mainly in the customer's mind and experience as opposed to written specifications. The movement of service

363

toward customers and total quality management (TQM) focuses that definition on the idea that quality is what the customer wants it to be. TQM is a philosophy and the principles that form a foundation for a continuously improving organization. W. Edwards Deming says, "Improve constantly and forever the system of production and service to improve quality and productivity, and constantly decrease costs." This mindset of continually striving for improvement often needs to be shaken by a more radical change called *reengineering.* Service organizations are especially prone to doing something "because we have always done it that way."

The opportunity exists to eliminate tasks, simplify procedures, reduce paper work, and to generally work smarter instead of harder. Benchmarking is helpful in comparing your functions to similar functions in other organizations. Those organizations do not necessarily need to be in product service. For example, one of the best pick/pack/ship operations in the USA is considered to be at L. L. Bean®, from whom many service parts organizations can learn. Both the numbers and the processes are integral to improvement. Many service organizations actively share information with others. In many cases, good ideas are only a start. The major challenge lies in the implementation.

The customer wants a product or service to be fit for use as defined by that customer. Why should we emphasize service quality? The following are main reasons:

1. Profit
2. Contract penalties and incentives
3. Customer demand
4. Legislation
5. Liability
6. Marketability

The reasons can be summarized in that one word at the top of the list—profit. The desired result of service quality is to make a profit. A few people may say, "But I'm not in a profit-making organization." Even if you represent a hospital, a school, or a municipality, you still should have an excess of benefits coming in versus costs going out. You're not going to stay in business as a hospital or anything else if you don't have positive income.

Another reason is the customer's demand for high quality. Quality is a very marketable thing. In the past, service has not received much attention, so the fact that service is now getting high recognition is a good thing. Competition stimulates quality. It's a positive thing to say, "We have fewer call-backs, we do the job right the first time, we get out there faster, and we satisfy customers to a higher level!" Further, it is necessary to match factual measures with perceptions so that performance can be benchmarked against both absolute and relative comparisons.

Those are all positive things. There are some things on the negative side. Because a few industries haven't regulated themselves as well as they should, government agencies in many states and nationally have passed laws that will regulate us all. Service charges and the speed with which things are done are issues in which society has a very large impact on what is happening in the area of service quality. Liability, no surprise to anyone, is emphasized by agencies of the government including the environmental Protection Agency (EPA) and the Occupational Safety and Health Administration (OSHA), and many ambitious lawyers. Service has a major impact on the liability of a product. If you are servicing something in the medical market and a patient gets a lethal shock, it may be the fault of the product, it may be the fault of the surgeon, or it may be the fault of the service organization, but that doesn't make any difference to the person who gets buried! And the product manufacturer, the doctor, or the service organization could all be involved in lawsuits and have a very expensive time of it. It could be your service representative, who may have had no influence whatsoever on the problem; but the fact that he had logged in as having serviced that particular item could be something that puts you into court with expensive litigation.

Penalties and incentives are included in several contracts that guarantee uptime on equipment, for example, 99.99+ percent uptime on a telephone directory assistance system or a file server. Patton Consultants' surveys show that over 90% of service organizations have response time targets in their service level agreements (SLAs). The next step needs to be uptime targets, from the time a capability fails until it is back up again. Customers really don't care how quick you get there. If you can solve the problem over the telephone or by remote diagnostics and a software patch, that is wonderful. But if you have to send a technician, customers expect that upon arrival the qualified technician will have the right parts, the right training, and the right tools, analytic devices, and documentation needed to rapidly restore the capability.

Differential superiority means that service quality is something people will notice and say, "Yes, ABC service is better than XYZ service for several good reasons." Do note that customer expectations set the standards. Advertising, a salesperson's comments, or actual delivery of service may create those expectations. Customers then intuitively compare their perceptions of achievement against those expectations and feel some degree of satisfaction. Service organizations must talk to customers frequently to determine the level of satisfaction, what might be done to improve it, and what other services might be provided to help the customer. The author recently ordered a top-of-the-line laptop from Dell Computer's web site on Sunday afternoon and received it via FedEx Second Day Air the following Friday, five days later. That is a good example of mass customization and customer happiness made possible by technology.

Plan

If you provide too much service, you will spend more money than you should, yet not gain proportionally from that cost. If you do too little service, the customers aren't happy and will complain or may quietly take their business elsewhere.

Put your money and resources where they are most important to the customer. Efforts should be concentrated to keep performance within the control limits. If a characteristic is not important to the customer, don't worry about the satisfaction level or performance. If you are delivering performance that is much above the upper control limit, you are wasting resources. Too much of a good thing doesn't really gain more benefits. It's nice to pat yourself on the back, but you are probably not gaining much extra business because of the excess, and it is going to cost a lot of extra money. An example is illustrated in Figure 17-1. Information was gained for 15 high-technology companies on what the specific percentage of fill was for service parts, and also how customers rated that level of performance.

The several companies that delivered less than about 83% fill rate were the subjects of ridicule and complaints about poor performance. At the high end of performance, several companies were reported to be delivering superior performance above what customers thought was efficient. One related observation is that a company with highly reliable products that do not fail very often is also regarded as having very good parts support. Apparently if it doesn't fail, you don't need parts so you rate very well. Another finding is that a service level in the low 90 percents is generally regarded as being much higher. In the middle range from about 83 to 93%, customers did not detect significant difference. This research should be replicated on your own products and customers before it is used in practice. However, evidence shows that unless you want to target high fill rate as a differential superiority, then stay low on your own curve to get the best bang for your buck.

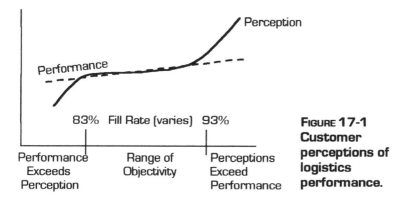

FIGURE 17-1 Customer perceptions of logistics performance.

Another illustration is managing response time. When signing contracts, customers often ask, "How good are you?" And you say, "We will give four-hour response time." Then, if response time turns out to be a faster two hours, you are probably very proud, but the customer's expectation changes to two hours every time. When business builds up and you have more volume for your technicians to take care of, you deliver the promised four hours and the customer says, "Your service has deteriorated; it's lousy now!" The idea may go against the grain of doing the best possible response, but, if you really want to perform to a four-hour target, you should manage to a four-hour target. There are some times when you may have a technician next door and you could easily have him there in 20 minutes. You might say to the technician, "Come back and work on the bench for a while so that you get to that customer just before the four-hour limit."

There will be companies that take issue with this directed response time. In areas of tight competition where customers rely on specific equipment, then you should restore that server as fast as possible. Customers will remember all the people sitting around and the amount of lost production, and hopefully they will recall the good job that your people did and sign up to renew their support agreement with your company.

It also depends on how you have specified response time. If you told customers that you are going to give them a maximum *average* of four hours, that allows you to go two hours one time and six hours another. If you tell the customer that you are going to give a maximum of four hours on any call, then manage to a four-hour time. A customer will be happier if you are consistently at a four-hour time than if you arrive in one hour today and seven hours tomorrow and vary from fast to slow. The US Postal Service has done a large amount of research in that area, and they find delivering the mail to be sensitive in the same way. Rather than having fast but erratic mail delivery, most of us would rather know that mail will arrive in three days every time. Managing to time is an interesting concept that is difficult for many of us to understand, but it allows service organizations to scientifically balance efforts and costs against results.

Customer-based situational goals are a step beyond universal goals. As customer targets become tighter, service managers realize that their organizations cannot do everything at equally high speed without spending excessive money on resources. It is better to provide very fast support when the need urgency is great and allow slower, lower-cost support when conditions permit. As a generality, conditions may be divided into either time-sensitive or cost-sensitive. If central equipment such as a file server fails, that affects many people; and all possible effort should be put to fixing that problem quickly. The target for down priority equipment might be maximum of one-hour response with two-hour time-to-restore. If low priority equipment (for example, a monitor in an area with many similar terminals) has a minor density problem, then that might allow a low-cost, next-day call.

Measure

Having planned the level of service that you want to provide, move to develop a measurement system. (Chapter 3 covers measurement in depth.) A measurement system will be a set of procedures that assigns numbers to events and items with the objective of providing relevant, valid, reliable, and economic information. There are two kinds of scales: absolute and relative. An absolute scale measures precisely, for example, 35 minutes. Relative scales relate the measurement as a ratio or percentage to other similar parameters, as in 99% or a 3:1 ratio. There are several service areas in which the relative rank is more useful than the absolute.

Installation quality reports are one way to measure quality, and one measure is hours and minutes versus the standard. For example, installation time measures how many hours it took to install the product as reported by the service technician. A poor quality product has to be fixed in the field before it can be turned over to the customer, and that takes time. In many cases, preinstallation is done, and then the product is taken to the customer. That's because quality wasn't built in when the product came off the end of the production line. How much time should it take to install a perfect product? An hour and a half? How long did it take to install this one? It took two hours, because the motherboard had to be replaced and some adjustments were necessary. Use a defect weighting system, because on most products the kinds of defects that can happen are not all essential defects that shut equipment down completely. Many systems code defects as "hard" or "soft," with soft items being things that merely degrade the operation and hard items being things that cause a complete shutdown of the system. Within that coding put weightings on the failures so that a total weight score can be calculated at the end. Then a product with a weighting of two may be acceptable and anything worse than two is rejected. That information should get back to the responsible people so that they can correct deficient areas. In the warranty return area, costs such as warranty dollars may be compared to the sales dollars, or the number of returned units may be ratioed over the number of units that have been sold.

Many examples exist of complex products that are shipped from several different locations so that all necessary, and often variable, pieces arrive at the customer at the same time. For example, if you buy a personal computer, it is quite possible that the CPU (central processing unit) loaded with the specific software you want comes from the production location, the monitor ships from a west-coast warehouse, speakers arrive direct from their manufacturer, and a printer or scanner might come from yet another source. Good quality enables all these pieces to be delivered in the same delivery van and all work together without requiring a service technician. The best service is often a process that allows the customer to help herself, knowing that a help desk backup is available in case of need.

Reliability is defined as "quality in the field." Quality, once equipment comes off the end of the production line, becomes reliability for our purposes. The main source of information is the number of requests for service. The number of times the customer calls and says, "Something is not working right, come and fix it," is a good measure of the mean time between failures (MTBF). Another measure is service technician reliability. The challenge is that low reliability people often service high reliability products. This is evidenced by using the first call fix rate (FCFR), which is the inverse of the number of broken calls out of the total number of service calls, to measure the reliability of personnel. Maintainability, again coming off call reports, will be primarily mean down time (MDT).

Technical performance includes product-specific things such as, in the copier or printer business, resolution and smears and how black the lines are and how white the background is. Or how many times you can dial the telephone and have the connection properly made, or how often the modem properly connects to your Internet service out of 100 tries.

Effectiveness, again measured from the call reports, uses two main measures: availability and down time. Availability is uptime divided by total time. Emphasize the positive. Talk about 99.9 percent uptime or availability, which is the inverse of 0.1 percent down time. Within those measures are parameters that are going to be much more critical in the future, as customers begin to become concerned beyond the issue of your service technicians responding in a hurry. Customer expectations are very important. One of the "fun" things about working with people is that others often perceive things differently than we do. The salesman describes all the wonderful things the customer will get.

Service often gets the results in complaint calls and letters. Every now and then service even gets a pat on the back, but people tend to register more complaints than render praise. Measure the number of complaints per the number of employees. The percentage should be very small. Also measure the messages of praise, and post the words on e-mail or the bulletin board for everyone to see and emulate.

The percent of responses that meets time targets should be measured. If the goal is a four-hour response time and you meet it 98 out of 100 times, then it is a good target and is met with good results. As response against goals begins to drop off it usually means that more people are needed, although it could also mean that the available people may not be managed effectively. The percentage of on-time deliveries of parts addresses how often parts are promised to arrive tomorrow morning and do arrive by the expected time. Naturally, the customer's expectation is that the part is going to be in their hands by then. If it's not there, then bigger problems arise. It is better to promise something on a guaranteed schedule to be met and then deliver it a little faster. Under-promise and over-deliver.

The percentage of service calls that are answered in time and the percentage of calls completed out of the total are a function of the telephone calls that come in to a customer service call management center. Assure that operators who are supposed to answer those phones do pick them up by the third ring (try for the first or second) and that calls aren't lost as they are being transferred to technical assistance personnel. Slow answers and lost calls are sources of additional aggravation to an already irritated customer. Another question is, "Do you have your best people with good voices and speaking skills and sunny dispositions in the first contact with callers?" Too often we select and train managers, but forget that the first impression about an organization comes from the person who answers the phone.

Costs and revenues are a clear measure in the service business. Sources of information include published prices, competitive quotes, and customer complaints concerning how expensive service is. That's based mostly on the number of comments about prices considered out of line with somebody else's, and the percent of return on investment (ROI) or the return on net assets (RONA). They really come together in business practices, which is where you can tell by repeat business whether the customers are satisfied enough to keep coming back to you. That really is the final decision point. How many contracts are renewed, and how many of the customers on the list for past time and materials (T&M) service are still coming back? Are there people in the records who haven't been heard from for six months and yet must have needed service in that time? Contact those customers and solicit them for future business. The percentage of new customers versus repeat customers is a good measure of satisfaction. It will cost at least eight times more to get a new customer than it will cost to keep an old customer happy. It's a lot better to keep present customers satisfied than to sell new ones.

Surveys

Conduct satisfaction surveys by mail, phone, and visits. One recommendation is a survey by mail to every customer at least once a year. Rank your customers in order to designate A-level customers that are big volume. If any of these get lost to competition, business will really suffer. B-level customers are the next most important group, and the rest are C-level. Use Pareto's 80/20 and 90/45 rule, which is also known as the "Principle of the Critical Few," so attention is directed to customers that have the biggest impact on your business. Those A-level customers should get a face-to-face visit. Give them everything and anything they want for a reasonable price so that everybody profits. The B-level customers should receive a telephone call on a regular basis and when there is any problem. C-level customers normally can just be mailed the surveys. This prioritized customer contact system can help keep a measure on how well customers are being satisfied. Little or no concern showed to a customer sends a message that you do not care about their business. Few customers leave due to excessive attention.

Control

Now that we have a plan we can measure performance and see if we are doing as well as we need to, or better, or worse. The next step is control. The following are some of the methods used to provide quality controls on service:

1. Goals—written, measurable, understandable, challenging, and achievable
2. Service help plan and design-in support
3. Service sign-off of all affecting changes
4. "Stop ship" if all resources are not ready
5. Product service council
6. Installation quality audits
7. Service call report evaluation
8. Failure report and corrective action systems (FRACAS)
9. Problem/cause/action analysis
10. Service hotline
11. Customer calls and letters
12. Service quality audits
13. Manager of service quality
14. Account reviews
15. Quality participation teams
16. Customer surveys
17. Managers phone top customers
18. Sales rate service
19. Service rate themselves
20. Motivated personnel

The last item, motivated personnel, is key to most elements of the process. Set your goals and write, "Here's where we are now, and three months from now we should be within these control limits," and people will work that way. It is important that service be involved intimately in planning and designing in support for new products. Service should have a sign-off on all affecting changes. Anything that influences a product—every engineering change order—should be approved by service. It may get to the point that you will have to stop-ship a new product if all the resources aren't ready. Some organizations, particularly those that have put enough emphasis on quality, will have designated someone as Vice President of Customer Satisfaction, Manager of Service Quality, or a similar title, who has the authority to stop any product from shipping until it will perform well in a customer installation. That delay will sometimes be overridden by a top executive who says, "Look, we'll be shot down in the marketplace if we don't get it out there. Yes, we know it's bad, but we must ship in order to get our chunk of the market and to demonstrate at the trade show." Nevertheless, bring the problem to the attention of responsible persons.

A product service council that looks at both existing and new products can say, "Here are the things that need to be done to be able to service it. We're having problems out in the field. We should be doing something differently."

An installation quality report system is vital to show that products are being installed smoothly. Installation is the most critical phase of the product's life. That's when the customer's perception of a lemon or an excellent product is determined. It takes a very long time to develop and nurture a good positive quality reputation. You can lose a reputation in service instantly.

Statistical process control (SPC) techniques are applicable to analyze service information. Evaluation of service calls requires a computer system that ranks calls and identifies problems and causes. The acronym FRACAS identifies a failure report and corrective action system, generally including both a reporting system and a task force charged with identifying the top problems on a product. Put short-range solution responsibility on the person or the organization that can alleviate the problem quickly, and then probably on a separate long-range solution, which may be a design engineering or a manufacturing correction. Quite often there is something in training or publications that can be done very quickly to get "Band-Aid" improvements, and then solutions can come later.

Problem/cause/action analysis is keyed to, "What was the problem? What caused that situation? What action made the customer happy again? What were the top ten causes? Are they material failures? If transformers are failing, is it because of loose connections? Are we spending most of the time board changing, or what?" Again, computerized information systems are a big help.

A service "hotline" is another good control. Particularly on new products, the speed and detail of mail isn't adequate. The normal reporting system isn't adequate. It is better to have the ability for tech reps in the field to call in and say, "We have real trouble, please come out here and help take care of it." As said before, customer calls and letters are a late indicator.

A DOA (dead on arrival) hotline is another good quality idea. Have a specific toll-free phone number for technicians to call if they encounter a DOA part. The phone should come direct to the Vice President of Quality or equivalent executive. One result will be that the number of alleged DOAs will diminish. Technicians who caused the DOA by ordering the wrong part will call the problem something else. The benefit comes from immediately identifying problems in production, repair processes, testing, shipping, and other functional areas. Those problems can be quickly corrected before any more bad parts go to the field. The DOA hotline also serves as a message telling both headquarters and field people that doing a job correctly the first time is expected performance, and anything less will not be tolerated.

Service quality audits are one of the best investments of the service manager's time. Have someone in your organization in charge of doing service quality audits measure how good customers think you are, how good employees think you are, and what the correlation is between those measures. A manager of service quality could head the process. Where a particular customer has a lot of equipment, get together with sales and service and review everything to support that customer. Quality teams, technicians, and in-house people know what most of your problems are. In many cases, we don't bother to ask for their advice. This idea is called participation circles, self-managed work groups, internally directed project teams, and similar management terms. They are very beneficial in identifying problems and helping people develop and implement solutions. Already emphasized is a prioritization system with the most important customers getting visits from your managers, the next group of customers each getting a telephone call, and everybody getting a mail survey. The survey questionnaire should be mailed to specifically named and addressed customer decision makers—

not just to the purchasing agent, but to the person who is really making the decision to buy your services.

Sending separate questionnaires to the equipment operators, the people who are using it all the time, helps to get their judgments. Even though the person who really makes the buying decision is the most important individual, the people who are using the product daily probably have some very good ideas and some influence and should be contacted. A mail survey will get about 30 percent returns in most organizations. The questionnaire should not be more than one page. If more than one page, fewer people will take the time to fill it out and send it back. Include a self-addressed stamped envelope so it comes directly back to you. Consider using double postcard forms sold prestamped by the post office. These cards can be typed by a word processor so that the request instructions and the customer address are on one card, and on the other card are the answer forms and return address. The cards are folded in half when they go out so that only the customer address and answer form sides show. The respondent just tears off the postcard and sends back the pre-addressed answer card. You can also reproduce the questionnaire as a letter, or even better, put it in e-mail. Busy executive will often take time to respond to e-mail better than they respond to mail or even voice messages.

Most customers are quite pleased that you ask them for their opinions. Leave space for any customers who want to complain or detail the problems, and flag those instantly. Don't send all these returning questionnaires directly to the computer people for processing. Make sure a responsible person looks at them quickly and pulls out any that have messages in bright red ink saying, "If it breaks again, your equipment goes out on the street." There is a very positive marketing advantage to this kind of survey. A few really dissatisfied customers will be identified at that point. Most service organizations are very surprised to find how well customers rate their service. In many cases the customers rate service better than internal organizations do.

Also, have sales rate service. Most of us have very critical things to say about our sales persons. How often have we asked sales persons to fill out questionnaires on the service of their accounts and general quality level? Our own people should be good critics of our operation.

The series brings us back to highly motivated personnel. There is no instant solution. It's not as easy to create motivated personnel as it is to do a good mail questionnaire. Of all the items that will help achieve high service quality, highly motivated people aimed towards unified service goals are the single most effective resource to achieve consistently high service quality.

Awards and Certifications

A wave of quality consciousness is sweeping businesses worldwide. Individual certifications that are applicable to service management include the Computing Technology Industry Association (CompTIA)'s *A+ Technician Certification*, Microsoft's *Certified Network Engineer* (CNE), the American Society for Quality (ASQ)'s *Certified Quality Engineer* (CRE), *Certified Reliability Engineer* (CRE), and *Certified Quality Auditor* (CQA); the American Production and Inventory Control Society (APICS)'s *Certified in Production and Inventory Management* (CPIM); the National Association of Service Managers (NASM)' *Certified Service Executive* (CSE); and the Society of Logistics Engineers (SOLE)' *Certified Professional Logistician* (CPL).

At an organization level, the national *Baldrige Award* has been emulated by most states for their own state quality awards. The *ISO 9000* series of standards is receiving major emphasis, especially for companies doing business in Europe, and is now managed in the USA by the American Society for Quality as *QS-9000* standards. Individual large corporations often have awards to external suppliers such as Ford's *Q-1 Award for Quality*, which can go to service organizations. Receiving such an award almost guarantees continued receipt of their business.

The Baldrige Award is presented annually to the top American manufacturing and service companies at the culmination of a long and expensive application and judging process. The preparation for the competition is valuable whether or not a company wins. Regional service firms may find more value in state quality competitions. The statement that your firm is "Winner of the New York State Excelsior Quality Award" could add powerful endorsement to your advertising. In the future, several states will change their quality awards from the selection of a relatively few top organizations in each category to an absolute yes/no rating that an organization has achieved the award criteria.

The ISO/QS 9000 series is applicable to service and maintenance organizations in hardware, software, and professional services. The standards require procedures, documentation, training, and consistency but unfortunately do not set levels of performance. Most organizations working toward ISO certification also set high standards of quality performance, so the effort results in definite improvement. External auditors typically do a prequalification audit, then the certification audit, and follow up at six-month intervals to assure continued effectiveness. Like the other awards and certifications, the ISO 9000 certification can provide a desirable goal toward which a service company's operations can be effectively directed.

The *American Customer Satisfaction Index* (ACSI) is a national rating that includes airlines, TV network news, electric service parcel delivery, the US Postal Service, hotels, hospitals, and more. ACSI is the only uniform, cross-industry indicator that links customer satisfaction with performance. Several sectors of the American economy are measured each quarter to update the rolling index. Presently the index, which started in 1994, measures US household customers. It contains elements of product service measures, and will no doubt expand in the future. It provides a relative measure for industries to compare within themselves and with other sectors of the economy. For example, airlines have dropped almost continuously from a 72 rating in 1994 to a 1999 rating of 63. During the same period hospitals have dropped from 74 to 70 and the US Postal Service has improved from 61 to 71. The *J. D. Powers Awards* are other, though commercialized, measures that provide stimulation for improvement across service. Companies want to be able to advertise that they have the highest satisfaction across the automotive industry for the fewest defects and the best service, and similar measures of customer satisfaction.

There can be high motivational value for your service people if you together select an award that you want to win and then stimulate everyone to strive for it. There can be significant cost involved, so make sure that the benefits will be higher than those costs. For example, a field service organization or a regional repair depot will probably find that the costs of ISO/QS standards are too high to bring a good return. Those organizations might instead try for a state or corporation award. Organizations doing business across national boundaries will find the ISO certification to be valuable, especially in Europe.

Questions

1. Why should service quality be emphasized in your organization?

2. Pick a product and describe how legal liability could be a concern to service.

3. What impact does the quality of service have on equipment uptime?

4. Should you reduce the level of service provided to customers if customers rate that service factor as unimportant? Why?

5. What should you do if customers rank a service characteristic as very important but rate your delivery as lower than the competition's?

6. Select a representative product that presently requires at least a few hours to install and discuss what can be done to improve the installation in terms of customer satisfaction and service costs.

7. Identify ten problems encountered by customers and recommend weighting for these defects that will focus attention on the items that most need correction.

8. Is it better to describe performance as 97% available or as 3% not available? Why?

9. Why are realistic expectations, even though undesirable, better than promises that are frequently not met?

10. What values do customer satisfaction surveys provide to a service organization?

18

Professional Services

The business of service is to effectively meet customers' perceived needs. Service is undergoing an evolution from primarily "hard" repairs to "soft" comprehensive support, now termed *professional services*. Transition is occurring due to the increased use of technology to meet customer expectations for computerized information support systems, phone fixes, help desks, remote diagnostics, applications assistance, logistics support analysis, training, network design, systems implementation assistance, and other aids. Many of these items have traditionally been provided to end-users at no additional charge.

Profits come to business in the form of money. Persons who claim that you can live on good will and a friendly smile and a possibility of added purchases need to better understand the present value of cash. Futures do not feed a hungry family today. At the same time, there is considerable short-term and long-term value in responsive, high quality support services. A major paradigm switch is necessary in the minds of both service personnel and customers to reevaluate service business economics and emotions. As open systems hardware brings commodity products and their repair needs diminish, comprehensive assistance over the entire life cycle creates happy customers and hard money profits.

Defining Professional Services

A typical maintenance contract involves a few thousand dollars a year. A user organization will spend at least 10 times that amount in related support services. Hard service infers installation and repair of durable physical equipment. Table 18-1 lists some of the soft support services that customers need. Some general characteristics of how these soft services differ from hard product-oriented service may be found in Table 18-2.

Unisys®, as an example of soft services, recently signed a $201 million five-year contract with the Department of Trans-

TABLE **18-1**
List of professional services.

Application Development	Network design
Asset Accountability	One Call Solves All
Backups	Operations Management
Benchmarking	Order Entry
Client/Server Planning	Outsourcing
Configuration	Product Integration
Contracts Management	Project Management
Data Conversion	Remote Processing
Diagnostics	Security Assistance
Disaster Recovery	System Administration
Documentation	System Design
Facility Planning	Systems Integration
Help Desk	Technical Assistance
Implementation Assistance	Telephone Support
Interoperability Assessment	Testing
Logistics Planning	Training
Moves	User Group
Needs Analysis	Warranty Administration

portation (DOT) to provide information services, research, engineering support, software development, operations research, strategic planning, demand and capacity analysis, and other "integrated services."

Why Promote Professional Services?

Alison Harris of *United Publications* states the condition well: "There are too many people in the field doing too little, for not enough money." Services in the 1990s are transitioning to a broad range of offerings along the total life cycle. Support is becoming highly customized and oriented to networks, with benefits of increased customer loyalty, total account control, additional product sales, and high margin revenues. There is also a general business move toward outsourcing functions that may better be done by external groups. In the fastest growing segment of computing today, personal computers, the traditional hardware maintenance revenue is estimated by Gartner Group Dataquest® at $2.9 billion with a 7.6% compound average growth rate (CAGR), while the professional services network support for the first time exceeds hard services with $3.4 billion revenue and a 21% CAGR. Network integration is the key data

TABLE 18-2
Comparison of hard versus soft services.

Soft Services	Hard Services
Intangible	Tangible
Perceptions	Facts
Emotions	Economics
People	Things
Improve Unknowns	Fix Known
Flexible	Rigid
Long Term	Short Term
Can Not Inventory	Carry Inventory
Perceived Possible Internally	Recognize Need Technical Help
Low Fixed Costs; High Variable	High Fixed Costs; Low Variable
Long Wait to Payoff	Short Payoff
High Profit Margin	Moderate, Declining Margin

center objective for 76% of the IS managers surveyed by IN-PUT®. Network integration CAGR for professional services is estimated at 37.7%, maintenance at 30.4%, and installation at 34.8%. The European market for computer-related professional services and systems is growing at an annual rate of over 15%.

For high-technology services, including computers, communications, medical, and utilities, we find that repairs and related hard services account for about half of the total US market, while soft services account for the other half. Note that hardware is projected to remain over 50% of service revenues, but soft services are growing at a faster rate than are the installation and repair hard services.

Before anyone gets too picky about the accuracy of these statistics, note that the markets and services are being cut differently from most analyses and the intent is to show that there is plenty of business opportunity for intelligent service strategists. Soft service is not yet a zero-sum market in which every sale must be taken from someone else. The major competition today is internal functions. You may ask, based on the previous statement that comprehensive support costs total many times more than just repair costs, "Why are the present revenues so close?" The answer is that user organizations' internal personnel today provide most soft services. Most of those costs are hidden from normal reports and receive little attention. These costs are a major target of opportunity.

Hardware sales and hard maintenance are still main revenue sources for computer retailers, but much of their margins comes from training, software, and professional services. Just five years ago, retailers were responsible for over 60% of the personal computers sold in the USA. Today the rate has shrunk to fewer than 30%. The salvation can come with providing customers with accurate information, customizing the total package to meet the customers' specific needs, and delivering on the promises with added value. Do note that there is synergism between hard and soft product sales. If you sell a computer, the customer may need installation assistance. If you sell new software applications, then you have the opportunity to further assist with training.

Determining Customer Needs

Too many products are pitched with the approach, "This is the answer to all your needs! By the way, what are your needs?" Talk to as many people in the prospect organization as possible to solicit their input. You will sell far more service with good questions and earnest listening than with the fanciest presentation. Obviously, you should begin with the top decision-maker who can additionally refer you to subordinates. Top-down needs determination is much more effective than bottom-up. A good screening question to ask is, "Who, besides you, will help make this decision?" Decision-makers for professional services are frequently higher level executives than the managers who can make buying decisions for hard services. The head of Information Systems (IS) or Service will be the minimum management contact level, with success directly related to the level of executive contact.

Service needs are based on both economics and emotions. Of the two, the more motivating is emotions. Help your prospect paint a picture of needs and pains. Use open-ended questions to gain the prospect's own concerns. It can be helpful to list the major needs so they can be factually reviewed with visual impressions added to hearing the words.

When prospects or customers say that they have needs, use money as a way of testing their commitment. For example, "Are you willing to pay $20 additional for two hours faster delivery?" If the need is painful enough, a customer will be willing to pay. If they are not willing to pay, then you probably want to take your efforts elsewhere.

Customers want choices, clarity, and confidence. You may have some of your services "productized" and a short handout prepared to guide decision. "Is this the type of thing you have in mind?" Do not expect to develop all your prospect's needs at one visit. It may take several meetings and follow-up discussions before all the true needs are on the table. Only then should you suggest solutions. It may help to have your prospect rate the needs by priority, with the most important at the top of the list.

A forced ranking system can be useful. Ask your prospect, "If you have $1,000 to spend on this list of items, can you help me understand how you would allocate the money?" The results should guide your offerings.

The following groups of customers require special attention in service organizations. Figure 18-1 illustrates marketing terms for classes of both hard product and soft product adopters.

1. *First purchasers as against repeat purchasers.* In many instances it is relatively difficult to forecast customer satisfaction with a product until it has been used under typical conditions. Although it is helpful to know how many potential customers can be persuaded to buy a new product, it will be difficult to determine the product's "staying power" until satisfaction is demonstrated by long-term use or repeat purchases. If the consumption cycle is long, the time lags encountered lengthen and complicate the test process to a very considerable degree.

2. *Test purchasers as against full-scale purchasers.* Buyers who want to determine how the product performs may purchase a new transistor or integrated circuit in small quantities. Once proven successful in application, a large order may follow when the product is adopted as a component. In the consumer field, a wholesaler or retailer may buy a small lot of a new product to determine acceptance among his customers. When an adequate level of sales to final buyers has been assured, larger normal orders will be forthcoming. In this form of repeat purchasing, order size and time lags justify careful investigation.

3. *Purchases by innovators and by non-innovators.* For some classes of goods, a distinct group of buyers are leaders or risk

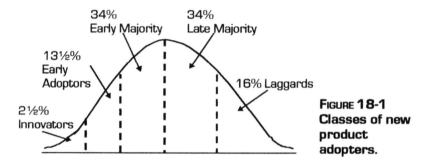

FIGURE 18-1
Classes of new product adopters.

takers, as is illustrated in Figure 18-1. Initial sales will be heavily concentrated in this group, and if sales reach a particular level the less adventuresome buyers can be expected to enter the market. The ability to forecast depends on knowledge of the types of buyers and the timing of their purchases.

4. *High-volume purchasers and low-volume purchasers.* Most types of goods are used in different quantities by different buyers. The extent to which a new product appeals to various segments of the market with different consumption rates can significantly influence the success of some new products.

5. *Loyal purchasers and fickle purchasers.* Other factors being equal, attracting buyers who can be expected to buy or use the product is more advantageous than gaining a temporary following. In some instances, buyers can be identified as one type or another. For example, in both the consumer and in the industrial goods fields, price-conscious buyers may be identified who tend to switch from product to product on short-run price movements.

6. *New purchasers and brand-switching purchasers.* In most cases, some buyers will be new entrants into the market and some will be former buyers of other brands. The number of new buyers and the market and sources of former buyers of another brand can be indicative of both the market size and share of market a new product may expect to attain.

7. *Purchasers requiring exceptionally high quality or levels of service.* Significant differences within customer groups should be identified to determine whether the proposed service package is acceptable to all or whether differences should be established. Some customers will require only basic functioning; others will require consistently high performance. The latter will cost more, but can also be highly profitable.

Although other market segments could be enumerated, the point of looking at these classifications should be evident. Knowing the characteristics of the users and buyers will enhance the value of sales information obtained from a test market. Of particular importance is the identification of decision-makers as possibly different from the product initiators or operators.

Most industries also have a "Best of Breed," "World-Class," "Superior Benchmark" company that sets the pace for others. Assuming normal exchange of information within the industry, if probability of test success is high, the product should be tried in this keystone company so that word of the experience will be spread through the industry as a credible positive occurrence. Conversely, if the test is high risk, perhaps the product should be placed where it will get a good test but possible failure will be kept quiet. A test often depends on the cooperation of the test company and its ability to properly do what is requested.

Packaging Offerings

It is better to manage services than to try and do it all yourself. The principles and practices for packaging soft services are similar to those used for hard offerings. Customers want options but will usually select the comprehensive package. If there are services that have major importance to a customer, use them as the foundation for your offerings.

A prospect's willingness to pay may not be directly proportional to the related pain. One mitigating factor is the availability of internal people to partially fill the gap. Another concern may be the administrative complexity of justifying the outsourcing. Keep your offering simple. Allow flexibility. Offer a cancellation clause. Do take a positive approach and promote the long-term solution with cancellation an option only if not fully satisfied.

Perhaps, rather than pushing to take over all support, you should offer to provide initial backup, with their people as first-line support and yours to fill in the gaps and help with peak activities or special skills. This "foot in the door" often leads to the customers' regarding your people as almost internal, and more business is likely to follow. Even a time and materials agreement can make it easy for the customer to call you first when a need arises.

Don't try to do it all yourself. No company can do everything well. Everyone needs help that can be available through subcontracts. Partnerships with experts can gain credibility for your organization. After all, you would just be practicing what you are preaching. Do, however, focus alliances to specific goals. Set mutual goals so that both you and the customer can measure progress and thereby better manage your relationship offering.

Niche Opportunities

Automated electronic services offer great opportunities that require few people. Electronic bulletin boards, e-mail, demand faxes, automated phone information, and similar electronic aides provide the opportunity for a few special people to multiply their talents. This contrasts with many people-intensive professional services.

There are significant professional service opportunities beyond computers. Banking, medical, telecommunications, plant automation, process control, and office automation are just a few areas in which expertise can be profitably developed. Vertical integration and narrowing specialization are paths to future success. Soft services put a premium on understanding the customer's business details. Aim to be the first company your prospects think of when they want experts in financial services or in logistics.

A personal example of soft services applied to logistics is Management Metrics Services, Inc.'s partnerships for "Almost Internal Scientific Inventory Management." Inventory management is both an art and a science. The place for the "art" is close to the customers and the marketplace. Internal persons who are familiar with the products and the customer's requirements best do it. The "science" is best done objectively with a view to total investment, technician productivity, distribution optimization, and inventory performance. Inventory planners often lack a complete set of scientific tools and are frequently too caught up in the crush of today's priorities to properly apply their limited skills in a timely manner. Also, in these tight business conditions, too few capable people are available, new products abound, organization changes are frequent and controllers are noticing the big financial investments tied up in service parts.

A solution is to outsource that function. Pricing can be very reasonable, and probably less than is being paid today for internal forecasting and planning people and systems. Options exist for incentives to reduce your financial investment at the same time that performance is improved. This partnership can be a stopgap aid, or it may be a long-term venture.

Agreements may be canceled any time on adequate notice, so you can take over the function as soon as internal people become qualified. You may say, "This is a core competency of my company; we can't have someone outside do that." Why not? You probably outsource payroll, insurance, travel planning, transportation services, warehousing, and even the data center operation. The deliverables can be quantified and measured. You remain in charge of your customers. You gain scientific inventory management information capability and the coaching to apply the results. Increased productivity, reduced operating expenses, and improved return on assets will easily pay the costs. This is just one example to broaden your thinking about professional services.

How to Succeed with Your Consulting Group

The idea of establishing a consulting group sounds wonderful from afar. Up close and personal, however, it requires special people. The position description for a successful service consultant requires formal training, years of experience, and continuous development in translating state-of-the-art management and scientific theory into practice. Consultants need to think and talk like your customers. Success comes not just from good ideas, but from good ideas implemented well. The typical service person's desire to help people is equally vital to professional services delivery. In fact, a challenge of the job is the balancing act between helping people and getting fairly paid for the value added. Good individuals with a team mentality must be empowered to help customers.

There are considerable opportunities for integration technology consulting as well as business process reengineering and strategy consulting. Watch out for the high investment costs required to hire or transition and train your own staff. Developing a consulting resource needs the same program plans and management and investment that should support any new product. Consider an initial arrangement with an established consulting organization that will help you get up to speed while you develop your internal staff.

Speaking from combined consulting experience of over 70 years, the authors can clearly state that you should watch out for newly minted MBAs from large do-everything consulting firms. Be sure that any people you hire have had practical experience with the type of service you handle. For example, someone from manufacturing will not do well in service parts until he has had time to listen to customers and associates and understand the 16 major differences between service parts business and production parts. It is possible to draw conclusions from triangulation that are entirely false in the real world.

Pricing

Added users should directly bear added costs, with a value-based price. Much like our tax system, the burden of universally used elements should be paid equally by everyone. User fees and specific contracts are more appropriate for people who require additional time or technology. A few companies like WordPerfect Corporation® and Intuit® judge that continued free 800-WATS phone support brings in enough business to pay for the large expense. That strategy will work well so long as new sales occur to pay for the cost of supporting the goods sold. The publicity to date, coupled with well-tested products, pays off in new sales. With this approach you must beware of resource and cash flow problems that come with an unexpected defect or slow sales revenues.

On the other hand, many companies, especially in software support, are searching for the right combination of charges for services rendered. The value of soft service is perceived as directly related to price. Software support agreements are typically 15% per year, with some discounts for overlap with warranty. Time may be purchased with advance contractual agreements or over a 900- phone line with automatic billing, or it may be charged to a credit card number. The general trend is to charge for the time involved, similar to the way hardware service is charged.

Research shows that, unfortunately, users are not always willing to pay for the support they need. IDC® surveyed users of operating support and found that 58% said they were not willing to pay for support. IDC's research in network support found 34.5% of respondents stating they were not willing to pay. Entitlement by customers trying to get free support is not generally a problem. Very few people state that they use the cheapest contact. Companies providing support generally state that it is not beneficial to try to eliminate cheaters.

Do not give your services away for free. Free anything is usually regarded as worth the cost. Your credibility is reduced if you give in on price. If the customer is not prepared to invest money in your improvement, then look for customers elsewhere, or perhaps a reduced or altered offering will gain monetary commitment. Whenever possible, charges should be based on the value gained. This allows the high investment in training and technology backup to be recovered against specific improvements rather than on a high-sounding charge per hour.

Marketing to Existing and New Customers

A key concept is to stop marketing your products and instead market solutions to specific customer problems, with whatever it takes to succeed. A major challenge is how to sensitize customers to the tangible advantages of your "invisible, seamless" support. Create typical scenarios of service problems. "I don't suppose this ever happens to you..." is a good way to present the potentially painful situation. Your objective is to get the prospect emotionally involved so he or she perceives your offer of help as complete salvation.

There is no question that the costs of gaining more business from existing customers is six to ten times less than the cost of acquiring new customers. Frequent contact with customers is critical. It is rare that a customer is turned off by too much attention. Prioritize your prospects according to their potential business. Class A top customers and prospects for more business should get a personal visit every month. Class B midrange prospects should get a phone call monthly. All others should get a call or letter at least quarterly, so they do not have a chance to forget your interest in helping them.

Since we are dealing with functions that are mainly supported today by internal people, you should expect concern over cutting staff. This is a two-edged sword. Many companies will survive only if they reduce overhead and trim costs for low-productive activities that can better be done by outside experts. At the same time, everyone is concerned about his own job and will also look out for the other people around them. Top managers are expected to look out for the company and will at least consider moving people to more essential tasks. The most mentioned resistance to outsourcing functions is higher-than-expected cost. Other concerns are loss of control and loss of inhouse expertise.

Expensive advertising is generally a waste. Your advertising and PR money is best invested in experienced service marketing people who can draw out prospect decision-makers' needs and gain financial commitment if solutions can be provided to meet the needs. Detailed presentations and written agreements can be provided at another time or even by less experienced sales persons.

Soft services, marketed by professionals to professionals, offer benefits to both and a major opportunity to earn hard dollars.

Questions

1. How do "hard" services differ from "soft" services?

2. Which type of services has more opportunity for growth? Why?

3. How can you make soft service offerings more tangible to prospective customers?

4. Why are soft services not a zero-sum business?

5. At a typical present customer, who will be your major competitor for professional service business?

6. How does consultative selling determine customer needs?

7. How should you best make prospects aware of your professional service offerings?

8. Why should you not supply your professional support services for free?

9. What factors determine a customer's willingness to pay for soft services?

10. Why are partnerships with other experts advantageous in supplying soft services?

Appendix

Related Professional Societies and Publications

APICS—The Educational Society for Resource Management
5301 Shawnee Rd.
Alexandria, VA 22312-2317
703-354-8851
www.apics.org
publications: *APICS—The Performance Advantage* & others

American Productivity and Quality Center (APQC)
123 North Post Oak Ln.
Houston, TX 77024-7797
800-776-9676
www.apqc.org
International Benchmarking Clearinghouse & other offerings

American Society for Quality (ASQ)
611 East Wisconsin Ave.
P.O. Box 3005
Milwaukee, WI 53202
800-248-1946
www.asq.org
publications: *Quality Progress* & others

Annual Reliability and Maintainability Symposium (ARMS)
www.rams.org

Association for the Advancement of Medical Instrumentation (AAMI)
3330 Washington Blvd., Suite 400
Arlington, VA 22201-4598
703-525-4890
www.aami.org
publications: *Biomedical Instrumentation & Technology*, standards, conferences

Association of Facilities & Plant Operating Engineers (AFPOE)
12334 Front St.
Norwalk, CA
562-929-6101

Association for Services Management International (AFSM International)
1342 Colonial Blvd., Suite 25
Fort Myers, FL 33907
800-333-9786
www.afsmi.org
publications: *The Professional Journal*, conferences; chapters

Computing Industry Technology Association (CompTIA)
450 East 22nd St., Suite 230
Lombard, IL 60148-6158
630-268-1818
www.comptia.com
A+ Certification testing program & others

Computer Service and Repair
2329 W. Main St., Suite 102
Littleton, CO 80120
303-797-8522
www.csrmagazine.com
publication: *Computer Service & Repair*

Council of Logistics Management (CLM)
2803 Butterfield Rd. #380
Oak Brook, IL 60521-1156
708-574-0985
www.clm1.org
publications: *Bibliography on Logistics Management* & others

Customer Support Management
203-857-8565
www.customersupportmgmt.com
publication: *Customer Support Management* magazine (ex-*Support Management*)

HealthTech Publications Company
10 Risho Ave.
East Providence, RI 02914-1215
401-434-1050
www.Healthtechnet.com
publications: *Medical Equipment Services Directory* & *24x7*

Help Desk Institute
800-248-5667
www.HelpDeskInst.com

Institute of Industrial Engineers (IIE)
25 Technology Park/Atlanta
Norcross, GA 30092
800-494-0460
www.iienet.org
publications: *IIE Solutions* & others; conferences

Institute of Electrical and Electronic Engineers (IEEE)
345 East 47th St.
New York, NY 10017
732-981-0060 (main)
www.ieee.org
publications: *IIE Spectrum* & others; standards; conferences

Instrument Society of America (ISA)
POB 12277
67 Alexander Dr.
Raleigh, NC 27709
800-334-6391
www.isa.com
publications: *InTech* & others; standards; conferences

International Customer Service Association
401 North Michigan Ave.
Chicago, IL 60611-4267
800-360-4272
www.icsa.com
networking, education, & research

Information Technology Services Marketing Association (ITSMA)
888-ITSMA92
www.itsma.com
conferences & training programs

IT Support News
United Publications
P.O. Box 995
38 Lafayette St.
Yarmouth, ME 04096
207-846-0600
www.itsupportnews.com
publication: *IT Support News* (ex-*Service News*)

National Association of Service Managers (NASM)
9855A Prospect Ave.
P.O. Box 712500
Santee, CA 92071
619-562-7004
www.nasm.com
publications: *Service Management*, conferences, training

Service Industry Association
494 Ansley Walk Terrace
Atlanta, GA 30309
404-885-9908, Fax -9909
www. Servicenetwork. com
publication: *Network News;* conferences

Society for Maintenance and Reliability Professionals
500 N. Michigan Ave., Suite 1920
Chicago, IL 60611
800-950-7354

Society of Logistics Engineers (SOLE)
8100 Professional Pl., Suite 211
New Carrollton, MD 20785
301-459-8446
www. sole.org
publications: *Logistics Spectrum* & others, conferences

Bibliography

Aguilar, Leslie; & Stokes, Linda. *Multicultural Customer Service*. ISBN 0-7863-0332-8, Irwin Professional Pub., 1995.

Amsden, Davida M. & Robert T; & Butler, Howard E. *SPC Simplified for Services: Practical Tools for Continuous Quality Improvement*. ISBN 0-5279-1639-0, Quality Resources, 1991.

Anderson, Paul. *A Call from the 21st Century: The Technology of Customer Contact*. ISBN 0-9653359-0-9, Doyle Pub., 1997.

Anton, Jon. *Callcenter Management: By the Numbers*. ISBN 1-5575-3112-9, Purdue University Press, 1997.

Armistead, Colin G. *Outstanding Customer Service: Implementing the Best Ideas from Around the World*. ISBN 1-55623-629-8, Irwin Professional Pub., 1993.

Beaumont, Leland R. *ISO 9001, the Standard Interpretation: The International Standard System for assuring Product & Service Quality*. ISBN 0-9636-0037-0, ISO Easy, 1995.

Becker, Hal. *At Your Service: Calamities, Catastrophes & Other Curiosities of Customer Service*. ISBN 0-471-25542-4, John Wiley & Sons, 1998.

Bell, Chip R.; & Zemke, Ron. *Managing 'Knock Your Socks Off' Service*. AMACOM, 1992.

Bentley, John P. *Introduction to Reliability & Quality Engineering*. ISBN 0-201-3313-22, Addison Wesley Longman, 1999.

Bergman, Bo; & Klefsjo, Bengt. *Quality: From Customer Needs to Customer Satisfaction*. ISBN 0-07-709016-0, McGraw-Hill, 1994.

Berry, Leonard L. *On Great Service: A Framework for Action*. ISBN 0-02-9185-556, Simon & Schuster, 1995.

Berry, Leonard L. *Discovering the Soul of Service: The Nine Drivers of Sustainable Business Success*. ISBN 0-6848-4511-3, The Free Press, 1999.

Blanchard, Benjamin S.; Verma, Dinesh; & Peterson, Elmer L. *Maintainability: A Key to Effective Serviceability and maintenance Management*. ISBN 0-47-15913-27, John Wiley & Sons, 1994.

Blohowiak, Don. *Complete Idiot's Guide to Customer Service*. ISBN 0-02-861953, Macmillan, 1997.

Blumberg, Donald F. *Managing Service as a Strategic Profit Center*, ISBN 0-07-006189-0, McGraw-Hill, 1991.

Brennan, Charles D. Jr. *Proactive Customer Service: Transforming Your Customer Service Department into a Profit Center*. ISBN 0-8144-0372-7, AMACOM, 1997.

Breyfogle, Forrest W. *Smarter Six SIGMA Solutions: Statistical Methods for Testing, Development, Manufacturing, and Service*. ISBN 0-4712-9659-7, John Wiley & Sons, 1999.

Brown, Stanley A. *What Customers Value Most: How to Achieve Business Transformation by Focusing on Processes That Touch Your Customers*. ISBN 0-47-16412-35, John Wiley & Sons, 1995.

Brown, Stanley A. *Breakthrough Customer Service: Best Practices of Leaders in Customer Support*. ISBN 0-471-64123-5, John Wiley & Sons, 1998.

Broydrick, Steven C. *Seven Universal Laws of Customer Value: How to Win Customers and Influence Markets*. ISBN 0-7863-0732-3, Irwin Professional Pub., 1996.

Buchanan, Richard. *The Enemy Within: Actions that Self-Destruct Companies and Customer Service*. ISBN 0-07-470324-2, McGraw-Hill, 1996.

Burke, Jack. *Creating Customer Connections: How to Make Customer Service a Profit Center for Your Company*. ISBN 1-56343-149-1, Merritt, 1997.

Burwash, Peter. *The Key to Great Leadership: Rediscovering the Principles of*

Outstanding Service: Lessons from the Front Lines of the World's Best Service Companies. ISBN 1-887089-01-2, Torchlight Pub., 1995.

Carter, Wendy. *Customer Service.* ISBN 0-07-011197-9, McGraw-Hill, 1994.

Cespedes, Frank V. *Concurrent Marketing: Integrating Product, Sales, and Service.* ISBN 0-8758-4444-8, Harvard Business School Pub., 1995.

Chaston, Ian. *Customer Focused Marketing.* ISBN 0-07-707698-2, McGraw-Hill, 1992.

Christopher, Martin. *Logistics and Supply Chain Management: Strategies for Reducing Cost and Improving Service.* ISBN 0-2736-3049-0, Financial Times Professional, 1999.

Clemmer, Jim; & Sheehy, Barry. *Firing on All Cylinders: The Service Quality System for High-Powered Corporate Performance.* ISBN 1-55623-704-9, Irwin Professional Pub., 1992.

Cleveland, Brad; & Mayben, Julia. *Call Center Management on Fast Forward: Succeeding in Today's Dynamic Inbound Environment.* ISBN 0-9659-0930-1, Call Center Press, 1998.

Colley, John L. Jr. *Case Studies in Service Operation.* ISBN 0-534-51126-0, Wadsworth, 1995.

Crego, Edwin T.; & Schiffrin, Peter D. *Customer Centered Reengineering.* ISBN 0-7863-0298-4, Irwin Professional Pub., 1994.

Cross, Richard; & Smith, Janet. *Customer Bonding: Pathway to Customer Loyalty,* ISBN 0-8442-3318-8, NTC Contemporary Pub., 1994.

Cusack, Michael. *Online Customer Care: Applying Today's Technology to Achieve World-Class Customer Interaction.* ISBN 0-8738-9383-2, 1998.

Czegel, Barbara. *Running an Effective Help Desk.* ISBN 0-471-24816-9, John Wiley & Sons, 1998.

Davidow, William H. *The Virtual Corporation: Customization and Instantaneous Response in Manufacturing and Service: Lessons from the World's Most Advanced Companies,* ISBN 0-88730-593-8, Harper Business, 1992.

Dhillon, Balbir S. *Engineering Maintainability: How to Design for Reliability and Easy Maintenance.* ISBN 0-8841-525-7X, Gulf Pub., 1999

Donnelly, James H. *Close to the Customer: 25 Management Tips from the Other Side of the Counter.* ISBN 1-55623-569-0, Irwin Professional Pub., 1991.

Ebeling, Charles E. *An Introduction to Reliability and Maintainability Engineering.* ISBN 0-070-18852-1, McGraw-Hill, 1996.

Edgett, Scott J. *Product Development for the Service Sector: Lessons from Market Leaders.* ISBN 0-7382-0105-7, PerseusBooks, 1999.

Elsayed, Elsayed A. *Reliability Engineering.* ISBN 0-2016-3481-3, Addison Wesley Longman, 1996.

Ferguson, Paul; Huston, Geoff; & Long, Carol (Ed.). *Quality of Service: Delivering Qos on the Internet and in Corporate Networks.* ISBN 0-4712-4358-2, John Wiley & Sons, 1998.

Ford, Lisa. *Customer Service Excellence: It's in the Details.* ISBN 1-884926-83-5, American Media, 1997.

Fromm, Schlesinger. *Real Heroes of Business—& Not a CEO Among Them.* ISBN 0-385-42555-4, Doubleday, 1994.

Furlong, Carla B. *Marketing for Keeps: Building Your Business by Retaining Your Customers.* ISBN 0-471-54017-X, John Wiley & Sons, 1993.

Gale, Bradley T. *Managing Customer Value: Creating Quality and Service That Customers Can See.* ISBN 0-02-91104-59, The Free Press, 1994.

Glanz, Barbara A. *Building Customer Loyalty.* ISBN 0-7863-0253-4, Irwin Professional Pub., 1994.

Greasley, Andrew. *Project Techniques for Product and Service Improvement.* ISBN 0-4506-3769-2, Butterworth-Heinemann, 1997.

Griffin, Jill. *Customer Loyalty: How to Earn It, How to Keep It.* ISBN 0-7879-0860-6, Jossey-Bass, 1997.

Gutek, Barbara A. *The Dynamics of Customer Service: Reflections on the Changing Nature of Customer Provider Interactions.* ISBN 0-7879-0101-6, Jossey-Bass, 1995.

Halbrooks, John R. *How to Really Deliver Superior Customer Service.* ISBN 1-

880394-28-6, Inc Pub., 1997.

Hanan, Mack. *Profits Without Products: How to Transfor Your Product Business into a Service.* ISBN 0-8144-5132-2, AMACOM, 1992.

Harrington, H. James; & Anderson, Les. *Reliability Simplified: Going Beyond Quality to Keep Customers for Life.* ISBN 0-07-027051-1, McGraw-Hill, 1998.

Harris, Elaine K. *Customer Service: A Practical Approach.* ISBN 0-13-436460-0, Prentice Hall, 1995.

Heil, Gary; Parker, Tom; & Tate, Rick. *Leadership and the Customer Revolution.* ISBN 0-442-01852-5, Van Nostrand Reinhold, 1995.

Heskett, James L.; Sasser, W. Earl; & Hart, Christopher W. L. *Service Breakthroughs: Changing the Rules of the Game.* ISBN 0-02-91467-55, The Free Press, 1990.

Hiebeler, Robert; Ketteman, Charles; & Kelly, Thomas B. *Best Practices: Building Your Business with Customer-Focused Solutions.* ISBN 0-6848-3453-7, Simon & Schuster, 1998.

Hill, Arthur V. *Field Service Management: An Integrated Approach to Increasing Customer Satisfaction.* ISBN 1-55623-547-X, Irwin Professional Pub., 1992.

Hinton, Thomas; & Schaeffer, Wini. *Customer-Focused Quality: What to do on Monday Morning.* ISBN 0-13-189630-X, Prentice Hall, 1994.

Horovitz, Jacques. *Total Customer Satisfaction: Putting the World's Best Programs to Work.* ISBN 0-7863-0108-2, Irwin Professional Pub., 1994.

Johnston, Bernice B. *Real World Customer Service: What to Really Say When the Customer Complains.* ISBN 1-5707-1062-7, Sourcebooks, Inc., 1995.

Keenan, Douglas. *Introduction to Computer Hardware, Theory, Maintenance, Troubleshooting.* ISBN 1-5687-02949, RonJon Pub., 1998.

Kessler, Sheila; & Westergard, Susan (Ed.). *Total Quality Service: A Simplified Approach to Using the Baldrige Award Criteria.* ISBN 0-87-3893-360, ASQ Quality Press, 1995.

Knod, Edward M.; & Schonberger, Richard J. *Operations Management: Team-*

work for Customer Service. ISBN 0-256-19406-8, Irwin-McGraw-Hill, 1996.

LaBounty, Char. *How to Establish and Maintain Service Level Agreements.* ISBN 1-57125-009-3, Help Desk Institute, 1995.

Leland, Karen; & Bailey, Keith. *Customer Service for Dummies.* ISBN 1-56884-391-7, IDG Books, 1995.

Leppard, John; & Molyneix, Liz. *Auditing Your Customer Service: The Foundation for Success.* ISBN 0-415-09732-0, Routledge, 1994.

Levesque, Paul. *The WOW Factor: Creating a Customer Focus Revolution in Your Business.* ISBN 0-7863-0386-7, Irwin Professional Pub., 1994.

Lewis, E. E. *Introduction to Reliability Engineering.* ISBN 0-4710-1833-3, John Wiley & Sons, 1995.

Locks, Mitchell O. *Reliability, Maintainability, and Availability Assessment.* ISBN 0-8738-92933, ASQC Qual., 1995

Lovelock, Christopher H. *Product Plus: Product Plus Service Equals Competitive Advantage.* ISBN 0-07-038798-2, McGraw-Hill, 1994.

Lovelock, Christopher H.; & Wright, Lauren. *Principles of Services Marketing and Management.* ISBN 0-1367-687-5X, Prentice Hall, 1999.

Lucas, Robert. *Customer Service: Skills and Concepts for Business.* ISBN 0-256-18742-8, Irwin-McGraw-Hill, 1995.

MacNeill, Deborah J. *Customer Service Excellence.* ISBN 1-55623-969-9, Irwin Professional Pub., 1993.

Martin, John E. *Command Performance: The Art of Delivering Quality Service.* ISBN 0-87584-562-2, Harvard Business Press, 1994.

Moubray, John. *Reliability-Centered Maintenance.* ISBN 0-831-1307-84, Industrial Press, 1997.

Naumann, Earl. *Customer Satisfaction Measurement and Management.* ISBN 0-538-84439-6, Thomson Executive Press, 1995.

Northwood University Press (Ed.). *Merchandising Parts and Service.* ISBN 0-8735-9006-6, Northwood University Press.

Orsburn, Douglas K. *Spares Management*

Handbook. ISBN 0-830-6762-60, McGraw-Hill, 1991.

Patton, Joseph D. Jr. *Maintainability and Maintenance Management* (Third Edition). ISBN 1-55-617510-8, Instrument Society of America, 1994.

Patton, Joseph D. Jr. *Preventive Maintenance* (Second Edition). ISBN 1-55-617533-7, Instrument Society of America, 1995.

Patton, Joseph D. Jr. *Service Parts Handbook*, ISBN 0-934623-73-2, The Solomon Press, 1997.

Pecht, Michael G. (Ed.). *Product Reliability, Maintainability, and Supportability Handbook*. ISBN 0-84939-457-0, CRC Press, 1995.

Ramundo, Michael. *Complete Book on Customer Service*. ISBN 0-13-399882-7, Prentice-Hall, 1997.

Reiche, Hans. *Maintenance Minimization for Copmpetitive Advantage: A Life-Cycle Approach for Product Manufacturers and End-Users*. ISBN 2-8812-4589-7, Gordon & Breach Pub. Group, 1994.

Reichheld, Frederick F. *The Loyalty Effect*. ISBN 0-8758-4448-0, Harvard Business School Press, 1996.

Rust, Roland T.; & Oliver, Richard L. *Service Quality: New Directions in Theory and Practice*. ISBN 0-8039-4919-7, Sage, 1993.

Sanders, Elizabeth A. *Fabled Service: Ordinary Acts, Extraordinary Outcomes*. ISBN 0-89384-270-2, Jossey-Bass, 1994.

Scheier, Robert L.; & Alter, Allen E. *Customer Service on the Internet: Building Relationships, Increasing Loyalty and Staying Competitive*. ISBN 0-02-911045-9, John Wiley & Sons.

Schneider, Benjamin; & Bowen, David E. *Winning the Service Game*. ISBN 0-87584-570-3, Harvard Business School Pub., 1995.

Schonberger, Richard J.; & Knod, Edward M. Jr. *Synchoservice! The Innovative Way to Build a Dynasty of Customers*, ISBN 0-7863-0245-3, Irwin Professional Pub., 1994.

Smith, David J. *Reliability, Maintainability and Risk*. ISBN 0-7506-3752-8,

Butterworth-Heinemann, 1997.

Spector, Robert; & McCarthy, Patrick D. *The Nordstrom Way: The Inside Story of America's #1 Customer Service Company*. ISBN 0-471-58496-7, John Wiley & Sons, 1995.

Stewart, Mark. *Keep the Right Customers: Five Key Steps to Profitable Customer retention*. ISBN 0-07-709139-6, McGraw-Hill 1996.

Timm, Paul R. *Customer Service*. ISBN 0-13-576695-8, Prentice Hall, 1997.

Tobias, Paul A.; & Trindade, David C. *Applied Reliability*. ISBN 0-4420-0469-9, 1995.

Tucker, Robert B. *Customer Service for the New Millennium: Winning and Keeping Value-Driven Buyers*. ISBN 1-5641-432-1X, Career Press, Inc., 1997.

Sviokla, John J.; & Shapiro, Benson P. *Keeping Customers*. ISBN 0-87584-333-6, Harvard Business School Press, 1993.

Unruh, James A. *Customers Mean Business: How World Class Companies Build Relationships that Last*. ISBN 0-201-59043-3, Addison Wesley Longman, 1996.

Vavra, Terry G. *Aftermarketing: How to Keep Customers for Life Through Relationship Marketing*. ISBN 0-7863-0407-7, Irwin-McGraw-Hill, 1995.

Wallace, Thomas F. *Customer-Driven Strategy: Winning Through Operational Excellence*. ISBN 0-471-13217-9, John Wiley & Sons, 1995.

Whiteley, Richard C. *The Customer Driven Company; Moving from Talk to Action*. ISBN 0-201-57090-4, Addison-Wesley Longman, 1991.

Willingham, Ron. *Hey, I'm the Customer: Front Line Tips for Providing Superior Customer Service*. ISBN 0-13-388158-X, Prentice Hall, 1992.

Wilson, Larry. *Stop Selling and Start Partnering: The New Thinking About Finding and Keeping Customers*. ISBN 0-471-13363-9, John Wiley & Sons, New York, NY, 1995.o

Wireman, Terry. *Computerized Maintenance Management Systems*. ISBM 0-83-11305-47, Industrial Press, 1994.

Index

ABOUT THE AUTHORS

JOSEPH D. PATTON, Jr. is chairman and CEO of Patton Consultants, Inc., the leading advisors to management on equipment service, logistics, and support systems. Before founding Patton Consultants in 1976, he was a Regular Army Officer and spent 11 years with Xerox Corporation. Patton was the founder, chairman, and CEO of Service InfoSystems, Inc. He is the founder and chairman of Management Metrics Services, Inc., and is the author of over a hundred published articles and eight books, including *Logistics Technology and Management* and *Service parts Handbook* (published by The Solomon Press).

Patton earned a BS degree from Penn State and an MBA in marketing from the University of Rochester. He is a Registered Professional Engineer (PE) in Quality Engineering; a Fellow of both ASQ (The American Society for Quality) and SOLE (The International Society of Logistics; a Certified Professional Logistician (CPL); National Association of Service Managers Life-Certified Service Executive; and has been a member of the Association for Services Management International for more than 20 years.

WILLIAM H. BLEUEL has been named executive director of the newly established Customer Institute at Pepperdine University. His expertise lies in the quantitative aspects of business. He specializes in measurement and analysis of business operations, customer satisfaction, loyalty, and retention.

Dr. Bleuel has held senior positions in engineering, marketing, and service management at Xerox, Taylor Instrument Company, and Barber Colman Company. He also has had experience as general manager in two start-up companies that he co-founded.

Bleuel is the co-author (with Joseph Patton) of *Service Management: Principles and Practices*, the landmark work in the field of customer service (printed here with major updating and revision). He is a nationally known lecturer and writer on management and customer service. He has an MS degree in statistics, a Ph.D. in industrial engineering, and in 1996 became a Luckman Distinguished Teaching Fellow at Pepperdine University, where he is Professor of Quantitative Methods.